TAKING SHOTS

TAKING SHOTS

TALL TALES, BIZARRE BATTLES, AND THE INCREDIBLE TRUTH ABOUT THE NBA

KEITH GLASS

HC

An Imprint of HarperCollins*Publishers*

Insert photographs courtesy of the author's personal collection, with the following exceptions: page 2 (bottom left) by permission of the Hulton Archive/Getty Images; page 2 (bottom right) by permission of Jim Gund/*Sports Illustrated;* page 3 (top) by permission of Heinz Kluetmeier/*Sports Illustrated;* pages 4–5 by permission of UCLA Athletic Department; page 6 by permission of UNLV Athletics; page 6 (inset) by permission of the *New York Post;* page 8 by permission of Andrew D. Bernstein/NBAE via Getty Images; page 10 (top) by permission of Nathaniel S. Butler/NBAE via Getty Images; page 10 (bottom) by permission of Ben van Hook/*Sports Illustrated;* page 11 (top) by permission of NBAE/Getty Images; page 13 (top) by permission of Jamie Squire/Getty Images; page 13 (bottom) by permission of AP Photo/Tim Larsen; page 14 (top) by permission of D. Lippitt/Einstein/NBAE via Getty Images; page 15 (bottom right), page 16 by permission of Louise Conover.

HarperCollins books may be purchased for educational, business, or sales promotional use. For information please write: Special Markets Department, HarperCollins Publishers Inc., 10 East 53rd Street, New York, NY 10022.

FIRST EDITION

Designed by Kris Tobiassen

Printed on acid-free paper
Library of Congress Cataloging-in-Publication Data

Glass, Keith.
    Taking shots : tall tales, bizarre battles, and the incredible truth about the NBA / Keith Glass.—1st ed.
        p.   cm.
    ISBN: 978-0-06-123185-8
    ISBN-10: 0-06-123185-1
    1. Glass, Keith.   2. Sports agents—United States.   3. Basketball players—United States.
4. Basketball—Humor.   5. National Basketball Association.   I. Title.   II. Title: Taking shots.
GV734.5.G53   2007
338.4'7796092—dc22
[B]   2006050447

07   08   09   10   11   10   9   8   7   6   5   4   3   2   1

TO CORKY AND JOE, WHO STARTED IT;
TO SAMI, TYLER, ALEX, MAGGIE, LUCAS, BRENT, AND JODI,
WHO HELPED ME THROUGH IT;
AND
TO AYLIN, WHO "COMPLETED" IT.

CONTENTS

THIS GLASS IS ALWAYS HALF FULL

I have known Keith Glass for most of my life and almost all of his. His older brother, Brent, and I were good friends from the third grade on and remain good friends today. For a few years there in elementary school—before their dad got rich and the family moved to a fancy house—I would go over to Brent's house nearly every day to shoot baskets in their driveway or to collaborate with Brent on some homework assignment.

Keith was there, and, having no brothers of my own, I watched him with some amusement—and from a distance. Keith also accompanied Brent to the summer camp my aunt and uncle owned, Camp Keeyumah in Orson, Pennsylvania. It was there that Keith first met Larry Brown, when Larry was Brent's (and my) counselor. Keith grew to be Larry's assistant, his confidante and, later, a prominent NBA agent. The agent business is what Keith has written this book about, and there are plenty of stories that connect Keith to famous and infamous basketball players, at home and overseas.

But when I knew Keith, he was just Brent's little brother. And for all those years of watching him in the neighborhood, in school, and at camp, if I was asked to use one word to describe Keith, the word would be "holler."

Keith was a holler guy. He was the guy on the basketball court who called out plays for the offense and cautioned his teammates about what the defense was doing. He was the loud guy in the infield who pumped up his own pitcher and chirped at the opposing batter. He was not always the best player, but he was always the loudest and most enthusiastic player. Keith was the "coach on the field" that coaches always talk about. He loved the games. He studied the games. He knew the games—and he saw the games as they unfolded. He was ahead of the curve. He didn't need instant replay to tell him what happened. He got it all the first time.

And, of course, he was incredibly competitive. I hear this is common for a little brother. I wouldn't know. But I could see in Keith something different, and maybe angrier, than in Brent. Brent liked to win. Keith *had* to win. I can recall summers at camp when Keith would have terrible scabs and scrapes on his elbows and knees from diving on a concrete court to capture a loose ball. He dove on that concrete the first day at camp, the last day, and every day in between. Truthfully, I thought he was nuts. I mean, come on, this was concrete he's diving on. But he knew that the only way he could possibly stick on a good team would be by outworking the more gifted players. Keith could appreciate that other players might be better than him. But nobody was going to play harder than him.

Looking back, I see now that Keith was a natural leader of a team. He led by being loud, being enthusiastic, and being dedicated. I can't imagine Keith is any good at any of the individual sports, like tennis or golf. He was born to be on a team, where he could summon the energy to lift up everybody.

As I said, I saw Keith regularly when we were kids. I was somewhat startled to learn that when he was in college, he was part of a folk-singing trio, Keith, Karen, and Mike. I found this out because "Mike" was my cousin. Mike was quite talented as a singer and musician, and I remember asking him somewhat skeptically, "Keith *sings*? Keith *Glass*? He has a voice? I'd have bet he sounds like a frog."

Mike said, "He sings quite well."

And I thought, "Really? What does he sing about—zone defense?"

I was so taken by the thought that Keith could actually sing that I asked the three of them, Karen, Keith, and Mike, to perform at my wedding. Mike and Karen did. Keith hopped off at the last minute to play in a pickup basketball tournament.

In my twenties, I became a sportswriter, and from time to time, I'd see Keith's name in the papers because of his connection to Larry Brown and other basketball clients. I always asked Brent about him, and occasionally—usually at a basketball game where Larry was coaching—I'd see Keith in the stands, and we'd chat. I was certainly aware of his career, as he was aware of mine. And it was always great to bump into him.

Just a couple of years ago, we both attended a camp reunion. And toward the end of it, Keith organized a mass softball game. Mass softball was a tradition at Keeyumah. At some point during the summer, all the kids gathered at the main softball diamond, where they were evenly split into two teams of about seventy-five people each. All seventy-five players batted for one team, and all seventy-five played the field for the other. People were wall-to-wall, so it was hard to get a hit. A special large and very soft ball was used, so no gloves were needed. First one full team got up, then the other. It was a one-inning game. And though there were seventy-five people on each side, usually neither team would score more than twelve to fifteen runs because, again, it was hard to get a hit with so many fielders.

Anyway, Keith organized the game and, of course, named himself captain of the team that was in the field first and came to bat last. Normally, you'd stack your team so the best hitters would all come up at the end, big bat after big bat. Keith stacked his lineup just that way at the reunion—though guys who had big bats in their teens now mostly just had big guts in their fifties.

I was watching from the sideline. I had no intention of playing. I hadn't picked up a baseball bat in over thirty years, and I was quite sure that if I did, I would strike out, make a total fool of myself, and embarrass my entire family.

With about three batters left and his team down by two runs, Keith hollered for me to come up and hit. I demurred, saying, "I'm just here to watch."

"Come on up and hit, Tony; we need you," Keith said.

"I can't hit," I said.

"Sure you can," Keith said, dragging me to the plate and putting a bat in my hands.

"No, I can't," I said. "Trust me."

And I proceeded to whiff mightily at the first pitch. It came in so slow I could count the stitches on the ball. And I missed it by at least four feet. I was mortified. Worse, I was sweating puddles.

Keith called time and approached me. He put his arm around my neck. And this is exactly what he said to me: "No problem, Tony, just hit it like we worked on in practice."

And I cracked up because of course we hadn't practiced at all.

We hadn't practiced in close to forty years.

I hit the next pitch hard on a line to right, and it fell cleanly for a single, driving in one run and putting the winning run on first for the big hitters. Then I immediately took myself out for a pinch runner, and I hugged Keith on my way off the field.

This is why Keith was the captain. This is why Keith was the coach. This is why Keith was the leader. He knew exactly what to say to me to calm me down in my time of stress. He knew exactly how to get the best out of me and out of hundreds, maybe thousands, of people over the years.

Just like we practiced, huh?

Oh, Keith's team won the game. But you already figured that out, didn't you?

—TONY KORNHEISER

PAGING DR. NAISMITH
What Have We Done to Your Game?

Basketball used to be a helluva game. It's not anymore, and that in large part prompted me to write this book. I know it's just basketball. I know that it's only a game. I also know that for me neither of those previous two sentences are true.

To me, basketball has always meant more. As a child, the game was my constant companion. As an adult, it has become my profession. It has supported my family in ways I could never have dreamed.

It is important to understand this because the tone of much of what follows may seem negative or unappreciative, instead of grateful. It is the exact opposite. I care deeply about the game, and for many years, I have grown to hate what has happened to it. Having come to the conclusion that I will no longer just take the money and run, I have decided to fight back the only way I can. I'll take the money and write a book, so here goes. The NBA is too powerful. Players make too much money. Teams charge too much money. The league sells too many products. Many coaches and administrators seem to have all the answers, and yet the game itself has become a selfish, tedious, and colossal bore.

This was not the plan.

The game's inventor, Dr. James Naismith, created basketball to instill a sense of responsibility in his students. He sought to have the players rely on themselves and one another. In fact, in 1910, the rules committee governing basketball, of which Dr. Naismith was a member, outlawed coaching entirely during games, and it wasn't until 1949 that coaches were actually allowed to speak during time-outs. The purpose was to teach the qualities mentioned above way before any spotlight shone on an individual player, since the lessons he was attempting to teach were meant for life, not just for basketball.

While Dr. Naismith's intentions were part of the rules of the game he created, the NBA's current gurus and nonvisionaries have turned the game on its head. The people who run the NBA are not evil. They have built an almost unreal marketing machine. They are responsible for generating untold amounts of money, not only for themselves but also for players, coaches, and agents like me. Along the way they have somehow lost the game itself. When the people who buy the tickets, buy ads, and pay ridiculous amounts of money for TV rights wake up and realize what they are really buying, the seemingly endless supply of cash is going to erode.

I have seen this coming for a long time. I have been the guy tilting at the windmills of the NBA for twenty-three years. I have had issues with the league itself, the players, the players' union, the fans, all the way down to my fellow agents. What follows in these pages will attempt to show how we got to this point. I'm not a great philosopher. I'm not an investigative journalist. I am a storyteller. I will not preach. I would rather make you think about something after I get you to laugh. I'm going to tell my stories and then leave it to you to figure out if there is a meaning. (I can't do all the work.)

P. T. Barnum is a man I greatly admire. While most of us think of him only as the creator of Ringling Bros. and Barnum & Bailey Circus, he was much more than that. He actually didn't begin his circus until he turned sixty. He had held political office as well. He was a two-term Connecticut state legislator, first elected in 1865. Barnum later served as the mayor of Bridgeport. Barnum's philosophy of life is evident in this quote delivered in the Connecticut State House during the debate over the ratification of the Thirteenth Amendment—freeing the slaves and giving them the right to vote: "A human soul is not to be trifled with. It may inhabit the body of a Chinaman, a Turk, an Arab, or a Hotentot—it is still an immortal spirit!"

Barnum was one of the greatest salesmen ever; he could sell you anything. He could have been a great agent or even better, the commissioner of the NBA. This is not meant in an insulting way. In fact, when naming him as one of the most important people of the millennium, *LIFE* magazine called him, "the patron saint of promoters."

In the 1840s, he took over Scudder's American Museum in New York City. One of his exhibits was the "SIX-FOOT MAN-EATING CHICKEN." Barnum advertised for months, teasing the public, building anticipation. When the exhibit opened, the line to see the phenomenon was around the block. When you finally got in, you found a six-foot tall man sitting in a chair, eating chicken. People laughed. They laughed at themselves and at Barnum. They were snookered, and they enjoyed the joke. It cost them ten cents a ticket. For a family of four, forty cents. Or about eight bucks today, adjusted for inflation.

There are subtle but critical distinctions between what P. T. Barnum affectionately referred to as a "humbug" and an out-and-out fraud. He sometimes flitted dangerously close to that line. He was, however, not the caretaker of a professional sports league. He was in the entertainment business, pure and simple, and he never cheated his customers. Even those who got snookered had to admit they had a good time. Even those who were "humbugged" knew that it was worth the money they had paid to get in the door. And if they were incensed, they could get their money back.

To go to an NBA basketball game today, a family of four gets the honor of the following: They park for ten dollars. The tickets cost around $400. If they didn't get hot dogs at Costco on the way to the game, they can purchase them for $4.50 each. If they then want something to drink. . . . You get the point.

Now on to the game itself. Even though they have already bought the tickets, paid for parking, food, and drinks, the selling continues. They are bombarded with commercials before, during, and after every game. They need to buy T-shirts, large foam index fingers, sweatshirts, shorts, and future season ticket plans, and so on. The introductions only continue the bombardment. After the obligatory introducing of the opposing team, the lights are shut off, fireworks begin, and the noise level from the public address system almost convinces the fans in the arena that now is the time for the excitement. This goes on for what seems like an eternity. When the smoke finally clears and the crowd is blasted with some more commercials, the game actually begins. It is at this point the family gets treated by and large to seventy-three post ups—isolations on the right low block. This is then followed up by the ever exciting fifty-two isolations on the left low block. In 91 percent of these isolation plays, the players perform the incredibly selfish act of finding any way possible to shoot.

Hopefully the game is competitive because if it isn't, it can get really ugly. That's when the players have what Marv Albert calls "garbage time." This is an expression used to signify the part of the game that *really* doesn't matter. The effort is not the same. The quality of play is not the same. The price of tickets, however, remains constant—no discounts. Imagine the thrill that Dad gets when it dawns on him that he has just shelled out $500 to watch garbage time. Barnum would be proud. Or maybe just a bit embarrassed. A family being snookered for forty cents will come again for the next joke even if it's on them. At $500 per game, people get a bit testy, and the NBA doesn't offer refunds to incensed customers.

But wait. It's not over yet. The next morning after sleeping it off and maybe calming down from the absurdity of the previous evening, the family members get to read the morning paper. They are bombarded once again by the comments of the players and sometimes even the coaches.

We just didn't show up tonight.
The effort wasn't there.

I didn't get enough shots.

I didn't get enough minutes.

I could go on, but you know the drill. All this coming from people who are being paid an average salary of $3.75 million per year. That is an average. Some are making $8 million per year, some $10 million, and some make $14 million and more.

ONE

FEEDING YOUR FAMILY ON ONLY $14 MILLION A YEAR

For the 2004–2005 season, Latrell Sprewell was paid $14 million. When he was confronted with an offer to extend his contract with the Minnesota Timberwolves, his response resonated across the country. He rejected an offer of $32 million for the next four years, saying, "I've got my family to feed." Yes, a $6 million a year pay cut is big, no matter how you slice it, but it still left him with $8 million on the table per season. At the time of this "insult," it should be noted that Latrell Sprewell was thirty-five years old, which meant that he would be "earning" the last of that money as a thirty-nine-year-old.

What?! How does something like this happen? It's way too easy to put it all on Sprewell. Call this an aberration if you want, but that is not the case. Latrell Sprewell merely embodies a general sense of entitlement prevalent in the NBA and throughout professional sports. You can look at the sports news on almost any day and find situations and comments that would never have occurred twenty or thirty years ago. These issues are not endemic to any one sport, or race, or nationality. They flow directly from a sudden and unnatural infusion of money into the human body.

During spring training for the 2006 baseball season, Alfonso Soriano of the Washington Nationals baseball team refused to go into a game as the left fielder instead of his normal second-base position. Soriano did this despite the fact that his manager was Frank Robinson, one the greatest players of his time. His time, however, was not this time. Robinson was (and I assume is still) a very competitive, proud, and, sometimes combative man. I could only wonder, even at his age, what was going through his mind that day. He would probably have liked to take Soriano "out back," but you can't do it that way anymore. And by the way, Alfonso Soriano "earned" over $10 million per year. Left field, my ass.

Back in the NBA, the year 2005 saw a relatively new and unusual development among players and their agents. When the Houston Rockets traded (or thought they had traded) Jim Jackson to New Orleans Oklahoma City Hornets, Jackson refused to report to his new team. In 1970 baseball player Curt Flood had refused to report to his new team when he had been traded. He was taking a stand and challenging baseball tradition. However, this was not a Curt Flood-type incident.

Alonzo Mourning, who had incredibly just signed a five-year contract with the New Jersey Nets worth $25 million, was traded to the Toronto Raptors for Vince Carter. I say "incredibly" not because of any lack of ability on the part of Mourning, but because he had a kidney transplant only the year before. The Nets' signing of him was a very strong show of support to say the least and was in part the idea of the Nets star point guard, Jason Kidd. Mourning's gratitude for this gesture was to refuse to report to Toronto. Mourning wanted to keep the $25 million, but not in Toronto. He wanted to make his deposits in Miami. So he never went to Toronto. His punishment for this behavior was that he now had to earn his $25 million with the Miami Heat. There were strong indications that the Nets paid a large part of that salary as part of the conditions of the Toronto trade. As of this printing, Jason Kidd has paid none of that salary.

Jim Jackson avoided the Hornets completely and ended up exactly where he wanted to be, in Phoenix playing for a fifty-plus win team and in the playoffs.

Hey, if the teams and league let players do it, then you have to try. This has actually now become part of my job. If I don't try to get away with this in the future, my players will find someone who will.

The roots of these types of situations are not a mystery to me. You don't need to be Sherlock Holmes to figure this out. Money is at the core of it all, specifically, too much money. Common sense should tell you that once any person has significant sums of money at his disposal, he doesn't have to do anything. In essence, the league has bankrolled the players into a position of power. Therefore, the league literally has to ask if their employees will acquiesce and play in a particular city. Heaven forbid requesting a player to go all the way out to left field, somewhere they don't want to go or do something they don't want to do. Whereas players of previous eras had to work second jobs to literally "feed their families," that era is long gone, and it is a good thing, too.

Don't get me wrong—today's players deserve to be paid. They work incredibly hard. They work on their games and their conditioning year round now. They are able to do this because, unlike their predecessors, today's players don't have to get second jobs. They have money in the bank. The benefits of this development are obviously better conditioned players and great athletes. These sums of money are not just given to them. It is not the lottery. However, like many other slices of our culture, the salaries given to athletes today are like a pendulum. That pendulum has apparently swung too far, and the salaries bear no resemblance to reality.

Both of my parents were born and raised in Brooklyn. My mother was an avid Brooklyn Dodgers fan. She would tell us that as she walked around her neighborhood, she would see Duke Snider in the candy store, or Jackie Robinson at the supermarket, or Pee Wee Reese at the cleaners. They were quite literally part of the community.

Today, obviously, this is not the case. Professional athletes are cloistered away, surrounded by their families, agents, publicists, business managers, personal assistants, drivers, and, in many cases, people from their past who are just hoping for some kind of title to justify their presence. Which of these people being "fed" by the player do you think is going to tell him about reality?

On March 23, 2006, Alfonso Soriano entered left field after all—the day after his refusal. I will interpret this for you at no extra charge. Some of the aforementioned enablers around Soriano—his agent, probably the players' union, and Soriano himself—realized that his salary was in jeopardy. The Washington Nationals made it plain that they were going to put him on the suspended list, which would not "enable" him to be paid. This seems logical and simple to me and to most people. However, this is not always the way it works.

Players have been stretching the boundaries of tolerable behavior for years, and management has, for the most part, caved. They caved first on the salaries, and this, in turn, has empowered the players to engage in behaviors and attitudes that no industry, business, or school should tolerate. In the instance of Soriano and the Nationals and in others, management is finally learning to say enough. The Philadelphia Eagles said it in 2005 with regard to Terrell Owens. In that instance, however, it took probably an erroneous arbitration ruling to uphold the Eagles' contentions.

Is it possible to stand up for what appears to the rest of society to be common sense? There should be standards of conduct. I'm not talking ethics and justice. It's about the money. Unfortunately, if Alfonso Soriano was sent home without his $10 million, that would have been considered unacceptable . . . to him.

As for Sprewell's comments and the reactions that followed, I look at them with a sense of hope. In 2006, Latrell Sprewell was unemployed. His rejection of that $32 million offer put him and his now ex-agent in a position where the best he can do financially is receive an NBA minimum for the rest of the 2005–2006 season. The fact that the minimum is over $1 million would ease that pain for most people. But it doesn't mean that we shouldn't have concern for his family.

Let's look at Sprewell's history to understand how this could have happened. He was the twenty-fifth draft pick in 1992—a six foot five inch shooting guard out of the University of Alabama. He had a very good professional career. "Spree" achieved more than most of us thought he would. He made NBA All-Star games and clearly was one of the best players at his position in the league. He had a certain reputation as well. Most of that reputation, however, centered around his temper.

This trait of his brought him to the general public's consciousness on December 1, 1997. During a practice with his team, the Golden State Warriors, Coach P. J. Carlesimo was instructing his team, which coaches do. It's actually in their contract. On this occasion, P. J. was demanding that Sprewell put more on his passes.

Sprewell basically informed his coach that he wasn't in the mood for his demands and told him to keep his distance. P. J. didn't. Sprewell threatened to kill Carlesimo and then grabbed his coach by the throat and pulled him to the ground. Witnesses said that Sprewell had his hands on his coach's throat for ten to fifteen seconds before other players could drag him off. It should have ended there, but Sprewell returned some twenty minutes later to continue his assault. He allegedly threw a punch at Carlesimo, which grazed the coach. Sprewell was again dragged out of the practice.

As over-the-top and incredible as this incident appears, there were signs of trouble before and after December 1, 1997. In 1994, Sprewell's daughter Page, who was four at the time, was attacked by one of Sprewell's pit bulls. Her ear was severed in the attack. Sprewell waited until the last possible day before having the dog put down. Sprewell, when questioned about his reaction to the incident, said "Stuff happens."

In 1995, Sprewell was involved in a fight with teammate Jerome Kersey, after which he returned to practice (sound familiar?), with a two-by-four and reportedly then threatened to come back again, with a gun.

In 1998, Latrell Sprewell served three months of house arrest for a reckless driving incident in California. In that incident, he allegedly forced another driver off the road.

Regardless of the details of the choking incident, that was an unheard-of occurrence, even in the NBA. You just don't choke your coach, or so I thought at the time. My initial instinct was that Sprewell would probably never play in the NBA again. I thought that the coaching and NBA community would rally around Carlesimo. I was ten years or so into the business, and now I'm amazed at how naïve I was.

There was rallying. It was around Sprewell! I specifically remember one of my colleagues/competitors, Arn Tellem, at the press conference with Sprewell. Tellem was Sprewell's agent at the time of the incident. My first thought was, *How do you defend this?* The National Basketball Players Association (NBPA) joined the fray as well. The league had suspended Sprewell for eighty-two games, and his agent and his union were fighting it. That was their job, and they did it well. An arbitrator later reduced the suspension to sixty-eight games.

I thought that the suspension was the least of their problems. When he tried to return the following season, who would sign him? What coach would want to have him? What general manager would want to subject his coach to that potential problem? What owner would want to have that image projected for his franchise? Hey, how about the Knicks?

During Sprewell's suspension, New York Knicks President Dave Checketts and Head Coach Jeff Van Gundy flew to Milwaukee to meet with Sprewell. These are men, by the way, for whom I have a good deal of respect. After spending an afternoon with him, the Knicks decided that he was a terrific guy and signed him. What always struck me as the saddest part of the whole incident was that upon his entrance into his first game at Madison Square Garden, Sprewell received a standing ovation from the 19,500 fans in attendance. An ovation that a local guy named P. J. Carlesimo could only dream of—what a disgrace.

Spree played very well in New York and attacked no one that I'm aware of. In 2000, he was subsequently rewarded with an extension of his contract by the Knicks. The total amount of the extension was for $62 million for five years, all guaranteed. When you get on the bad side in the NBA, watch out!

In his own feeble attempt at a defense for his attack on Carlesimo, Sprewell told *60 Minutes*, "I wasn't choking P. J. that hard. I mean, he could breathe." With that brilliant defense, I'm surprised in a way that P. J. wasn't suspended for getting his neck in the way of Sprewell's hands.

On October 2, 2002, it was the Knicks' turn. Sprewell reported to training camp with a broken hand. He had not informed the Knicks of the injury. He claimed that he broke it falling on his yacht. New York fined him $250,000 for not reporting the injury. Interestingly, they also banned him from using their practice facility. After the *New York Post* suggested that Sprewell may have injured his hand while fighting, Sprewell sued the paper for $40 million.

Spree was traded to the Minnesota Timberwolves in July of 2003. On his return to Madison Square Garden, Spree gave the faithful fans of New York one last display of inappropriate conduct. The background on this one was that the owner of the Knicks, James Dolan, had come out publicly to say that Spree had in essence been banished because the Knicks were interested in the character of their players. Spree took this comment as a personal affront. James Dolan, as he always does, sat on the floor, under the basket almost adjacent to the Knicks' bench. Spree turned the evening into a personal vendetta and attack on Dolan. His language was expletive-laced to say the least. Dolan simply had to take it. I did some work for Lon Kruger, who was the coach of the Atlanta Hawks and is, as of this writing, the head coach at UNLV. On this night, he was an assistant coach with the New York Knicks. Since none of the players intervened in any way on behalf of the man who signed their inflated paychecks, Lon had the temerity to confront Sprewell.

"Hey Spree, knock it off; just play." That is what Lon told me he said. Sounds reasonable to me. The result of that comment served only to have Sprewell shift his vulgarities toward Lon. The rest of the night Lon had to deal with F-this and F-that. I remember the following day reading comments from Isiah Thomas, the Knicks' newly minted GM, about how unacceptable the behavior of his own team was. He was referring to the fact that Lon was the only one to stand up in any way on the owner's behalf.

About a month later, Lon and I had dinner with our wives across the street from the Garden. The Knicks were playing that night. We walked across the street to go to the game. It was about 5:30 p.m. with the tip-off at 7:30 p.m. At 5:45 p.m., Lon emerged from the locker room and asked if we wanted to go out for dessert. He had just been fired.

With this as a history of Latrell Sprewell's dealings with the league, it is a lot easier to understand how a thirty-five-year-old player who had already received close to $100 million in income, between his NBA contracts and shoe deals alone, could say and believe that there was more out there. Someone would come to his aid as they always seemed to do. This time there was no Tellem—he had been terminated, and no team was willing to back him up. The only thing that stopped his sense of entitlement was time. His age precluded another team from proving him right again. I am extremely confident in saying that if he was, let's say, even thirty years old, the line of NBA teams waiting to sign him would have been out the door. In today's world, it doesn't matter what you do. It doesn't matter what you say. It doesn't matter how much you insult our intelligence. The bottom line is: If you can play, you get paid. You don't need to look far for verification of that concept. Does Terrell Owens ring a bell?

The list of NBA players alone who have either been arrested, charged, and even convicted of offenses is extensive. Yet it is obvious that as long as a team thinks a player can make a contribution on the floor, they will sign him. The sound of general managers speaking as legal correspondents echo in everyone's ears every season. The tired refrain that the arrested players are only accused and not convicted is more of an excuse to retain them than an ode to the law. There is little regard in the ignoring of these transgressions for the effect on team chemistry and, more important, on the effect that these constant second, third, and fourth chances have on the public and our children. The message is clear. As long as a player can shoot it, or rebound it, or block it, the league will give him another look. It is also obvious that the better players can get away with more.

In the early 1990s, I represented Marlon Maxey of the Minnesota Timberwolves. Marlon was a six-ten power forward and was a rookie in 1992. Marlon got in trouble with the Minnesota police for having a gun in his trunk. He was suspended for this. He was very confused and told me that he didn't understand the suspension. His reasoning was typical of the thought process in the NBA. He informed me that Scottie Pippen had the same thing happen to him, and he wasn't suspended. It was my job to inform him that Scottie Pippen was a better player than him. The public's reaction to the Spree statement about feeding his family was predictable and widespread. It was treated mainly as a joke, and in fairness to him, was hopefully meant in that vein. However, it also became the ruler for measuring how far the disconnect between the players and the fans who paid to watch them play had grown. When they arrive in the NBA, players don't suddenly appear before our eyes as defined people with defined personalities. Athletes in general, however, have always—for whatever reason—been treated differently. By virtue of their abilities or sheer size, they have been given extra opportunities and myriad chances. They have received grades they didn't deserve, fame and glory that was disproportionate to the results attained, and, in my case and many others, dated women we otherwise never would.

I don't pretend to have known Latrell Sprewell in his formative years, but I did meet up with players and people who illustrate for all of us how this system of extra benefits works during my travels in this business of basketball. These people also demonstrate how this system can destroy our culture, and I don't just mean in the NBA.

TWO

I'M BICOASTAL—
NOT THAT THERE'S ANYTHING
WRONG WITH THAT

When I was a kid, my brother, Brent, and I would religiously watch *The Twilight Zone; Championship Wrestling* with Haystacks Calhoun, Killer Kowalski, and so on; and *The Adventures of Ozzie and Harriet.* In 1964, however, there began an annual series featuring the UCLA basketball team, starring then coach John Wooden. This series started innocently enough but developed into a ritual, the likes of which had never been seen in college basketball. From 1964 through 1975, UCLA won an unprecedented ten NCAA championships. Believe me, it will never happen again. For instance, Duke has named the basketball court after the wife of coach Mike Krzyzewski, and there is an area where they play around Cameron Indoor Stadium called Krzyzewskiville. Impressive. But Duke has only won three titles.

Brent and I grew to really resent John Wooden and his teams. Coach Wooden didn't even look like a coach. He looked like a teacher, and from 3,000 miles away, it seemed as if he had reduced our game to just another classroom. The players seemed almost mechanical. Where was the passion? Where was the excitement?

We also were suffering from a severe case of regionalism. As kids we played basketball on the asphalt playground courts of Long Island and in the mountains of Pennsylvania during the summers. We in New York felt that basketball was our game. A city game. Clearly an eastern-part-of-the-country game. Coach Wooden and his Bruins were quickly destroying that foundation. It was bad enough in 1964 and 1965, but when they had the nerve to then come to New York City and recruit away possibly the best prospect in the history of the city, Lew Alcindor (who later changed his name to Kareem Abdul-Jabbar), well, that was the last straw.

Year after year that scholarly man with the glasses would make his way up to a hastily constructed podium to receive the NCAA championship trophy. He also would be given a box and would shake hands with whomever while receiving it. Brent and I always asked each other what the hell was in that little box.

The years between 1964 and 1975 also saw me grow from a thirteen-year-old kid to a twenty-four-year-old man. I managed to avoid the Vietnam War by receiving a very low draft number: 337. Women and children were called to serve before a guy with the number 337. I later found out that I would only be pressed into action if the Vietnamese were on the Throgs Neck Bridge. Fast-forward to 1975, during Coach Wooden's final run, when I found myself in, of all places, Los Angeles, California. I was enrolled at the University of San Fernando Valley College of Law, to which I arrived after driving across the country in my Chevy Vega station wagon. The law school was situated in between an apartment house and an Earl Scheib auto painting store. In other words, no campus. It was basically the last hope for guys like me who had too much fun in college. People ask me why I went all that way to go to a law school that was accredited only in California. The answer was simple: It was the only one that would take me. My applications to other bigger, better, and actually legitimate law schools were met with a variety of reactions, from hilarity to disgust. Not only was I summarily rejected from those schools, but I think one of them sent back my application fee. So off to California I went.

I settled into a mobile-home park in Northridge, which years later became the epicenter of the catastrophic Northridge earthquake. I was the youngest resident of Northridge Park by about sixty-three years. They were great people out there, and they sort of adopted me. I got cakes every week from the female residents of the park and played poker with six eighty-something guys who I am still convinced let me win to help me through law school.

My best friend was Bill Richter, who was eighty-six and was known as the park Don Juan. One of my first cases was to defend Bill against being thrown out of the park on a sexual harassment charge. During a park social, Bill, who was happily married to Myrt, asked a female neighbor to dance. All was well until Bill told his partner, "Honey, don't worry if you feel something hard down there; it's my pipe." Bill and I also got to watch UCLA every Thursday and Saturday as they played in the Pac-10 Conference.

As in some other years for Coach Wooden and his UCLA Bruins, they were not supposed to win it all in 1975, but they did. They beat Louisville and Kentucky in the Final Four, and Coach Wooden announced his retirement before the final game against Kentucky. Three months later, I was offered a job working at Coach Wooden's summer basketball camp in Thousand Oaks. Coach Wooden ran six weeks of camp and had three hundred kids every week. I was a coach at the camp for $150 per week. I had experience in camping, having worked for seven years at Camp Keeyumah in the Poconos, but a phone call from Larry Brown clearly helped get me the job as a coach.

Anyone reading this last sentence must be asking, "How or why is NBA Hall of Fame coach Larry Brown calling John Wooden on behalf of a law student living in a mobile home in the San Fernando Valley?" Some family history will help. In the late 1950s, Larry Brown worked at Camp Keeyumah in the Poconos. Larry had the prestigious position of camper/waiter. He also got to play basketball. In later years, he was promoted to counselor. It was in this capacity that he would change our family. One of Larry's campers was my brother, Brent. Brent was then about ten years old. Larry was seventeen, and I was six and back in New York. Brent was a good athlete, but not great. He was, however, the hardest worker in the entire camp. (Just as a show of brotherly pride, today, Brent is the director of the Smithsonian Institution's National Museum of American History in Washington, D.C. He apparently got the bulk of the brains.) Brent would do whatever you asked of him. In other words, he would try. Suffice it to say that Brent became Larry's favorite camper, and when they both returned home to Long Island, Brent was miserable. He missed all of his friends, but he missed Larry the most. My parents arranged for Larry, who lived in Long Beach, to come for dinner. He never left. From my perspective as a six-year-old living in Lynbrook, all I knew was that there were three in our room now, and I had to sleep on the cot whenever Larry was "home." I didn't even know we had a cot!

At that time, Larry was about to embark on his collegiate days at the University of North Carolina. My parents had no idea that Larry was a great basketball player. They were not basketball people. They were quite simply the best parents and caring people that ever lived. They cared about Brent; my little sister, Jodi; and me. Now they cared about Larry as well. Just to illustrate this arrangement a bit further, Larry was not the only counselor that Brent brought home. Mike Huberman also became an integral part of our family as well, and he and his family still are. Not as famous as Larry would become, but "family" nonetheless. In our house, if you wanted in, it wasn't too hard.

I was still a few years away from being allowed to go to Keeyumah with Brent, Larry, and Mike. When I finally got there, I was a little different than Brent in my approach to Larry. I had more talent, and the games came easier for me. I also never looked at Larry the same way others did at Keeyumah. By the time I got there, Larry could do no wrong. He was like a god. To me, he was another older brother, nothing more than that. I remember that it was actually an honor to be able to sit with Brent's group at dinner because you got to eat with Larry. I was given this honor even though I didn't apply. At Larry's table, as on Larry's teams when he's coaching, you had to do things "the right way." One of the rules was that everybody had to eat their vegetables—not fresh vegetables, but overcooked canned vegetables as anyone who has ever attended a sleepaway camp will attest to. I didn't like them, and I had no intention of eating them simply because I found myself in a chair at Larry Brown's table. The solution was simple to me. Being only eight and having very little power to speak of, I lied. On the spot, I concocted the tale that I was allergic to vegetables, and whereas I would eat them, it would be on Larry's head when I died. I was excused from eating anything I didn't like for the next four weeks.

It was a glorious four weeks sitting there and watching Brent and all of his friends struggling with their peas, carrots, and lima beans. I say four weeks even though we were there for eight weeks. The only flaw in my plan was that I did not factor in parents' visiting day. Larry apologized to my father for even attempting to make me eat my peas due to my allergies. The scam was over. Larry didn't take it well either. The day after visiting day, I was physically accosted by Larry, Mike, Brent, and others. Shaving cream was applied to my body in massive quantities. This was in approximately 1959, and I finally got all of the shaving cream out sometime in early 1993.

Apparently, Larry got over this incident because sixteen years later, I found myself working at Coach John Wooden's basketball camp in Malibu, California. Just being around Coach Wooden was bizarre. I actually was feeling some guilt due to the dark thoughts I had about him way back when, but I figured I could always lay those off on Brent. It was during the first week that I noticed that one particular guy spent the most time with Coach—the commissioner of the camp. He was in charge of the counselors, but one of his duties was to pick up Coach and drive him back to his town house in Encino. The job was a step below mine and paid only $75 per week, but that was the job I wanted. During the next five weeks, I managed to get myself demoted to commissioner and off we went.

Spending two hours a day with John Wooden in my Chevy Vega station wagon was one of the greatest experiences of my life. Once I got past the 5:30 a.m. pickup time, I was fine. At 5:30 a.m., Coach Wooden had already walked his five miles and was in a great mood. "Good morning, young man," he used to say. I did not always share a similar disposition at that time of the morning, and occasionally, I would be picking him up straight off the night before, if you know what I mean. He would just laugh at me and enjoy my crabbiness.

For those five weeks, I basically became a sponge. I asked him every question I could think of. And he answered them all. Occasionally, he would get upset with me, and once, when discussing the Vietnam War, he proclaimed angrily that I had a little too much Bill Walton in me. Bill, besides being one of the greatest college basketball players ever, was known to be extremely inquisitive by nature. Coach Wooden told me on one of our rides to camp that the only difference between coaching Bill and his other great center Lew Alcindor was a subtle one. When he told Lewis to do something, he just did it. But when he told Bill the same thing, Bill would do it as well, but he needed to know why.

Coach Wooden and I discussed everything from his disdain for facial hair to family and, of course, some basketball. I found him to be the most interesting person I had met. A truly great man, not just a great coach. Coach Wooden would polish the water fountains and remove the chewed gum that the campers would spit out. He believed that you should leave a place a little bit cleaner than you found it. He had time for everyone. He was hands-on at his camp. He wasn't just collecting a check. At the end of each week's session, Coach would give a talk to close the camp. He would always challenge the parents as well as the kids. He would remind the parents of their responsibility to set good examples. He always finished with an admonition to the parents that came in the form of his reciting a poem by rote. I even remember some of it.

A careful man I want to be
A little fellow follows me.
I do not dare to go astray
For fear he'll go the self-same way.

Like me he says he wants to be
This little guy that follows me.

I do not once escape his eyes
Whatever he sees me do he tries.

I came to understand that my perceptions of him and his teams were wrong. That lack of emotion I perceived on Long Island was really discipline. The seemingly mechanical nature of the winning was due to practice and preparation. To quote another of his favorite poems, "How to Be a Champion" by legendary sportswriter Grantland Rice, "Most of it is practice, and the rest of it is work." One of my biggest honors was when Coach Wooden invited me into to his home in the San Fernando Valley. He asked me only that I not divulge anything that I saw there. He trusted me, and it was, I think, well placed. I never talked about what was inside, and I won't now either.

The world as we know it is full of mysteries and wonders. Moses parted the Red Sea, the 1969 Mets won the World Series, and in 1978, I graduated from law school.

I passed the bar exam and was sworn in May 1979. I opened my own practice immediately. I had a small office in my house—I was out of the trailer park, much to the chagrin of my neighbors—and I literally took any case I could get. I did divorce cases (an ominous precursor for my own marital configurations), wills, accident cases—anything and everything. Coincidentally in 1979, the head coach at UCLA, Gary Cunningham, resigned his position. UCLA, through legendary Athletic Director J. D. Morgan, hired Larry.

So how did Larry go from sleeping in my bedroom to becoming the head coach of UCLA? Well, after winning a gold medal in the 1964 Olympics, Larry became an assistant coach at North Carolina. My father, who was building discount stores at the time, got Larry a contract with the New Orleans Buccaneers in the American Basketball Association in 1967. Remember the ABA with the red, white, and blue basketballs? Larry went on to play for the Oakland Oaks, Washington Caps, Virginia Squires, and Denver Nuggets, where he ended his career. He then started his head coaching career in 1972 with the Carolina Cougars in the ABA, moving to the Denver Nuggets in 1974. When the ABA and the NBA merged, Larry became an NBA coach with Denver, where he was before moving to UCLA. He then moved on the the New Jersey Nets, the University of Kansas, the San Antonio Spurs, the L.A. Clippers, the Indiana Pacers, the Philadelphia 76ers, the Detroit Pistons, and the New York Knicks. More on that later . . . believe me!

I picked Larry up at the airport and drove him to Mr. Morgan's house in the Valley. They finalized the deal with help from my father, who by this time had become Larry's advisor on all business decisions, as well as his surrogate father, and Larry became the new head coach at UCLA. My father isn't a lawyer, but he thinks he is, and I haven't had the heart to tell him. With a sudden influx of free T-shirts and warm-ups, Brent and I started to soften our opposition toward the Bruins. Now they were all right. My family was constantly having to adjust our loyalties to whichever team Larry happened to be coaching in a particular year. Once we learned who was on which of his teams, we were fine.

Larry started at UCLA with his usual dose of enthusiasm and dedication. I was happy to be pursuing clients and the law. I was also always coaching kids in the recreation leagues of L.A., to preserve my sanity and enjoy myself. I loved it.

During a law school basketball league game one Tuesday night, I came down with a rare rebound and felt something strange in my lower back. I actually spent the next seventeen years fighting off surgery to repair a herniated disk, which I finally surrendered to in 1996. I can hear the concern, but thank you, I'm fine.

In September 1979, I was informed by a surgeon in California that I needed to have at least ten days of bed rest. No getting out of bed for anything—flat on my back for the ten days. This was bad enough, but at the time, my real fear centered around the fact that I was married to my now ex-wife. Nice person, but not exactly a speed demon. If she were added to the race between the tortoise and the hare, she would get the bronze medal if you know what I mean. A sandwich was out of the question, and I couldn't even count on the occasional glass of water. My solution was simple and obvious—pack up my firstborn, Sami, who was a year old and run home to my mother in New York. It was really a good decision, as the ten days unfortunately turned into twenty.

Around day nineteen or so, I received a phone call from Larry in L.A. He asked me to do him a favor. He made it sound like he needed a ride to the airport or something. To my shock, he offered me the assistant's job at UCLA. I was taken aback and flattered at the same time. I knew that this had a lot to do with Larry's respect for my father, but I also felt that Larry must have had at least some respect for me as well. To Larry's shock and mine, I turned him down. I had worked too hard, and it was too miraculous that I had become a lawyer in the first place. I was just really getting into what I thought would be that adult phase of my life, and I didn't want to go back. Larry called again. I said no again, at which point my dad came upstairs to talk it over. I was surprised that he wanted me to take the offer since I knew that he was proud of the fact that I had become a lawyer. He reasoned that this was really a once in a lifetime thing and that the next time Larry called, I would say that I would love to accept, so I did. I cut short my bed rest by a day or two and went "home" to Los Angeles. There was, however, one piece of negotiating left to do with Larry. I knew there was a junior varsity (JV) team at UCLA, and I wanted to coach it. Despite my lofty legal aspirations, coaching was what I did best. Even though I was thrilled to be an assistant with the big team, I knew Larry well enough to know that would be his baby. I wanted my own.

On October 18, 1979, three days after practice had begun, I walked in to Pauley Pavilion to begin my job as both JV head coach and assistant coach to Larry Brown with the varsity. I don't get awestruck because I have met many famous people and have been around them all my life, but I have to admit to feeling awestruck the first time I entered Pauley Pavilion as an actual employee. It's one thing to go to a game there, but it was hard for me to comprehend the fact that I now belonged there. Naturally, I thought first of Coach Wooden and then of all the great teams and players that had made this building the shrine of college basketball.

I was given some equipment by one of the eight managers and shown to my locker room. I immediately noticed that the shorts and golf shirt that said "UCLA Basketball" could have been traded at Keeyumah for an entire camp wardrobe. After getting changed and heading out to the court, I was met by an older gentleman named Mr. Ducky Drake, the head trainer. He was, at the time, about seventy-five. He was also almost as big a legend at UCLA as Coach Wooden. He had been there for fifty-three years—since 1926. He was the track coach not only at UCLA but also at the 1960 Rome Olympics where he coached Rafer Johnson and C. K. Yang to the gold and silver medals in the most stirring decathlon competition in Olympic history. The track stadium was named after him. He was the trainer on all ten of Coach Wooden's championship teams.

When I first met the legendary Ducky Drake, I was a little bit unnerved. I said "hello," and Mr. Drake noticed the metal back brace that I was wearing. He felt around back there and immediately proclaimed in a gruff and direct way that I was to remove it at once. I tried to explain that I had just spent almost twenty days in bed, and I didn't exactly want to do it again anytime soon. He was unimpressed and off came the brace. He then instructed me to lay on the floor of Pauley Pavilion, so he could crack my back and stretch me out. It actually helped, and Mr. Drake said that I was not to wear it again in his presence. I didn't. He said as nicely as he could that my real problem was that I was lazy and needed to stretch every day. I know you won't believe it, but I had very few problems with my back after that little episode, at least for the time while I wasn't lazy.

It was a strange way to meet the person to whom I would become closest at UCLA. Ducky was so interesting to me. For example, when I first visited him in his office at the training facility, I noticed that in spite of all his accomplishments and honors, the walls of the office were bare except for two unframed black-and-white 8 × 10 photos. One was a picture of a man with a big bulbous nose and a hat on his head. Ducky explained that the man in the photograph was his high school coach. I guess the fact that some sixty years had passed wasn't the point. The respect he held for this man who had taught him exactly what he needed to know was incredible.

The other picture was of a broad jumper laying face down in the sand, covering his face in horror. When I asked Ducky what this was doing as the other half of his collection, he responded that he had been coaching this young man in the broad jump in the Olympics and that had been his final jump. He had instructed the young man not to foul, and he fouled. I said, "That's great, Duck, but why is it up there?" He replied, "I keep it there to remind myself always to listen."

I hung out with Ducky as much as I could, and I listened. To me, it was like being best friends with the library. He was a fountain of knowledge and not just about sports. We had fun together. I recall one time when we were asked to both speak at one of the sororities on campus. He didn't want to go, but I told him I wasn't going if he wasn't. He begrudgingly went but on the condition that we leave quickly. I agreed. About an hour or so later, I went to get Mr. Drake and take him home. I found him surrounded by about a dozen UCLA sorority girls, and when I said to him that it was time to go, he waived me away and said, "I'll get a ride."

Every player or coach who ever had the honor of working with or for Mr. Drake has his own stories. My favorite occurred during my first year and involved two players who were freshman at the time and whom I ended up representing during their pro careers, Michael Holton and "Rocket" Rod Foster. They were roommates, and we had just beaten the University of Arizona by one point at the buzzer. Michael decided to take the opposing coach's daughter out after the game. He also ended up breaking curfew. It just so happened that Ducky was in his bed-checking mode that night.

He went to Michael and Rod's room, banged on the door, and when Rod answered, Ducky asked where Michael was. Rod lied and said he was in the bathroom. Rod was quick only on the court, apparently. Ducky marched into the bathroom, checked, and told Rod that he didn't blame him for lying to protect his teammate. Ducky then proceeded calmly to take off his shoes and go to sleep in Michael's bed. Michael returned an hour later and was faced with the horrifying discovery of Mr. Drake asleep in his bed. His decision now was to either be later than he already was or to wake up Mr. Drake. He decided on choice C, which was to call Coach

Glass. I said that he was on his own with this one. He woke up Ducky, and Mr. Drake just calmly got out of his bed, put on his shoes, and went back to his room. Michael was now in a state of panic. He called me again and said that I had to speak to Mr. Drake for him. He said Ducky wouldn't even speak to him and that if Larry found out, he knew that he was finished.

I called Ducky and said, "Duck why won't you just talk to Michael?"

Ducky said, "Let him think about it!" and hung up the phone.

Ducky never did say a word to Larry, and Michael Holton not only started the next game against Arizona State, but also every game for the rest of the year. He never broke curfew again. Today, Michael is the head coach at the University of Portland. I represented him for his entire nine-year career in the NBA.

When I began this adventure, it was never clearly laid out for me what my actual job description was. I sort of just figured it out as we went along. I was the head JV coach, and that was what I was most excited about. I was also at varsity practice and was beginning to understand that recruiting was also going to be a major part of the job.

Our first road trip was in December 1979 to South Bend, Indiana, to play the Fighting Irish of Notre Dame. It was at Notre Dame that Coach Wooden's and UCLA's eighty-eight-game winning streak was stopped. Try for a moment to understand the preceding sentence. That is not a typo. The UCLA Bruins won eighty-eight consecutive games over a three-year period. It's a mind-blowing achievement, and one sentence isn't enough.

Larry Farmer and Kevin O'Connor were two of the assistants with me. Farms, O'Connor, and I became very close. They were both extremely knowledgeable and very helpful to me. Farms was a big part of those teams, and he, in fact, told me that during his playing days under Coach Wooden, his teams were 89–1, with the only loss being at Notre Dame. Farms also added that if Sidney Wicks had played any defense, they would have been 90–0. As Farms always used to joke, "We were 89–1, and I had no help!"

This was quite an experience for a kid from Long Island. I had made up my mind that even though I basically had no business being there, I was going to enjoy the experience. I mean, two months earlier, I was studying to pass the bar exam and living in a trailer in the San Fernando Valley. Basically, I enjoyed anything and everything I could. I went to the Notre Dame pep rallies; I walked the campus and saw "Touchdown Jesus" looking over the football stadium. I was thrilled when we came out for warm-ups and were roundly booed and had toilet paper thrown at us. It was fun. I always knew no matter where I ever played that this kind of reaction wasn't hatred; it was respect. Why else would people get so excited if we weren't a threat? Larry actually looked at me right before the game, and seeing my joy, said, "You love this, don't you?" When I said, "You bet I do," he asked me to pass it along to our freshman players because they were scared to death.

The game itself proved to be an ugly encounter. Our first five that afternoon were Kiki Vandeweghe and James Wilkes at forward, Tyren Naulls and Tony Anderson at guard, and Gig Sims and Darrell Allums sharing the middle. This was our initial starting group, as Larry wanted to give as many seniors an opportunity as possible. This wouldn't last, but he tried. One by one they played their way out of the lineup, some never to return to active duty.

Notre Dame lined up with Kelly Tripucka and Tracey Jackson at forward (both of whom I would later represent for some time), Rich Branning and John Paxson at guard and Orlando Woolridge at center. It was a close game that was marred at the very end by an incident involving Wilkes, Tripucka, and Notre Dame's coach Digger Phelps. With about two minutes left, down at the far end from where we were sitting, all I saw was Tripucka go down in a heap. The play happened right in front of Digger. He saw the whole thing. It wasn't until we saw the films that we saw what really happened. The ref had smashed Kelly in the mouth in the act of signaling for a time-out. As ridiculous as that sounds, the camera doesn't lie. Digger, even though he saw the incident, used it to accuse James Wilkes of fouling Tripucka. He was flailing around pointing at

James and getting the crowd crazed. The rest of the night was difficult for us, and the crowd became really ugly. We were all more than a little pissed with Digger from then on.

The team headed back to L.A. without me. I was to embark on my first recruiting trip. It would, by the way, be the last one I would overpack for. I took four bags for a ten-day trip, and Kevin O'Connor was nice enough to take three of them back to L.A. for me, right after he stopped laughing. Travel light became my mantra while in recruiting mode. My trip was an ambitious one, and I was ready. I would see Sam Perkins in Albany, New York; Melvin Turpin at Fork Union, Virginia; Sam Bowie in Kentucky; Kenny Perry outside of Chicago, Illinois; Derek Harper in Florida, Earl Jones in Washington, D.C.; and last but certainly not least, Gary Springer of Benjamin Franklin High School in East Harlem, New York.

Ben Franklin was the number-one-rated high school team in New York City and ranked in the top ten in the country, and Gary Springer was supposedly their best player. He was a six-seven small forward who could really play, according to the reports I had. They were undefeated and coached by a thirty-three-year-old guy named Stan Dinner, who was quite a character. Coach Dinner, or "Dinner" as he was disrespectfully referred to by both players and students, also owned a fairly successful deli in Manhattan. The journey from Coach Wooden to Coach Dinner cannot be measured in miles alone, but I will try.

I arrived at LaGuardia airport in the afternoon and, being a former cab driver, I realized that to recruit a kid from Ben Franklin, there was no way around Harlem. I had, or so I thought, arranged with Coach Dinner to meet with him and Gary at the school. They had a game that night at St. John's in Queens. When I entered the imposing colonnaded building on East 116th Street, I saw a student, and I asked him if he knew where I could find Coach Dinner. He said "I don't know where the hell Dinner is; what the hell are you asking me for?" Little did I realize that this would be the winner of the congeniality award at Ben Franklin High School.

After about twenty minutes, I found Coach Dinner. I introduced myself, all prepped out with my tie and jacket, and Dinner said "Oh shit, I forgot you were coming."

Let me just break here. Throughout the writing of this book, I'm trying to avoid expletives. I want my children to be able to read this. However, to tell this story, I've got to give you the flavor. Therefore, anytime you see *F*, do me a favor, and use your imagination.

Dinner started right in. "I don't know where my *F*-ing kids are. I haven't seen my *F*-ing kids all day." I found that interesting because they were supposed to be in school. "I don't know where the *F* Springer is. Let's go down to the *F*-ing principal's office to try and find *F*-ing Springer." You get the point. This went on and on. The principal had no idea; the people in the guidance office hadn't seen him. If I didn't know better, I would have thought this was all a big joke at my expense. Dinner told me to sit down with the "*F*-ing guidance counselors" for a little while, so he could find "*F*-ing Springer." Forty-five minutes later, as I was trying to talk about academics at UCLA, Dinner burst back into the room and said ". . . you got an *F*-ing rental car? I found my *F*-ing kids." We headed out the front door of Ben Franklin with Dinner mumbling "if I ain't the *F*-ing White Shadow, no one is."

He still hadn't told me where the *F* (excuse me) we were going. We drove a few short blocks to 119th Street and started up the steps of the 25th precinct police station. There were three twelve-year-olds on the steps, and when they saw the esteemed coach of the number-one-ranked team in America, they started laughing and said, "Hey man, hey Dinner, they got your Franklin boys in there." Dinner shot back with a no look *F*-you and we entered. The desk sergeant recognized Dinner, and the coach diplomatically asked, "Where's my *F*-ing kids?" The sergeant replied that he had them all in a holding cell. It was then that it started to dawn on me that his whole team was in there.

Dinner requested that he be given the forms to sign the kids out of jail. I mean, after all, they had a game that night. The sergeant, looking like the cat who swallowed the canary, said that he didn't know that Dinner would be so anxious to sign them out this time. He asked, "Why not? What did they do this time?" When informed that they had stolen a car, Dinner looked positively relieved. This was apparently nothing. Dinner said, "So what's the *F*-ing problem?" That's when the sergeant alerted Dinner that it was *his* car that they had stolen. This news unsettled him somewhat, but not for long as he proceeded to sign them out of jail.

We entered the holding cell area. The first thing Dinner noticed was that a young girl about fifteen or sixteen was handcuffed to a chair outside the cell itself. Dinner obviously knew this young woman and demanded to know what the *F* she was doing there. She cried, "That's what I'd like to know. I'm walking down the street, and they said I was with them." This elicited hysteria from the holding cell proper. I looked up to see the number one high school basketball team in the land staring at us through iron bars. Walter Berry yelled out, "Hey Dinner, get me out of here, man. I have to take a leak." More laughter. Dinner walked me over to the inmate all the way to the left with a smile on his face and said, "Gary Springer, say hello to Coach Glass from UCLA."

Gary's head just dropped. He realized, correctly I might add, that this was probably the end of his recruitment by the UCLA Bruins. Now if I had been from UNLV, he probably would have shot up on their list, but there was no chance in Westwood. It was a shame we didn't have a photographer present: They could have taken a team picture. There was Gary; Berry, who would later star at St. Johns, and become a first round draft choice; Kenny Hutchinson, who went on to play at Arkansas, and Donnie Green, another future Division 1 player. There was also a young man named Richie Adams.

The story was this. Dinner had given Springer the keys to the gym and told him to make himself a copy. I have actually done this myself while coaching at Mater Dei High School in New Jersey, so the kids have access to the gym if they want it. The difference in my case was that my players had never taken the liberty of making fifty sets of my car keys as well and passing them around the school. Dinner's car became the means for joyriding, lunch, and other errands for the students of Ben Franklin for several weeks. One day, Dinner noticed that his car was missing during the lunch hour, and he reported it stolen. When he came out of practice, it was back, but he had never canceled the stolen-car report, and it remained in the police computer. Dinner's starting five was driving around Harlem during the lunch break and attracted the attention of the NYPD. When the plates were checked, they came up as stolen.

I had earlier arranged to meet with one of my best friends from high school and college at Rockefeller Center, where he worked. Alan Zweibel, or Zwebe as all our friends called him, had taken a job as one of the writers on *Saturday Night Live*. Zwebe has gone on to win several Emmy awards and has done great work out in Hollywood. I drove my *F*-ing rental car over to NBC and went up to see Zwebe. I couldn't help but tell the story that had just happened to me. The room was filled with other writers as well, like Buck Henry and Al Franken, and members of the cast, like Bill Murray and Jane Curtin. They were rolling as I told it. All except for Zwebe. He never laughed, never said a word. I said my good-byes and headed back to LaGuardia to catch a plane to Chicago to see Doc Rivers play.

I checked in at the Hyatt Regency O'Hare, and to my surprise, the message light on the phone in my room was already lit. Nobody knew where I was staying . . . except I had told Zwebe. The message was that I should call Zwebe immediately. The reason he hadn't been laughing was because he was planning. He told me that everybody thought the story was a riot and that they were going to do it that Saturday night on the show. I cancelled the Rivers recruitment. I went right back to the airport first thing in the morning and flew immediately back to New York. All I needed was to have people tie the university to this fiasco.

I explained to Zwebe that there could be no way that I or the university could be associated. He said he would protect us. For example, the coach's name would be "Coach Keith." Thanks a lot. They made the necessary changes and away they went. Two months later, on February 16, 1980, Elliot Gould played me. A bit taller, not nearly as good-looking, but a better actor. Zwebe, thankfully, had altered the story slightly. Those of you who saw it might remember that they did open with a short film of a university. The clip was being shown on a wall of some kind, and a man was talking about the library and how many volumes they had. When the lights went on, they were both in jail. You get the point. The rest of it went according to the story. No one ever connected me to the skit.

Since I was back in New York, I decided to catch a Ben Franklin High School game. I witnessed something that was obvious to me right away. The best player on the best team in the country was not Gary Springer at all. His teammate Richie Adams appeared to me to be, without exaggeration, a reasonable facsimile of Bill Russell. He was a left-hander, and at six feet nine inches tall, he was blocking or at least altering every shot in the paint. He was not what I would call a major threat offensively, but it looked like he could be. His presence on the defensive side, however, was enormous and would transform our team at UCLA, or any other for that matter.

After the first quarter, I had seen enough. I thought I had just discovered America. I would be a genius—and on my first trip, no less. Good centers are harder to find than a cab on a rainy day. I couldn't wait to call Larry at home. I told him that I didn't think Springer was good enough for us, and I went on and on about this other kid who I had originally met earlier in the holding cell. Larry, matter-of-factly said, "Oh you mean Richie. He's the best, but we can't recruit him because of his grades." There goes my genius tag. I have to admit that my second thought after speaking further with Larry was: *How can we let a 0.8 grade point average get in the way of our defense?*

Luckily, I came back to reality, but since I was in New York, I decided to set up a visit with Richie and his mother. This meeting took place in a world where I don't wish to return. Again, I found myself in Harlem. This time I went to Richie's apartment, which was located on the sixth or seventh floor of a housing project in one of the city's most blighted areas. All of us have heard or read about the living conditions of poor people in our country. The reason that I cannot give details of how they were living is because I tried not to look. I was there trying to sell our program. I was trying to see if there would be any incentive for Richie to work and pull his grades up so that we could recruit him. Even though I found Richie and his mother both to be very nice and cordial people, I also got the feeling that what I was hoping to accomplish was never going to get done.

During the visit, I started to smell smoke. There was no getting around it. After a couple of minutes, it was getting stronger, but Richie and his mom never flinched so I thought maybe it was me. Finally, when I was no longer able to see them due to the gray cloud in the room, I casually mentioned my concerns. They both blew it off as something that happened every day and said that I really shouldn't worry about it. Not only was I worried, but I began looking for a window to jump out. Hey, I'm from the suburbs—you know, fire drills just for the hell of it. But I sucked it up and stayed. Richie walked me out, thank god.

When I got back to campus, I was firmly informed that UCLA was never going to be able to recruit Richie Adams. My master plan was over. His grades were just unacceptable.

One year later, Richie Adams was the starting center for UNLV. He would become the two-time MVP of his conference and be drafted by the Washington Bullets (now the Washington Wizards). Two days after the NBA draft, Richie was arrested for car theft. Only this time, it wasn't a car belonging to Stan Dinner. He never played for the Bullets or any other team in the league. The car theft landed Richie and an accomplice in prison. I would periodically hear of him. Richie was in trouble constantly for fairly minor offenses, but it periodically got worse. He was heavily into drugs. I had heard that he was homeless after his release.

On Thursday, October 17, 1996, while having lunch in Red Bank, New Jersey, I opened up the *New York Post* to read the following:

EX-HOOP STAR NO. 1 SUSPECT IN TEEN SLAY

A former high school and college basketball star—who gave up a shot at the NBA for a life of crime—is the prime suspect in a beating death of a popular Bronx teenager, police said.

Richie Adams, 33—who is on parole until December 1997 for a series of muggings and purse snatchings—was questioned yesterday in the brutal murder of 14-year-old Morris HS student Norma Rodriguez.

I went on to read that bloody shoeprints were found on the victim's body, and that detectives were checking to see if they were from the size $13\frac{1}{2}$ black and green Adidas sneakers—believed to belong to Adams—found about 50 feet from the building.

My eyes scanned further down the page.

Adams, a star forward at the University of Nevada—Las Vegas after attending Benjamin Franklin HS in The Bronx [actually, the school was in East Harlem, but the school was closed in the early 1980s], was arrested for grand larceny the day after being drafted by the Washington Bullets in 1985.

A police source described him yesterday as a "crack addict."

I don't want to be pretend to be overly close to Richie Adams. I wasn't. But reading this article gave me this incredible sick feeling. Part of it was that Richie was, at the time I met him, a good kid. He had limited choices and therefore limited chances, but he was not a malicious person. What had happened to him in the intervening years may have changed all that. Richie was arrested the day after the girl's death.

The enduring effect on me of the death of this poor young girl is that I fully realize that the only reason I even became aware of her was because her alleged killer was a former basketball star. It makes for a good story in the *Post* and for that matter in this book. What about the countless other lives that we never read or hear about? The thousands of other drug addicts and deaths that are not related to sports? Something really odd is going on here.

I have often wondered since learning of this murder why things couldn't be different, both for people like Richie, and, more importantly, for the victims. Would the results of these tragic lives turn out differently if athletes like Richie were treated and educated the same as nonathletes. I wonder how many times Richie was excused for being late to things like practices or classes. I wonder how many times his grades were overlooked if not altered. They actually couldn't have been altered too much since when I went to recruit him his GPA was 0.8.

I wonder at how young an age these players are identified, thereby beginning this cycle of nonresponsibility. I wonder if we realize how damaging that can be to a young person—to not be aware of the right or wrong way to go to school, apply for a job, or interact with society. I wonder what it's like not to experience and, thereby, learn from failure or rejection because you are constantly being told how great you are. I wonder if, after all of the adults in an player's life have gone away because the players are not the saviors people thought they were, how these athletes deal with truly having to make it in the real world.

The teammates who watched them play and cheered for them all of those years *learned*. They learned what the "star" was just starting to understand—that all of us struggle to make it. The "stars," however, never had to learn that lesson. Guys like Richie Adams and the others who don't make it into the NBA are fifteen years behind the rest of us. Many of them can't make that adjustment. What may have looked like favorable treatment for all of those years often turns out to be no favor at all.

THREE

THINKING *INSIDE* THE BOX

At last, my trip was over, and the Bruins were now full swing into the season. I was having a ball coaching my JV guys. We had a strange type of schedule. On one hand, we were supposed to beat all of the other JV teams, which we did. On the other hand, we weren't supposed to be able to compete with junior colleges. The junior colleges, in many instances, were where players from high school who did not earn the required grades or test scores to enter four-year universities could hide out for a year or so and then enter a big-time program. College rosters, and for that matter, NBA rosters, are full of these types of players.

We were beating many of these junior colleges, and it was fun. Larry, however, had inherited a very tough situation. We had several veteran players, but the trouble was that we quickly could see in practice that our four freshmen recruits were better. Larry was sensitive to the plight of the upperclassmen and tried to give them their shot. It didn't work. We struggled big time. One by one, Larry made the agonizing decision to replace them in the lineup. The first two to go were the guards, Tyren Naulls and Tony Anderson. They were replaced by the roommates that Ducky had busted, Mike Holton and Rod Foster. This was radical enough—starting two freshmen in the backcourt. But Larry wasn't finished. He then took the wild step of putting six feet five inches tall Mike Sanders at center, relegating Gig Sims and Darrell Allums to backups the rest of the season.

The team was struggling. To make matters worse, Larry was attacking every group in sight. He chastised the alumni for showing up late for games and leaving early. After our trip to the Oregon schools, he complained that the crowds up there were so enthusiastic, he would rather play on the road. He lashed out at the students for not providing a home court atmosphere for us. He even verbally assaulted the band for not playing the right music to get our guys ready to rock. I started to have lunch in the office; it was getting dangerous crossing campus.

After fourteen games, we were eight up and six down. At UCLA, that's the same as being 0–14. Larry and I were leaving practice on the Friday night before our return engagement with Notre Dame and Digger Phelps. As we exited Pauley Pavilion, we were surprised to find about a hundred students in sleeping bags. We stopped to ask what was going on. We were informed that they always sleep out on the night before big games since the seating in the student section is on a first come, first serve basis. Larry never knew this, and I could see that this really touched him. He promised the students that if they were out there before the USC game in two weeks that we would sleep out there with them.

You have to understand that Larry was not what they were used to at UCLA. He was different in many ways from the coaches that preceded him. Coach Bartow and Coach Cunningham were excellent coaches, but not in Larry's mold. Even Coach Wooden had a laid-back image, at least, though I doubt that that was really the case.

This incident has always (at least to me) marked the beginning of our turnaround at UCLA that season. The next afternoon, on national TV, we trounced Notre Dame and somewhat avenged our earlier tough loss at South Bend. We won by thirty-something, but it was the way we won that was important. Our young kids were starting to blend in with Kiki and James Wilkes, and we were really defending. It wasn't that we caught fire at this point, but we were now a tough out.

Word of our encounter with the hundred or so students spread as well. Sure enough, the night before the USC game, the students were there, and they were daring Larry to keep to his word. They didn't have to. Larry was planning on it all along. The only difference was that this time there weren't a hundred students—it was more like three thousand. Larry and I got air mattresses, and Larry ordered out for about three thousand donuts and coffee from Stan's Donut Shop in Westwood. Larry Brown was about to become a cult figure in Los Angeles.

He kept up his attacks on everybody, but now he did it with a purpose. When I told him that the band was really upset with his criticisms, he was genuinely surprised. Rather than leave it there, he went to band practice. He told them that they didn't understand, that we really needed them. They were important to our success. I don't think any former UCLA head basketball coach attended band practices.

The following day during our JV game, I heard a commotion, and the band launched into the UCLA fight song. Larry, in shirtsleeves, had come out to watch our game, and the four thousand fans erupted. This would continue, only louder, for the rest of the season. The student section went wild for him. Every time he showed his face, they went crazy. All the fans, alumni, and students stayed for the whole game, no matter what. And they got there on time, too. Whatever happened on or off the court the rest of the season, it seemed to further magnify Larry as "The Man." In our last home game of the season, with an NCAA tournament bid possibly in the balance, Larry went back to the seniors for their final home game. He didn't just start them for show. They played. He started Kiki and James as usual, went back to Darrell Allums in the middle, and started Gig Sims, the backup center at one forward and Chris Lippert, who never played, at the other.

The students went nuts. The seniors played their asses off. We lost at the buzzer on a thirty-five-foot shot. The NCAA tournament, which Larry Farmer had not-so-jokingly referred to as the "UCLA Invitational Tournament," was now in serious jeopardy, which was unheard of at UCLA. We went back solemnly to the locker room. We heard a lot of shouting and commotion outside on the court. Eight thousand students— the entire student section—were standing and cheering and wouldn't leave until Larry came out to speak to them. He did. Farms just shook his head in disbelief. He had seen many major events at this place, but never anything like this. Think of it this way: We had come in run the program into the ground, and Larry was becoming the most popular coach they had ever seen.

We were now 15–9, with our last two games being Pac-10 games on the road at California and Stanford—not easy, especially on the road. We won both to finish at 17–9 for the year. The NCAA, however, only seeded forty-eight teams in those days—not today's sixty-four. A 17–9 record was shaky at best. If it weren't for the past glory of UCLA, I doubt that we would have been the forty-seventh team invited, as we were. Thanks, Coach Wooden.

From a purely basketball point of view, let's examine how things got turned around. Larry had always been a passing-game type of coach in the pros. In all of his stops along the way in his coaching career, that has always been his preference. In fact, as a player, Larry was the all-time leader in assists for the ABA. And he is the linear coaching descendant of Dr. Naismith—via Phog Allen and Dean Smith at Kansas.

The passing game is designed to allow players to make plays. There aren't many rules. You can pass and cut, pass and screen off the ball, or pass and replace yourself. Pretty basic stuff. It was the offense he installed at UCLA. The only trouble was that we discovered we didn't have passing-game type players. We did not have the type of guys who could make a play for themselves or anybody else.

We had some shooters, but not creative guys. We had no true center. Mike Sanders, who I would later represent throughout his eleven-year NBA career, was a center in name only. He was not an inside presence. He was as great a kid to coach as there ever was, but his game was defending bigger guys and drilling fifteen-foot jumpers. We called Mike "Slew" after the famous racehorse Seattle Slew because he was a thoroughbred. He listened to everything all of us told him, and we realized that he was trying to please the four of us and was being driven crazy. Larry told us to leave Mike alone—"Slew" was his.

Recognizing that this was not the way this team should play, Larry approached Farms about Coach Wooden's high-post offense. One of the many keys to being a great coach is the ability to recognize and, therefore, change according to the type of players you have. Larry Brown is a great coach. He has his faults as far as actually fulfilling the lengths of his contracts, and that leads to questions regarding his loyalty, but no one can ever dispute that he was and is among the finest coaches in the country.

He realized in the middle of the season that our players were better suited for a more structured offense. He decided to try Coach Wooden's UCLA high post. The high-post offense enabled our shooters who were having trouble getting their own shots to get the ball where they were comfortable and score. Kiki, Wilkes, Sanders, Holton, and Foster started to thrive because they knew when and where they were going to shoot the ball. When you had Kiki, Rod, and Slew coming off a double low screen for a jumper, it was "money."

In addition, as well as with all Larry's teams, everybody defended. (Well, maybe not Kiki.) Everybody also knew their role. Holton became a tenacious defender and a converted point guard. The Rocket scored on everybody, and Kiki basically carried us offensively.

It was in this image that we entered the tournament. For the second to last team invited to the "Big Dance," we were surprisingly confident, especially when you take into consideration the fact that we were starting a sophomore "center" and a freshman backcourt. We had to play a preliminary game against Old Dominion to see who would advance to play the number one rated team in the nation, DePaul, and we handled Old Dominion pretty easily. It was a thrill just being in the NCAA tournament, but after that first win, we wanted more. We were no longer 17–9, we were 1–0, and it was nice to have a fresh start.

Next up was DePaul. Not only were they the top-ranked team in the tournament, but also they had embarrassed us in our own building just a few months before. The article in *Sports Illustrated* that week read THE BRUINS ARE IN RUINS. DePaul was led by Mark Aguirre, who would go on to be the first pick in the 1981 NBA draft and last year was one of Larry's assistants with the Knicks. DePaul also had future NBA all-star Terry Cummings, as well as a great supporting cast and the venerable and classy coach, Ray Meyer. The contrast between Larry in his first year and Coach Meyer in his ninety-third or so was interesting enough. The game would prove to be even more so, at least for us.

The details of the contest are not that important. What I do remember clearly is that toward the end of the game, we had all four of our freshmen playing. Cliff Pruitt and Darren Daye joined Foster and Holton to form what had to be a preview of the Fab 5 from Michigan. They were incredibly poised freshmen. Larry and the rest of us coaches felt that they really didn't understand what they were into and that was why nothing seemed to bother them. At any rate, with those four, plus big boosts from Kiki and Slew, we pulled off the upset. This time the headlines had changed. When we got home, the *Los Angeles Times* blared out: WITH THE RISE OF THE BRUINS COMES THE FALL OF DEPAUL. I liked that headline better.

The players headed home, but the coaches stayed to scout the next game, which pitted Ohio State against Arizona State (ASU). ASU had played us twice and convincingly beaten us twice. The second time we played in Arizona, they basically humiliated us. We were getting used to that. Even though Ohio State was loaded with talent, we just assumed that ASU would beat them—after all, look what they had done to us. In fact, the ASU lineup boasted five future NBA first-rounders. Their backcourt had Fat Lever, who would be the eleventh pick, and Byron Scott, who had a great career and is currently the head coach of the New Orleans/Oklahoma City Hornets in the NBA. He was the fourth overall pick in the draft. You throw in Alton Lister, their seven-foot center, and you get the point. Ohio State beat them by thirty.

I remember Larry feeling and saying sincerely that at least we had accomplished something. The huge upset of DePaul was going to help us in the future, and the kids could at least be proud of that accomplishment. In other words, we had no chance. Right after all of us agreed that we couldn't beat Ohio State, Larry started to figure out how we were going to do it. The first thing he said to the team at practice the next day was that for the sake of the university, they should keep their warm-ups on as long as possible. You see, we were a bunch of skinny young kids for the most part and suffice it to say that OSU was made up of men. They had Herb Williams at the power forward slot. Herb was six feet ten inches, and would become a top-twelve selection in the upcoming draft, and was, incredibly, Larry's top assistant with the Knicks. The guy in the middle, Jim Smith, was even bigger, and the small forward was freshman Clark Kellogg, who was a great player and would later become the eighth overall pick in the draft. In the backcourt, stocky Kelvin Ransey would actually be the fifth pick in the draft some three months after this game.

We flew back to Arizona for the next set of regional games. There were now sixteen teams left, and we were, naturally, the lowest seed remaining. We had our usual pregame meal at 3:30 p.m. We noticed that James Wilkes, one of our captains and starters for that evening, was missing. James was very reliable, and we were a little concerned, but no big deal yet. About ten minutes later, in walks James soaking wet with a bewildered look on his face, his basketball shoes in his hands. It seems that as James was coming to pregame, he noticed a little boy falling into the deep end of the hotel's pool. The kid's mother hadn't even noticed, and the kid was going under quick. James, a great defender, but not a great swimmer, in-stinctively jumped in, went to the bottom, and saved the kid's life. Little did we know that James's heroics weren't over.

In the second half of the game that night, James Wilkes played the best defensive half of basketball that I have ever seen. He played post defense on Herb Williams to the point where Herb never even got to touch the ball. Again, Kiki and the kids rose up. We made all of the big shots and all of our foul shots and pulled off another upset. We were, incredibly, in the Elite Eight. If we won one more, we'd be going to Indianapolis for the Final Four. It was such an improbable occurrence. Just two weeks ago, I re-ally didn't know where the thing was being played.

I also remember a fairly private incident that happened after the game between Larry, Mr. Drake, and myself. Ducky, as usual, was trying to clean up the locker room to make it, as he and Coach Wooden would say, a little bit cleaner than when we got there. Unbelievably, there had actually been some talk that Ducky was going to be under some pressure from the university to retire. He was having some trouble with his duties, but Larry and I found it hard to believe and had actually discussed what to do if it ever really got going in that direction. Larry respected and loved Ducky. With just the three of us in that locker room, Larry just blurted out that he basically didn't know what Ducky was trying to pull, but we weren't going to come back to UCLA if he wasn't there. Larry said that if it was money or whatever, Ducky should just say it, and Larry would take care of it. Mr. Drake was indignant. He said that he would never leave UCLA and that we should have known that. In all my dealings with Larry, that was the nicest thing he had done.

Ducky had promised the kids that if we won, they could "order off the menu." This was a thrill for our guys. Instead of getting one standard meal, they could actually order. I guess the thought of a scholarship athlete at UCLA paying for his meal was out of the question. Anyway, the bus after the game was a little wild. The team was ecstatic, as you could assume. They were yelling and joking in the back. One of our key freshman, Cliff Pruitt, a six-eight forward and team comedian, was the ring leader. Ducky asked Larry if he could address them. Larry said, "Duck, it's your team, say whatever you want." Ducky quieted the bus by simply standing up and in his firm voice saying, "You've done a pretty fair job in there today, but you haven't won anything yet. At UCLA, we don't cut down the net unless it's the last net. Now it's time to come down." He was angry, but the kids knew he was proud of them.

The silence was broken ten seconds later when Pruitt yelled out, "But what about those steaks?"

Ducky jumped back up and yelled, "We'll have steaks in Indianapolis! Bus driver—Jack in the Box." The team, as one, screamed, "All right, Jacks!" and off the UCLA team bus went for our victory dinner of burgers and fries. The incredulous looks on the faces of the other patrons at Jacks was a memory I will never forget.

As crazy as it was to even think about, we were one game away from the Final Four. To make matters even more bizarre, I was worried because I felt that we *should* beat our next opponent, Clemson. They had a very formidable club and were led by six feet eleven inches tall Larry Nance, who would go on to be a great pro. I simply felt that we were playing so well. We were the best defensive team left in the tournament, and defense usually wins games. The whole experience was remarkable, and I was trying to learn and remember everything I could from it.

In a total team effort, we beat the Clemson Tigers, with a freshman named Cliff Pruitt making the key foul shots down the stretch. We were, incredibly, heading for Indianapolis, the Final Four . . . and steaks. The teams with us were Purdue, who would be our next opponent in the National Semi-finals, the University of Iowa, and Louisville. Louisville was coached by Denny Crum, a former assistant with Coach Wooden at UCLA.

I set as my goal for that week to not only try to make any contribution I could to help us win, but also to suck up the entire experience of being in the Final Four. I somehow knew that I would never be back in this situation as a coach again.

People often ask me what it was like to be able to participate in this event, but the truth is, when you're in something like that, you are too caught up in the event itself. It strangely is almost more exciting to watch it on TV than to be a part of it. It was hectic with ticket requests, the travel, and obviously, the game itself. My parents and Brent came, and this made it even more special. I wanted to get Brent's special insight into my being in this situation, but it was so hectic, we never got to it. Still, it was a thrill having them all there. The irony of the situation was that in 1966, when I was fifteen, Brent took me along to the Final Four in Louisville to watch the University of North Carolina play against Dayton. North Carolina had an assistant coach named Larry Brown. Brent and two friends suffered through my tagging along and, in fact, had to deal with the fact that I lost my ticket. In 1980, I was giving Brent his ticket. I guess we were even.

The day before our semi-final game against Purdue, all four teams practiced. This was an incredible experience for me. Market Square Arena was filled to capacity with fans watching practice. One of my lasting impressions of the whole weekend was the site of head coaches from all over the country having to stand behind ropes to watch us go through our drills. Heaven forbid Dean Smith or Bobby Knight should somehow get too close to me. Remember that six months prior to this weekend, I was living in a mobile home park in California and getting bed rest on Long Island. The improbable ride was not lost on me.

Purdue was next. They were lead primarily by Joe Barry Carroll. He would become a first pick in the 1980 NBA draft. An interesting note regarding Joe Barry is that the Boston Celtics had the first pick in that draft. Red Auerbach, the late Celtics legend, was at this point their GM. Red, not wanting Joe Barry Carroll, traded him to the Golden State Warriors. The Celtics received the third pick in the draft and the center that the Warriors didn't want, Robert Parrish. With the third pick, the Celtics selected a six-eleven power forward named Kevin McHale. They teamed Parrish and McHale with Larry Bird, and Boston had assembled the greatest front line in the history of the NBA. By the way, we beat Purdue and Joe Barry Carroll the same way Red beat the Warriors.

Sunday was spent preparing for the final and disposing of tickets (in that order). I didn't really see any signs of nervousness from our players at all, but it was still sort of a weird kind of day. I guess it was a classic case of the calm before the storm. The situation on Monday would change with the arrival of our unrequested police escort, which I really believe scared the crap out of the freshmen. Whereas, before that escort they were basically unaware of the importance of the event they were in, the sirens and lights served as a direct indication. There was a strange quiet that enveloped the bus, which included Cliff Pruitt. To make matters worse, we miscalculated what time we should arrive at Market Square Arena. There was, in those days, a consolation game between the losers from Saturday: Purdue and Iowa. It was also strange that we were actually watching that game from our hotel and realized that we were headed for the National Championship in a little while. In any case, we left way too early and had way too much time to just sit around and think at the arena. Larry asked me to try and tell some stories to lighten things up, but I don't remember them working very well. I wasn't too much concerned with taking in the scenery anymore; I was just thinking about winning it all.

Things went pretty well during the initial stages of the game and through to the half. The one problem we were having was that at this point of our season, the freshman, Pruitt, was clearly a better player than James Wilkes, the hero of Ohio State victory. Wilkes was the better defender, but there was no comparison to what they could both do with the ball. The problem was that James was a senior, one of the only two remaining, who had survived Larry's purge during the year. In James's case, however, Larry was particularly loyal. He felt that James, in a significant way, was responsible for our being where we were. James was clearly struggling in this game with Louisville. We, as assistants, had discussed this with Larry, but in the end, I knew that we would either win or lose with James in this game. Pruitt would help as much as he could in a relief role.

The key play in that game occurred with about four minutes remaining. We were up by five, and Kiki had a semi-breakaway lay-up. This would have given us a seven-point lead, which I don't believe we would have ever surrendered. In these situations in the tournament, we would spread the floor and invariably get fouled and put teams away. This was, you should know, preshot-clock days in college basketball. Instead, a Louisville guard Jerry Eaves sliced in front of Kiki just enough to throw him off balance. Kiki, who had carried us throughout, missed the easy opportunity. Louisville came down the floor and got the ball in the right corner to their best player, Darrell Griffith, who went up over Michael Holton, made a tough jumper, and was fouled. When he made the free throw, we were only up two.

We never scored again. I did, in fact, say at our UCLA banquet that for those of the people who didn't really know who I was, I coached the first thirty-six minutes of the Louisville game. Everyone laughed except for Larry. We lost by five points and, therefore, the National Championship. I remember the game, but I have never watched the tape even though it has been over twenty-five years since it happened. It simply would hurt too much. We were, as one could imagine, devastated. It is easy at a time like that to feel sorry for yourself even though you're one of the luckiest people on Earth. Larry cried. He actually asked me, "When is it going to be my turn?" I found that question strange, as he was forty-one years old and in his first season of collegiate basketball. (His turn did come eight years later in Kansas City as the coach of the University of Kansas. I would be there along with my parents and Brent. We would wait for him in the tunnel, and Larry and I felt something special.)

However, there I was now after the devastating loss trying to console Larry as best I could while being crushed myself.

I happened to turn and saw workmen hastily constructing a platform at half court of Market Square Arena. I realized that they were going to award the National Championship trophy to Louisville. I also realized they were going to give out some other stuff, too. I desperately looked for Brent and yelled, "Hey, I'm going to find out what the hell is in that little box!"

FOUR

EIGHTY-ONE FEET OF WHITE CENTERS

Agents travel the world in search of clients or prospects. They go to games in remote places: to high school gyms, to college gyms, to Europe, to Asia, to Africa. They employ "runners" just to track down these prospects and make introductions to the agent. This can take years. My first client was found under a car in a Mark C. Bloome Goodyear auto center somewhere in Southern California.

Mark Eaton was seven feet five inches tall at the time of this discovery. He was also, at that time, apparently the world's largest auto mechanic.

Mark, though being of obvious basketball height, had one problem with the game. He hated it. He didn't play in high school, which is not exactly the way to build a future as a professional basketball player. Because of his size, everyone expected him to play and pushed him in that direction. Sometimes this can be a great way to push someone in the opposite direction. That was the case with Mark.

Mark had other interests, like automobiles. After high school, he became a seven-five mechanic. One day, while lying on his back doing an oil change on a '75 Montego, a man named Tom Lubin came into the garage and decided to change Mark's life. Tom was lost, but more importantly, he was an assistant basketball coach at Cypress Junior College. He saw feet, went around to the other side of the vehicle, and saw a head. Thinking there were two guys working on the car, he asked for the directions. It was shortly thereafter that he realized Mark was indeed one guy. After demanding Mark get out from under the car, he persisted in having him enroll at Cypress. I imagine the idea of Mark playing there was the main point.

Mark did enroll and began playing—not too well, but playing. When you are seven feet five inches tall, people tend to stay with you as a basketball player. There just aren't that many who are that tall. In addition, Mark was strong. He also had what I call a "good feel" for the game and good timing, which, coupled with his height, posed serious problems for the opposition on the defensive end of the court. He started to get better and developed a little bit of a reputation as a prospect.

I was in my first year at UCLA. I had been sent to scout Mark several times. The other assistants did the same. By the time signing day came, we were of the opinion that while we really liked Mark as a kid, he was not good enough as a player for UCLA. The consensus was, I remember, that since our players were so fast, Mark would look even slower than he already was. Mark was being recruited by the University of Washington and Pepperdine University, out in Malibu—good schools and good places to play. We advised Mark that he couldn't go wrong attending either place.

The problem was that Mark Eaton only wanted to play at UCLA. I guess growing up in the L.A. area and watching Coach Wooden and his teams perform can do that to a youngster. Mark then started recruiting us, me in particular. He told Larry and me in person that nothing had ever come easy for him and that he was going to work and get better. Knowing Larry and how he thinks, I knew that was it. Mark was offered a scholarship to UCLA, and he arrived in September 1980.

He was awful. He just couldn't keep up with our players. There was no shame in that, though, since several of them would go on to careers in the NBA, but it was discouraging. Maybe to get back at me for being the guy who wanted to sign Mark in the first place, Larry sent him down to me for a tournament the JV was playing in the California desert somewhere. We had won the first game without him. He arrived for the semi-final, and we lost. He was the main reason. I was instructed by Larry very specifically to play him no matter what. Larry knew I didn't want to because I didn't think it fair to my other guys who had practiced for weeks getting ready for our season. I also didn't want to play him because I wanted to win.

Every time we threw to Mark, he walked. At the other end, every time he tried to guard, he fouled. We lost that game and the next one with him. Mercifully, Larry cancelled the experiment and recalled Mark exclusively to the big team. The JV won its next six in a row.

In spite of my negative experience from a won-lost point of view with Mark, there was something about him that wouldn't let you quit on him. The main thing was how hard he was willing to work. I noticed that his biggest problem on the offensive end was that he actually could catch the ball when it was thrown his way, but he always caught it with his two feet together. He then would jump and move both feet at the same time. That's a traveling violation—a walk. That's a turnover. That's not good.

To combat this, I started throwing him 300 lob passes a day after practice. We were only trying to get him to catch it with one foot down. He could then gather himself and actually make a play, which he was good at. I just wanted to get him in a position where he could do what he was good at. The unexpected off-shoot of this activity was that I easily became the best lob passer in the country, but there was very little practical application of this unusual skill set. I thought this was working. I started to push the thought that Mark could help us. This was met with resistance the entire season. Mark Eaton played twenty-three minutes for UCLA his entire junior year.

At the end of that year, the year after we made it to the national championship game, we lost to a BYU team with Danny Ainge, currently the general manager of the Boston Celtics, and Greg Kite. It was a huge upset in the NCAA tournament, as it was in the first round and we were a very high seed—the ironic exact reversal of our improbable upsets the year before. On the bus back to the hotel after the loss, Larry called me up to the front to sit with him. He leaned over and said, "You know kid, we should have played the big guy!" I switched seats.

That loss to BYU in the NCAA tournament was mine and Larry's last game at UCLA. Larry left to become the head coach with the New Jersey Nets. I stayed in L.A. The coaching, however, remained very much in my veins. I was asked by a friend who happened to write for one of the papers that covered us at UCLA to meet with the principal of Venice High School. This was just to give him some advice on the hiring of a new head coach at Venice. They hadn't won in twenty-seven years, and they just wanted a little direction. After an hour meeting, I found myself as the head coach of Venice High School.

Mark Eaton, however, remained as a player at UCLA. He met the same basic fate as the year before. His total minutes for his UCLA career topped out at sixty-one (not exactly NBA numbers). This was, however, 1982, and the NBA draft still went ten rounds. Today, it is only two. Based solely of his size, the Utah Jazz drafted Mark Eaton as the seventy-second pick in the fourth round.

I was not in agent-mode in those days. I was thinking about it with my father, but I was still taking on legal cases and was happy coaching at Venice. Mark and I had stayed in touch when I'd left UCLA. He knew that I was always the one in his corner. In fact, Mark and I had just played a lame round of golf a few weeks after the draft. He said "Coach, I've heard from about forty agents and lawyers who want to represent me. How come you haven't called?" I told him that he knew me and he knew how to find me, and in fact, I didn't see what there was to represent. Not many make it out of the fourth round of the NBA draft. Mark proceeded to tell me that I was the only one he trusted and asked me if I would represent him. I said fine, not really knowing that this would change my vocation and life forever.

The thought of getting Mark any type of guaranteed money as the seventy-second pick was far-fetched. I decided to try anyway. I met with Frank Layden, who was the general manager and coach of the Jazz. Frank was an extremely engaging and humorous guy. He was a good solid coach, but he was actually better known for his sense of humor. He was once asked why he only carried eleven players on his roster when the NBA allowed twelve. He said, "Even Jesus had trouble with twelve!"

I told Frank that I wanted a guaranteed deal for Mark, mainly because of his potential, but also I recall a veiled reference on my part of a deal in Spain for $50,000. Frank came right at me with a very logical line of questions. Specifically, he wanted to know why I would possibly think that Mark could play for the Jazz in the NBA when I actually helped coach him myself and we wouldn't play him in college.

I thought that might come up. My response might have sounded flippant, but I was very serious. I told Frank that we couldn't play Mark because, "Every time we threw it to him, he walked and every time he defended he fouled. In the NBA, they let you walk and they let you foul! He's perfect!"

This line of reasoning worked, and Mark Eaton became the first and last player in the history of the NBA to receive a fully guaranteed contract in the fourth round of the draft. The terms of this signing made the rounds. I ended up signing all of the big white centers that nobody else seemed interested in. I signed the previously mentioned Greg Kite from BYU, who had helped beat our brains in during the NCAAs. I signed Blair Rasmussen from Oregon; Mike Smrek form Canisius; Stuart Gray from UCLA; Chuck Nevitt from North Carolina State; Alan Bannister, who was seven feet seven inches tall and played his college ball somewhere in Utah; Scott Meents from Illinois; Mike Peplowski from Michigan State; and Marty Conlon from Providence. And there were more. All of these guys somehow ended up on NBA rosters; most of them for a long period of time. It was either the greatest coincidence in the history of the NBA or maybe I had figured something out.

It was Greg (Kite) who actually got me my baptism in dealing with the late Red Auerbach. Greg was relatively unheralded coming out of BYU in 1983. Just another one of my eighty-one feet of white centers. Greg should have been taken in the second round or later in that upcoming draft. At six-eleven and 250, he was big and strong and set a vicious screen but could not do much on the offensive side.

As he had done many times before, Red didn't care much for what everybody else saw or thought. To the surprise of everyone, the Celtics drafted Greg in the first round at number 21. The following day I received a call from Red. I should point out that I began the conversation calling him Mr. Auerbach but clearly finished with Red. It went something like this:

KG: Hello, Mr. Auerbach. This is Keith Glass.

RED: Yeah. Now Glass, that big stiff of yours—understand that he can't play. Don't think about anything cute here. If you threaten that overseas crap, just send him there. He can't play.

KG: Well then *Red*, if that's true, then yesterday that was my problem. Today it's yours.

RED: (After a long pause) Glass, you're probably going to have to get up here.

It really didn't take a genius to realize that for some inexplicable reason the league seemed almost to have a rule: Every team had to have three white centers. They didn't have to actually play, but they had to have them. I am not alleging this in any racist or quota sense. It is just that the league is a copycat league and trends develop. There have been other trends as well. They are based more on types of players rather than color. There was the recent high school trend that also coincided with the European trend. If one team has success with a Kevin Garnett or Kobe Bryant, then the rest of the league follows suit. If one team has success with a Dirk Nowitski, the rest fall in line as well. My niche became my eighty-one feet of white centers.

Jack McCloskey, who was the architect of the two Detroit Pistons championship teams in the 1980s, went so far as to tell a magazine that if one of their white centers gets hurt, he doesn't call the NBPA to find a replacement; he calls Keith Glass. What a reputation to have. But don't get me wrong, I loved my eighty-one feet of white centers! They got me started.

So Mark Eaton made the Utah Jazz. He couldn't play at UCLA, but the NBA—no problem. In fact, within a very short period of time, Mark was the starting center for the Utah Jazz. At the end of the year, Mark was third in the NBA in blocked shots. I believe he was behind Bill Walton and Tree Rollins. (Rollins is credited with a bit of fame from his NBA rookie questionnaire. When asked on the form to fill in the box that said "church preference," he supposedly wrote "red brick.")

Some years later, Mark Eaton ended up becoming the NBA defensive player of the year. He was also a participant in the NBA All-Star game, which has now become NBA All-Star weekend and is threatening to become NBA All-Star month. I have heard a rumor about making the all-star game an entire season, like spring.

That initial contract foray that I negotiated with Frank Layden was for $55,000. Our last one was negotiated directly with the current owner of the Jazz, Larry Miller. We did this one at one of his many car dealerships in Salt Lake City. This one was a little trickier, and I actually, for the only time in my career, had my client come into the room with me while I did it. I did this for a specific affect. Since Mark did not put up huge scoring numbers, the Jazz negotiators, not Larry Miller but others, were constantly attacking those lack of stats to drive my asking price down. Mark Eaton and other players who make their contributions in less tangible ways are harder to negotiate for. The other side tries to put you in a defensive posture by pointing out irrelevant numbers or the lack thereof. I knew that with Mark in the room, none of that nonsense would go on.

I guess we were right. The former world's largest auto mechanic signed a four-year contract for $8 million. It was guaranteed in full, and I did not even have to invoke any foreign entities to get it done. Today, if you visit the Delta Center where the Jazz play, look up to the ceiling, and you'll find Marks' retired number, 53, hanging there. It sits right in between numbers 12 and 32. Those are the retired numbers for John Stockton and Karl Malone. What a thrill . . . for them.

FIVE

AGENTING—THE TRUTH, THE HALF TRUTH, AND NOTHING BUT BALONEY

Agents did not begin with *Jerry Maguire* and *Arli$$*. Their history, besides being checkered, is a very short one. Let's just say that agents have never exactly been embraced by professional clubs, in any sport.

In the 1960s, the Green Bay Packers ruled the NFL. Their leader was the legendary Vince Lombardi. Lombardi was not only the coach, but also the club's general manager. The center on that team was one of Lombardi's favorites, Jim Ringo. He was the anchor of their offensive line. He was an all-pro center. He had played hurt, as all of his teammates had. They had won championships together.

On this particular day, Jim Ringo was a free agent. Or to put it in terms of that time, let's just say he was without a contract. He had to negotiate a new one with Lombardi. Jim Ringo showed up in Lombardi's office. He wasn't alone. With him was a little guy with glasses and a briefcase. Lombardi, I'm sure, very pleasantly asked, "Jim, who the hell is this?"

Ringo answered, "Coach, this is my agent."

Lombardi excused himself from the room and came back eight minutes later. He told Ringo, "Jim, you and your agent have just been traded to Philadelphia."

Welcome aboard! The reason for this attitude toward agents or anybody trying to help a player is simple. For so long, the leagues had it their way. It was time for the pendulum to not swing but maybe get pushed into motion. Players negotiating their own contracts were easier for management. They had no idea what the actual finances of these clubs were. They knew they were having success in the sport, but how did that quantify in their particular case? This was a beautiful situation for the owners. And why not? At this point in the history of professional sports, the owners, general managers, coaches, and scouts were also, many times, its founders.

These leagues did not begin with Super Bowl I. They struggled mightily for years. The owners lost money for years. They had the vision, and they took the risk. Their initial views that these players were given the opportunity to continue playing a sport they loved was true and understandable.

It sometimes seems that the notion of fairness, once an envied American cultural trait, has faded to the point of disappearing, especially in business. People seem to have a problem understanding what is fair. Most times, that concept needs to be explained. People need outside help. That is the beginning of the need for agents. I still tell clients and prospective clients that if the teams were fair with them in the first place, I wouldn't have a job. Simplistic? Maybe. But isn't that what an agent is supposed to do—watch out for our clients so they don't get screwed?

The NBA and the players union have both been trying to reduce the impact of agents for years, if not get rid of us entirely. They have created rules designed to eliminate agents. They have insulted us, vilified us, and made it plain that we are not welcome.

Nothing works! I was widely quoted after one of the many battles between the owners and the players. The new collective bargaining agreement included provisions that would lessen or totally eliminate the need for an agent, as if this was specifically the goal. There were pay scales for rookies. There were higher minimums for veteran players, with specific dollar amounts for each year. I was asked on my way out of the settlement negotiations about how I felt about the apparent discounting of an agent's ability to negotiate. My response was, "Agents are like city rats; we can survive in any environment."

I said that in 1998. Agents in the NBA have never made more money than they do now. Can't we all just get along? The salaries are so astronomical that agents don't need to negotiate as many deals as they used to. The players' union has knowingly, or unknowingly, joined the effort of the league by reducing the fee that an agent can charge a player for one of these "minimum" contracts. Instead of the standard 4 percent, the maximum fee for a minimum contract is 2 percent.

I have argued long and hard for ten years on this one. The NBPA still does not acknowledge what an agent has to do to get a player a "minimum" contract. Believe me, I have done all types of contract negotiations in my twenty-four years of agenting, and getting a player a guaranteed minimum is the toughest. Whereas the league will almost give away money at the top, they become very tough with the guys that they feel they can bully at the bottom. This is understandable on some level. However, some of these players down below rise to what the league believes is the top and then watch out! My issue is not so much with the league's approach but with the union's.

An agent spends ten times the effort representing a player trying to receive a minimum contract. He receives half the fee. The union allows an agent to receive conversely 4 percent on a contract for $15 million per year. In short, if you take a player from nowhere and work hard together, you can expect to receive 2 percent of his minimum, which, in the first year, is approximately $400,000. The agent receives $8,000, instead of $16,000 if the regular 4 percent fee was allowed. However, if you "recruit" the $15 million per year player, your fee rises to $600,000 per year. It seems a little ass-backward to me, but what do I know.

By using this model of rewarding efforts, the union has unwittingly placed the emphasis of agenting not with representation, but with recruiting. There is a big difference between the two. This has led to the situation we now take for granted today. Agents steal one another's clients constantly. Agents buy players while they are in high school. The most impor-

tant item has obviously been made clear even by the players' own union—
do whatever it takes to hit the mother lode. Being an agent in 2006 is 90
percent recruiting and marketing and 10 percent actual representation.
Many times the better actual job you do of representing, the less you earn.

A GET-OUT-OF-CONTRACT-FREE CARD

Let's couple that concept with the following tidbit from the union's set of
rules governing the agent-player contract. In the contract I sign with the
player, there is a little clause allowing the player to terminate, at will, the
contract he has just signed. In other words, the agent-player contract is basically worthless. While "representing" this player, there are hundreds of
agents certified by the union who are trying to steal your client. While not
being actually sanctioned by the union, client theft is allowed through
practice and is subliminally encouraged through the priorities set above.

To illustrate this point, let me give you an example. In 1991, I was introduced to a junior from the University of Alabama named Robert
Horry. Today, after six NBA championships, the country refers to him as
"Big Shot Bob" due to his proclivity for making huge shots in the NBA finals.

Before all that, Robert asked me to advise him on whether or not he
should enter the 1991 NBA draft. The NCAA allows me, as an attorney,
to give this advice. Technically, a person who is solely an agent cannot,
though today this happens all the time. Most prospects will test the waters
before they are seniors. My conclusions on Robert's behalf were that he
would be a late first to early second round draft choice. I came to this conclusion after spending a great deal of time polling people throughout the
NBA on where he would go. I, therefore, told him to stay at Alabama for
his senior year, since I thought he could develop his game further and go
higher the next year.

At six-ten, Robert was an unusual player. He was forced to play inside
at Alabama and twice a year, had to bang heads with a monstrous center
from LSU named Shaquille O'Neal. However, Robert had great skills for

the game. He not only could score inside, but he also could step out and even shoot threes. He was tough and fearless and could pass and handle the ball extremely well for such a big man. To top that off, he was very intelligent on and off the court. I also found him to be an engaging person. Therefore, I couldn't imagine him not getting picked higher in the first round in 1992.

I was right. Robert had a very good senior year and was projected after the season to go in the area between twenty and twenty-five in the upcoming draft. I truly believed that he was better than that. Robert signed an NBPA contract with me right after his eligibility ended with Alabama. Now it was my turn to perform. I badgered teams constantly for the three months leading up to the draft. On draft night, the biggest surprise of the evening was when Commissioner David Stern announced that with the eleventh pick in the draft, the Houston Rockets selected Robert Horry of the University of Alabama.

Most people, and even draft experts, were stunned. I thought he should have gone two spots higher. A month later, Robert came to New Jersey to spend time with me and my family. He was great to be around. I have fond memories of him lying on the floor with my son, Alex, watching cartoons and laughing. He also took turns holding my colicky daughter, Maggie. It actually was Robert who came up with the only idea that stopped her from crying, however briefly, during the first year of her life. He somehow discovered that if you held Maggie at a particular angle with the water running, her incessant wailing would subside, at least for a little while.

After negotiating with the Rockets, we signed a five-year contract for around $5 million. I also secured a shoe contract and numerous basketball trading card deals for him. He and I were thrilled.

During his first season with the Rockets, I was warned that a pair of brothers from Houston who were registered agents with the Union were trying to get close to Robert to steal him as a client. However, I trusted Robert and didn't mention it. During the second year of our contract, the rumors kept getting back to me that through people known as "runners," these guys were either directly or indirectly taking Robert clubbing all over Houston. I'm not and have never been a big clubbing type of guy. In short, they were recruiting him while he was being represented by me.

It did get to the point where I asked Robert about it. He admitted spending time with these people, but indicated that they were friends and that I had nothing to be concerned about.

Because of my relationship with Robert, I never doubted him but I didn't trust what was going on either. Everything between us was fine. The rumors, however, continued. Now I decided to contact the NBPA. This is not supposed to happen. Their reaction was that I needed proof, or in the absence of that, I needed Robert to rat out the brothers. Not having a video of the club-hopping at my disposal and understanding that Robert had already indicated to me that they were friends of his, I knew I was not going to get protection from the NBPA.

Robert and the Rockets won their only two NBA championships during his first contract with them. They accomplished this while Michael Jordan was unsuccessfully attempting to hit a minor league curveball, but championships they were. They were led by the great Hakeem Olajuwon, and Robert was a key and valuable member.

He was valuable enough that during his last season, the Rockets and I started to negotiate an extension. The final offer I received was for $21 million over a seven-year period, an average of $3 million per year. At the time, the Rockets were playing the Philadelphia 76ers, and I drove down to meet with Robert to discuss the offer. We sat in Roberts' room and talked about it for a good while. Finally, he asked me what I thought, should we sign or not?

I told him that I thought it was a good offer, a good contract, but I honestly thought we could do better if we waited until the end of the season. He agreed, and I informed Houston that we appreciated the offer, but we were going to wait.

Three months later, I received a letter from Robert Horry terminating me as his agent—no phone call. Fifteen days after that letter arrived, Robert signed another NBPA contract with two brothers from Houston.

A month or so later, Robert signed a $27 million deal with the Los Angeles Lakers. I guess there is a fine line between trying to do the right thing and being an idiot. The verdict on this one is slanted very much toward the latter in my case. That fine line cost me 4 percent of $21 million or $840,000. Just think of the fun my ex-wives and their lawyers would have had with all of that money.

THE EMBRYO AGENT

In 1956, Mickey Mantle of the New York Yankees won the triple crown in the American League. In others words, he led the league in home runs, runs batted in, and batting average. To say the least, this was a staggering achievement and one that is rarely accomplished. In 1957, Mantle "only" led the league in two of those three categories. When he opened his mail that winter to see what his new contract for 1958 was, he was greeted with a $5,000 cut. The rationale was that he didn't have as good a year as the year before.

Again in the 1950s, Ralph Kiner of the Pittsburgh Pirates led the league in home runs for seven years in a row. One year, when he went in, alone, to negotiate his contract with the Pirates and get rewarded for leading the league in homers, he was asked one question by crafty GM Branch Rickey. "Ralph, where did we finish last year in the standings?" Kiner's reply was "Last." Rickey's response was "Well Ralph, we can finish last without you!"

Enter the agent! It is ironic that the very teams that want to get rid of me have enabled me to earn a living. Some of the things they have made me and my players fight for are ridiculous. The previously mentioned Michael Holton, who found Ducky Drake asleep in his bed, is an example.

When Michael graduated from UCLA in 1983, he asked me to represent him. Mike was drafted in the third round by the Golden State Warriors. In other words, since today there are only two rounds, he wouldn't have been drafted at all. He was drafted in June. I spent the next three months fighting, and fighting hard, to secure a $5,000 roster bonus for Michael. Understand that Michael's contract was $45,000. Also understand that none of this money was guaranteed in any way. The Warriors could release him at any time and owe him nothing. I was merely trying to get him to $50,000 *if* he was on their opening day roster.

We got this done. Instead of taking five minutes, it took three months and caused plenty of animosity. When Michael made it, and made it for nine years in the NBA, who do you think he felt loyal to? Who do you think he was grateful to? It was silly and petty, and there was no reason for it, except that it does justify my existence, and it always has. This existence has been questioned and challenged on numerous occasions and in many different ways. Since the landscape of professional sports has dramatically been altered, the need for agents in the first place is in question.

"HOW CAN THEY HEAR THE TRUTH ABOVE THE ROAR?"
—"Razzle Dazzle" from *Chicago*, by Kander & Ebb

Today, clearly we do not have a situation where the players are being screwed. However, this does not mean that there is not a need for an agent. The ironic part of this questioning of the relevance of an agent is that the players and the people around them are not the ones doing the questioning. They clearly recognize the need. It is the agents that are panicking because they do not truly consider themselves to be advocates or representatives of their clients; they are constantly searching to provide a reason for their existence.

They have consciously tried to complicate the process. They create new roles for themselves. Today, being that advocate is not enough. Now, they are training their clients for the draft. Incredibly, now they are not only agents, but also basketball gurus who can take a player that has already obviously been identified as a prospect and teach him how to play and get ready.

Imagine the gall of this position. You have some guy who probably wouldn't know a basketball if it fell out of the sky and hit him in the head pontificating about the game. The assumption is that he is recruiting this player who has had a great career, but incredibly, this player has, up to now, not been trained or coached properly: not in grade school, not in high school, not in college. It leads one to wonder why these agents are not just set loose on the general population to teach and spread the word of basketball to the masses.

The truth of the matter is, as always, a little different from the spin. The real deal is that these agents are just recruiting. They are justifying their presence in the players' world. The incredible part of this is that the players buy into it. For them, these phony training camps are merely ways for them to get away and drop out of classes on somebody else's dime. What a world. To me, they deserve each other. The idea of the poor exploited athlete died a long time ago. They know the scam, and they are willing participants.

Just in case this training doesn't get the desired result, specifically signing the player, the agent goes further. He is not only the best agent and basketball sage, but also he has almost miraculously compiled the best financial advisors, money managers, media consultants, and marketing people in the country. In short, this is quite possibly the most gifted citizen in the land. If you are buying that, then I can't help you. If representing a player isn't enough or if you really don't understand how to do it, then why not camouflage that fact with some pure unadulterated bull crap.

In fact, the pendulum I often speak of has now swung so far in the direction of the players that the screwing is now being done, in large part, to the teams and its fans. The problem has gotten to this point because the owners have misread the entire scene. To counterbalance the situation they have created, the owners invoke rule upon rule to save themselves from themselves. They have created salary caps, rookie wage scales, minimums, maximums, escrows, luxury taxes, and so on.

Nothing works. They have, in essence, choked themselves on their own rules. In their effort to control spending, their rules have promoted spending. Rules alone cannot do it. Rules without common sense don't work. In the NBA, a maximum salary provision is now really a slot that is given to anyone coming close to qualifying for a contract. Let's take one of their rules and illustrate what I'm talking about.

Several years ago, through the efforts primarily of the agents, in the NBA, we were able to institute an exception to the salary cap called "the mid-level exception." The purpose of this exception was to enable a team to exceed the set salary cap by adding a way to pay a player the average salary in the league at the time.

When this exception was created, the average salary was under $3 million per year. The teams could use this exception, or they could choose not to use it. Additionally, the teams could split up the exception into two parts by splitting the money whichever way they wanted. In other words, they could negotiate with the agents. Lastly, and most illustrative of my point, the average salary would rise each year so that today, for instance, it is in excess of $5 million.

From the very beginning of this exception, the teams have merely turned this opportunity for some form of flexibility in the cap into another slot that they give out to whoever happens to be lucky enough to be a free agent at the time. Quality means nothing. As an agent, you don't negotiate the mid-level exception as was intended. You merely demand it. How else can one explain the following situation. In the summer of 2004, separate NBA organizations negotiated identical contracts for the following very disparate players: Adonal Foyle, Brian Cardinal, Marquis Daniels, Mark Blount, and more. The going rate gave each player a total of $37 million over a period of six years. No differences. Amazing. Forget the issue of whether they were all worth that kind of money. That's another chapter. But why all of the identical deals? Do you really mean to tell me that if Brian Cardinal was offered only $34 million he wouldn't have signed?

The reality of it was that Daniels signed his contract first for the full mid-level exception, and all of the rest just fell in line. The final question to answer is what would have happened if, heaven forbid, Brian Cardinal or Mark Blount turned down those offers and signed somewhere else? The answer is equally disturbing—their teams would have been a lot better off.

THE CESSPOOL!

I obviously have issues with this notion of recruiting players rather than representing them. Let's be straight here. I have been in this business of agenting for twenty-six years. I have also made a terrific living from it. To survive in this business, you can't be pure as the driven snow. I have done my share of recruiting as well. In today's world, these forms of distasteful activities are a given. It's a tough business, and if you want to survive, you have to fight back, and I have.

My problem with the recruiters is the disingenuousness of their entire approach. Most, if not all, of the agents that the media and the public view as superagents employ runners to do their heavy lifting. Runners are guys who can get to players through various means. None of these means are sanctioned by the NBPA.

There really is nothing the NBPA can do about it because the runners are not part of the NBPA. The NBPA is not the FBI, and it would need to be to police these goings on. Therefore, the agents avoid any sanctions from the union that they do belong to. Agents are nothing if not clever and devious. If a runner gives anything to a prospect, the agent simply disavows any knowledge or contact. If a runner gives anything to AAU coaches or the kids' high school coaches, so what!

I know the general perception of these AAU coaches and programs. People assume that these are all inner city teams from poor neighborhoods. That may well be the stereotype, and it obviously does apply, but it doesn't stop there.

I was personally involved with an AAU coach from the suburbs. He enlisted my aid to advise one of his former players. I did so for about two years. He wanted me to give advice to this kid, a major college player, on whether the player should enter the NBA draft. The understanding in these cases is that after giving this advice, the player will sign with you when his eligibility is over. I must have met with this coach fifteen times and did what was asked.

After advising him to stay in school through his senior year, he was drafted in the top fifteen picks of the NBA draft. I never got the opportunity to speak directly with the player, only with his AAU coach. He signed with an agent known for providing incentives to do so. I heard from several reputable sources that the price was $250,000 to the AAU coach.

Can I prove this? I don't have any video of the actual transaction. I also don't have the time. You suck it up and move along. What gnaws at me through all of these incidents and the dishonesty is the fact that we are, in many of these cases, talking about coaches. I was a coach. I was proud of it. I coached high school kids for sixteen years while I was representing basketball players. When asked why I coached since I apparently didn't need the extra money, my response was, "I have to do something honorable." I meant that!

The thought of cashing in on any of my own high school players' abilities or opportunities is a leap I just can't make. I know the world is a corrupt place, but coaches were always different to me. They were above it. Not anymore. Obviously, this doesn't apply to all coaches. There are still great ones out there. There are still many coaches who truly care about the players entrusted to them. These guys have gone way beyond what was expected of them when they agreed to coach a high school or college basketball team. In fact, the vast majority would never get involved with any of this. There are enough though to make this cesspool of activity smell even worse.

The power that certain AAU programs have over top basketball prospects is not a good thing. The power that certain sneaker companies have is not a good thing. These entities have eroded the power or influence of legitimate high school coaches and administrators throughout the country.

The fact that the major sneaker companies openly flaunt their ties to major college coaches is a stain on the game. It is totally unregulated by the NCAA as well. The reason for this is simple. These contacts with elite players begin before they enter college, thereby putting them out of the reach of any NCAA rule. Therefore, literally every major college basketball player that you see playing in the NCAA tournament in March is probably eligible only due to the timing of his infractions.

This is a damaging thing. The lack of respect for the high school coach has become epidemic. It is in part due to this erosion of his influence. What this has fostered is quality coaches fleeing from the schools. It's just not worth it anymore. They not only deal with AAU teams, but also now parents throughout the nation know more than their kids' coaches.

What is even worse is that since many coaches in high school have had it, the quality of coaching itself has disintegrated. My youngest son, in fact, just finished his eighth-grade basketball season. After suffering through a bad coach the year before, the school hired a new one. This one didn't know how to call a timeout. I am not exaggerating. It took five games for him to figure it out. Substitutions I guess will be discussed next year. Our schools today are filled with coaches and referees just collecting a check. It's not hard to figure out where the respect has gone. At least in most AAU programs, they know the game. It's the side games that are troubling.

SIX

THE SCALES OF JUSTICE
The Houston Rockets
versus Chuck Nevitt

The issue of the necessity for having an agent versus not having an agent revolves, in part, from one's own particular perspective. Let's take my perspective first. Of course, you need an agent. I've got five kids and countless wives to deal with. Everyone needs an agent! I am currently trying to represent my gardener.

My own selfish agenda aside, I also found Isiah Thomas's perspective interesting as well. Isiah, as most will know, was one the greatest point guards to ever play the game. He also was the president of the players' union and, as such, appeared to be extremely antiagent. To agents, he seemed to be urging players to keep more distance between themselves and their representatives. He implied that they really didn't need their agents quite as much as they thought. This made us a little bit testy. When your livelihood is threatened, people get a little testy.

At this same time, one of my favorite and most unique players, Chuck Nevitt, was playing with Isiah on the championship teams of the Detroit Pistons. Somehow Chuck and Isiah became very close friends. They didn't exactly seem destined to become close friends, but they did. That is one of the beautiful things about sports. Their paths to Detroit could not have been more opposite. Isiah Thomas was the second pick in the NBA draft. I think Chuck was 137th. Isiah was a prospect; Chuck was a suspect.

After both of them retired from playing, Isiah became the first president of the expansion Toronto Raptors. Chuck went home to North Carolina to begin his real life, which we had somehow managed to delay for about nine years or so. The Raptors had no players. One of Isiah's main functions was to prepare for the upcoming expansion draft. This was one of the ways the Raptors would start acquiring players. An NBA team could "protect" eight players from their roster and had to expose four players to the expansion teams. The Raptors could choose one of those four unprotected players from any team.

Isiah was trying to assess which players might be unprotected around the league. In that effort, he called me to inquire about one of my players, Mahmoud Abdul-Rauf. Mahmoud was a tremendous talent, but he was struggling with the Denver Nuggets. He also was earning over $3 million per year off a contract we had just negotiated with the Nuggets.

I informed Isiah that I thought there was a good chance that he could get him in the expansion draft. I also told Isiah that Mahmoud made a lot of money and that he had a great agent, meaning me, of course. Isiah shot back quickly, "No Keith, Mahmoud's a great *player*; Chuck Nevitt had a great *agent*!"

When I look back at my relationship with Chuck, I guess I should have realized that everything that had to do with him was going to be at least a little unusual. I first met Chuck Nevitt, all seven feet five inches tall and 225 pounds of him, in Las Vegas in 1981 at the Las Vegas Pizza Hut Invitational Basketball Tournament. This showcased the best college seniors in the country for the NBA scouts for the upcoming draft. When I met Chuck, he was on his knees in the casino shooting crap, so he was really only about five feet ten inches tall, or eye level to me, at that point. Everything that happened since then in terms of my relationship with Chuck has followed suit.

A lot of big people have problems with being so large. They have issues with being so different from everyone else. Not Chuck. He always appeared to be comfortable in his own skin. I'm sure he had his moments, but not publicly. Not only can people be insensitive when they see a person over seven feet tall, but also they can be downright rude and insulting. The mere size of some players unnerves many people, and to level the situation, they say some pretty stupid things. After Kareem Abdul-Jabbar was asked one time too many "how is the weather up there," in an elevator, he supposedly spit on the guy and told him "It's raining."

Chuck was the polar opposite. We were in an elevator also, and an unsuspecting woman asked Chuck, "How big are you?" Chuck's response was, "Standing up or lying down?" Different approach for different men. Chuck was the most personable of people. He never carried himself like an NBA player. Maybe that was because he barely was one. Although we managed to stay in the league for nine years, Chuck averaged 1.2 points per game over that time. Suffice it to say, when the Hall of Fame ballots were tabulated, we didn't check the papers the following day for Chuck's name.

Personality-wise, he was an all-star. At our fund-raiser for six years, it was always Chuck to whom everyone gravitated. It was always Chuck who every golfer wanted in his foursome. It was always Chuck who helped with the auction.

In 1982, during a North Carolina State practice when Chuck was a senior on the team, he appeared extremely nervous. His coach, the late Jim Valvano, asked what was making him so nervous. Chuck said, "My sister is having a baby, and I don't know if I'm going to be an aunt or an uncle."

I signed Chuck several years after he had graduated from North Carolina State University and had been cut three or four times from different teams in the league. My brother, Brent, worked with his mother-in-law and put us together. So, the unusual nature of our relationship got off to that kind of a start. My normal way of attracting clients is not by having their mother-in-law work with my brother in North Carolina. But that fact, coupled with the reputation I was developing with backup centers, clinched this deal.

I sent Chuck to nine or ten different NBA training camps, summer leagues, rookie camps, or whatever you could think of that first year. And he was sent back every time with a different demeaning, negative reaction. One suggested a career in insurance; others weren't so kind. I finally sent him to the Lakers and got a phone call from Jerry West, who said, "You know, Keith, he's not that bad."

Armed with that unbelievable endorsement, we proceeded to go back to the Lakers because certainly nobody else wanted him. Instead of releasing him, they gave him a job selling tickets in the ticket office. And he was a darned good one. What they did from there was when they had an injury, Chuck was put on the roster. As a matter of fact, he filled in and did a fairly decent job. From there, we went to Detroit, New York, Houston, San Antonio, and back to Houston. And it is in Houston, that his story takes its most interesting twist.

Earlier in this book, I discussed agents in their negative forms. However, there are naturally occasions and events where an agent is not only necessary, but also essential to protect and fully service his client, almost like a real lawyer. Chuck Nevitt and the Houston Rockets gave me the opportunity to impersonate an actual lawyer when his case was finally heard in 1992.

The circumstances, like the client himself, were unusual to say the least. Chuck had played for the Rockets, if you want to call it that, the season before. He averaged 1.6 points per game, scoring a total of sixty-five points for the season. He averaged 1.5 rebounds per game after grabbing a total of sixty-four. He managed to accomplish these feats while playing a total of 228 minutes in forty-three games for the entire season. As usual, I was prepared to begin my search for a new team for Chuck. This was a yearly occurrence for me, like the coming of spring.

Ray Patterson was the general manager of the Rockets that year and in June he was vacationing in Europe. I don't know if it was something in the food or if he was disoriented from the trip itself, but when he returned in early July, he called to discuss a contract for Chuck Nevitt. Believe me, I love being a hero. However, the truth was that without any prodding from me at all, Ray offered me a two-year contract for Chuck. This was great, but the really unbelievable part was that they were willing to fully guarantee the two years.

For a player like Chuck, this was unheard of. I was legitimately shocked. After taking a few seconds to get up off the floor and compose myself, I naturally asked for three years guaranteed. The beauty of being an agent is being able to justify almost anything. By the time that phone call ended, I was positively indignant about the Rockets not guaranteeing that third year.

After calling Chuck to inform him of the offer and Chuck checking the calendar to make sure it wasn't April 1, I proceeded to try and accomplish my goal of the third-year guarantee. Ray and I discussed and argued to a degree over that third year. What I try to do in any negotiation is to establish what the concerns of the other side are. Ray basically informed me that the reason they wouldn't do the third year was because of Chuck's weight. Actually, because of Chuck's lack of weight. At seven feet five inches tall, Chuck weighed in at about 225 pounds. There were times that he was in danger of disappearing completely. The Rockets' concern was that because of his slight build, he could not compete in the post against the giant centers that roam the NBA. What was particularly troubling to the Rockets was that they did not believe that Chuck could ever gain the weight.

This is where they volunteered a bit too much information. This was my opening. I asked Ray how much they wanted Chuck to weigh. They said ideally 255. My logical inquiry was that if Chuck did indeed weigh 255, would they therefore have no problem guaranteeing the third year? Ray said that was true, but how could we determine that?

Enter the now infamous Chuck Nevitt weight clause. I simply stated that in addition to the $300,000 annual salary for the first two years, Chuck would be given a bonus of $25,000 pending a weigh-in after year one if he had gained fifteen pounds and, therefore, weighed in at 240 pounds. He would also be given another $25,000 bonus if he weighed the requested 255 pounds after year two. One last point that we added was that in addition to the bonuses, if he reached the required 255 after year two, then the entire third year worth $350,000 was to be fully guaranteed as well.

Houston went along with this proposal, and we signed a three-year contract with the first two years guaranteed and the third year contingent on Chuck gaining weight. I can't tell you how many women have approached me about getting them similar deals.

It was at this point in time that Ray's son, Steve Patterson, took over the general manager's job of the Rockets because Ray retired. Steve is a good guy and currently is the president of the Portland Trailblazers.

Everything was fine. Chuck and I were thrilled. It was the first real security that Chuck and his wife, Sondra, had ever enjoyed—three years in Houston. There was only one small glitch. In December of the *first* year, they waived Chuck. To the uninformed, you can translate *waived* as *cut, released,* or *don't let the door hit you in the ass on the way out.*

This was a blow. We didn't see it coming either. You clearly don't expect to be waived a month after you sign a three-year deal for a million dollars. Chuck's final statistics for the 1990–1991 season were three games played, four total points, and three rebounds for the season. I knew that the Rockets would automatically pay for the first two years. They were guaranteed. The third one was different since it was contingent on Chuck's weight, but it was down the road a bit, and I wasn't that concerned.

The weigh-in dates were for June 1 of each year. Around May 15 of the first year, I called Steve Patterson and innocently asked: "Where's the weigh-in?" Steve's response was, "What weigh-in?" After I informed him that it was for Chuck Nevitt who they had not seen for six months, I admit Steve got a little testy. He said basically, "Keith, you have pulled a lot of crap in this league, but you're not going to pull off this one!"

I realize that this may sound strange and certainly self-centered, but I honestly never thought that I was trying to pull anything in this situation. It was very clear to me. We were prepared to play in Houston. We didn't want to be released. We signed a contract in good faith, and a major part of that contract was contingent on Chuck weighing 255 pounds. We had every intention of him doing exactly that. Steve's view was specifically,

"Keith, we don't give a shit what he weighs!" I said that I did and also that he was bulking up on the pasta as we were speaking.

Realizing that the Rockets were probably not going to provide the place or the scale for the weigh-in, I had to improvise. We went to a doctor in Houston after the first year and had him certify that Chuck indeed weighed 242 pounds on June 1, 1990. The second year was more of a problem. We had signed Chuck to the Miami Tropics of the United States Basketball League (USBL) for the summer. This was Chuck's forty-third team, but he had to play somewhere. I told Chuck to get himself to the emergency room in Miami to be weighed on June 1, 1991—257!

To me, this was open and shut. I understood that Chuck was no longer in the league. He was still, however, a person. A person has a weight. Chuck's was 257. He was required to weigh 255. Show me the money! (Did I just write that?)

What I subsequently discovered was that I was literally the only person who felt this way. The players union, which has defended everybody from Latrell Sprewell for choking his coach to Ron Artest for beating up paying customers, thought I was crazy. They laughed and thought it was a good story, but they said we had no shot.

I filed a grievance with the league and waited for a hearing. We waited a long time. Two years in fact. I think all of them felt that I would, at some point, just go away. I had caused some trouble, and that would probably be enough for me. It wasn't. The Rockets delayed, as most defendants do in these matters. Some key witness was always sick or some such thing, but the day finally came.

On its face, it seemed like a mismatch. Chuck flew in from his home in North Carolina. I drove into Manhattan from the Jersey shore with Bob Susser, who was an attorney I shared office space with in Red Bank. That was our side. The league had three attorneys, and the Rockets flew in their general manager, Steve Patterson. The arbitrator was a nationally known contract law professor, Daniel Collins.

The main attorney for the league, and therefore Houston, was the NBA's lead lawyer, Gary Bettman. He had others with him, but this was clearly his show. All of them had one thing in common. They viewed Chuck, me, and our case as a joke. The overall attitude was one of *what are we even doing here?* I was made to feel like more of an annoyance than an adversary.

I don't practice law for a living. Therefore, I don't get an opportunity like this very often, especially when I believe in my case. I wasn't going to let their disdain for me get in my way. I had to focus on the fact that Chuck had been denied the opportunity to earn his third year. He was released before the weight clause could even go into effect. The truth was that Houston obviously felt that they had made a mistake in signing Chuck in the first place. Why else would you release a player after three games? Whatever the rationale was, Chuck really had nothing to do with it. He accepted an offer. Now the Rockets, in my opinion, were merely trying to get out of 33 percent of their error.

Gary Bettman took over. He called Chuck as his witness. He then proceeded to display why lawyers are so reviled in our society. He never discussed or questioned Chuck about anything that might shed some light on the understandings or intentions of the contract. He sought, instead, to focus on any piece of minutia that could possibly distract the arbitrator from finding out what actually had gone on in the negotiations. Anything to get away from the truth. This was a revelation to me as it was pre-O.J. We were not so blatantly subjected to this type of deception until the Dream Team successfully distracted Judge Ito and a jury away from the issue of how three people's blood ended up on a glove on O.J. Simpson's lawn.

Today, Gary Bettman is widely known as the commissioner of the National Hockey League. He was groomed, however, in the NBA offices. He is also widely credited with forcing the elimination of an entire hockey season. I don't believe this has ever happened in any major sport before. He is obviously a very driven and stubborn individual. If he could cancel a season, you know that Chuck and I would be a piece of cake.

Let me just take this occasion to defend Gary Bettman. People have said that since he became commissioner, he has changed. He has become arrogant, pompous, and condescending. I disagree with that. Being elevated to the position of commissioner didn't change him at all. He was *always* arrogant, pompous, and condescending.

Incredibly, Bettman's approach to this case dealt with what type of scale Chuck got weighed in on. He did this line of questioning for a very long time. When that was mercilessly over, he continued with a new attack on whether Chuck knew the last time these scales had been checked and maintained. I could not believe it. That was it. Nothing else.

Now it was my turn! I realized that in spite of Bettman's attempts to distort the case to a ridiculous argument over scales and maintenance, Professor Collins was too smart to decide this case on that. I realized that the issue here was that the Rockets felt that Chuck's weight wasn't the issue. The fact that Chuck was no longer on their roster was the issue. Under that assumption, I called Steve Patterson as a witness, and the following scene played itself out:

KG: Steve, you're basic premise here is that it was a very important thing for Chuck to be on the actual Houston Rocket roster to collect his bonus and third-year compensation.

SP: Absolutely.

KG: This was a very critical part of your contract.

SP: Yes.

KG: Were there other elements to this contract? For example, was there a minutes bonus as well as the weight clause?

SP: Yes.

KG: Was that important to the Rockets?

SP: Yes.

KG: Was that more important to the Rockets than him being on the roster in order to make his weight bonus?

SP: No, no, it was more important to us that he was on the roster for the year in order to have the weight clause go into effect.

I then proceeded to enumerate every other clause in the contract and question Steve on the issue of whether that particular clause was more or less important than the weight clause and the necessity of Chuck being on the roster in order to collect it. In every instance, the answer was the same. Chuck's being on the roster to put the weight clause into action was more important to the Rockets than any other clause in that contract!

KG: Now, Mr. Patterson, if this issue of Chuck being on your roster to meet his weight bonus was more important than every other clause in your contract, then why didn't you put it in the contract when you put all of the other less important clauses in the contract?

SP: I don't know.

KG: One last question. Who drafted this contract? (Never ask a question you don't know the answer to.)

SP: Well, honestly, obviously we did. The club drafted the contract.

KG: You know, Professor Collins, I'm not even a real lawyer. I'm licensed and everything, but not like Mr. Bettman and these other real ones. I'm just a basketball guy, and basketball players like me and trust me to protect their interests when they think they're getting screwed. But it's funny, the *only* thing I remember from law school is this: Any ambiguity in a contract is to be construed against the drafter of that contract.

Professor, I didn't draft this contract, the Houston Rockets did!

I rested my side, and we took a break. I went out to get some water in the hallway. In front of me was Professor Collins. When he finished his turn at the fountain, he saw me and had a knowing smile on his face. He said, "You know son, the next time you are before me, I'll bet you remember something else from law school."

About ten days later, I was faxed the decision. Chuck was to receive his entire $350,000 salary for the third year. The bonuses were eliminated. I still don't understand why, but I am a forgiving guy. I heard that the Rocket's owner was not thrilled making out that check, but a copy of it is hanging on my office wall.

Eight days after that decision came down, the Houston Rockets drafted Robert Horry, my client. Not that I needed the lesson, but it at least showed me that if you fight the good fight and believe in what you are doing, things work out. The Rockets didn't hold it against me for fighting. In the end, I think they respected me for it. Agents are scumbags, but once in awhile, we do the unexpected.

"Always do right. This will surprise some people and astonish the rest!"

MARK TWAIN

SEVEN

LEAVE THE NAPKINS; TAKE THE CANNOLI

In March 1986 while I was sitting in my den and watching the NCAA tournament, the phone rang. It was Larry Brown. He was at the press table of the game I was watching between Georgetown and Michigan State. Georgetown was the favorite, but the point guard from Michigan State guard was terrorizing them. Larry was then the coach at Kansas and his team, having just won their game, was to play the winner of this one in the next round of the tournament.

This point guard for Michigan State had just completed one of the great passes in NCAA history and had given his team an improbable lead toward the end of the game that Michigan State would ultimately win. The kid was not only good, his competitiveness almost came right through the TV at you. He was battling, and he was having fun.

Larry called only to say, "Keith, I'm watching a kid that you have to sign! He's the only kid I've ever seen as obnoxious as you!"

Enter Scott Skiles into my life.

It wasn't that easy. It never is. Naturally, there is a story. This one began some time before. I had wanted to try and sign a very talented player from Michigan State University. The only trouble was I didn't know anyone associated with the school. One of my closest friends then and now is George Irvine, who was at the time the vice president of the Indiana Pacers. George had mentioned that he had been friendly with the coach at Michigan State. He said he would call to introduce me, and then I'd be on my own. George also warned me that the coach could be a very gruff and blunt guy.

Coach Jud Heathcote is one of those guys who you look at and realize you don't want to piss him off. He and Magic Johnson had led Michigan State to a watershed win over Larry Bird and Indiana State for the National Championship in 1979. This game has long been credited with starting the craze that has become March Madness today. The appeal of Magic and Bird continued into the NBA and actually saved the league from itself. The unselfishness and dedication of both of these players spread throughout a selfish league and elevated the quality and style of play for years.

When Magic and Bird were joined a few years later by Michael Jordan, David Stern and his marketing people took it from there. The problem in my eyes is that they miss these three so much that they have been trying to recreate them ever since. That never works. This holy trinity was a unique occurrence. To attempt to try and make the public believe that you can duplicate it by merely substituting names is insulting, or should be. I suggest trusting the fans to make that decision based on actual performance rather than by some fabricated marketing plan.

Kobe Bryant is the next Michael. Lebron James is the next Magic. Dirk Nowitski is the next Bird. I always find it interesting that we are still, in the twenty-first century, not able to compare Bird to a black player or Magic to a white one. I guess that will be our acid test for when we are really making some progress in that area.

With this as a backdrop, I called Jud Heathcote. Even with George's warning, I wasn't totally prepared for Jud—I don't think anybody ever really is. "Coach, my name is Keith Glass, and I'm a friend of George Irvine's." I explained that I was interested in one of his players. He said that would be fine, and we could meet out in Hawaii, which was after his season was over. Jud was going to be coaching one of the teams in the Aloha Classic, which unfortunately doesn't exist anymore.

I thanked Jud very much for that opportunity, but knowing the business better than Jud, this was October, and Hawaii was some seven months away. I realized very well that the kid was going to be approached long before he got to sit down with me in Hawaii. Therefore, I would have absolutely no chance at all to sign him. I informed Jud of my concerns in that area. "Coach with all due respect, I appreciate the chance, but I think you guy will probably be signed by the time we get to Hawaii." Jud's response, typical of Jud, was, "Well then, he'll be signed." He then hung up the phone.

I realized right then that I was going to have to do this his way or no way. In the agent business, there is always another way. Simply, say the hell with the coach and go behind his back to get to the player. That never crossed my mind. I had and have too much respect for coaches and coaching. Also, in this case with my baptism into Jud's nature, I also wanted to continue to live.

Seven months later, out to Hawaii I went. A twelve-hour flight from New Jersey. I never contacted the player; I maybe sent Jud a letter or something to indicate that I still wanted to have the meeting. The meeting was scheduled for Jud's suite. I walked in, and the kid was sitting on the couch facing me. Jud was sitting in the chair, and he said, "Okay, Glass, you're a lawyer—start talking." So, I talked. I talked for an hour and ten minutes, rambling along, as I am known to do. In the middle of a sentence, Jud stopped me:

JUD: Let me tell you something, Keith; I've been involved in about ten of these meetings with Earvin Johnson, and Gregory Kelser, and the Vincent brothers, and everyone else, and I gotta tell you, you're the most impressive guy I've listened to yet. If I was him, I'd sign with you right now. But I can't play anymore, and you have absolutely no chance of signing him, and I don't wanna waste any more of your time. Thanks a lot for showing up.

KG: Well Coach, I appreciate the words—the kind words—but just out of curiosity, why do I have no chance?

JUD: Well, you're not what he wants. . . . you're just an honest guy. Where's the car? Where's the broads? Where's the money under the table? Don't you have a black guy that works for you?

PLAYER: Aw, it's not like that, Coach!

JUD: It's exactly like that!

With that little exchange, I realized that Jud was trying to educate his player. I understood now that Jud was that rare breed of coach or person that truly gave a crap about "his kids." Even though I was not going to get him, I felt good about, if not a bit shell-shocked from, the experience. I got up to leave, and Jud walked me out of the suite. He said, "You know, I meant everything I said in there. I appreciate the way you went about this, appreciate the way you did it, and someday, I'll need you, and you won't have to come and find me. I'll find you! Now let's get something to eat!"

A year later, I'm watching Jud and Scott Skiles battle Georgetown when I get the above mentioned call from Larry. With Michigan State winning, it set up a NCAA tournament game between Larry's Kansas Jayhawks and Jud and Scott's Spartans. The stakes were obviously very high. The winner would go on to the Elite 8 with a chance for the Final Four in Dallas while the loser went home. I decided that this was one game I wanted to see in person. I traveled to Kansas City for the game. It was a terrific contest that was actually marred by a clock error in the second half. The clock had stopped or ran inaccurately and there was quite an outcry from the Michigan State bench. Jud in particular.

The game was close all the way with Kansas winning it at the end. An incident caught my attention as well. Scott had just hit another long jumper. It was his eleventh consecutive point for his team, and he also brought Michigan State to within three points. While running back on defense after the shot, there was an exchange between Larry and Scott. It was clearly initiated by Scott. After the game, the reporters were curious about what was said during that exchange. Normally, a player doesn't have too much to say to the other coach. Larry informed the media that Scott said "Coach, you better call time-out!"

They asked Larry what he did in response, and he said: "I called time-out. The kid had the rest of the game figured out!"

Larry and Kansas beat Jim Valvano's North Carolina State team two days later, and they were on the way to Dallas and the Final Four. While walking across the lobby of the Anatole Hotel, which was the NCAA headquarters for the Final Four, I heard a familiar voice paging me from across the lobby. In the middle of a crowd was Jud. And he said to me, "Glass, I need ya."

On Jud's say so, and coupled with the knowledge that Scott Skiles could really play, I'm back in Hawaii. From the beginning, the kid started to demonstrate why he was and is different. We met for dinner the first night in Honolulu. Since we had just arrived and I was tired, I told Scott that we should just have dinner and relax. We could talk business the next day at lunch.

The following day all of us went to practice. There were at least fifty agents in the gym, all of whom wanted a shot at any potential first rounder. They don't discriminate. Scott qualified. I was standing with a bunch of NBA people when Scott simply made a bee line for me through the other agents and said, "you said we could talk at lunch; how about today!" Any other player in that position plays it differently. They wait to be recruited. They play it cool and make you go to them. Not Scott. No games, no nonsense, and that's the way it's been ever since.

We had lunch that day, and I started to talk to him and casually mentioned that if he signed with me, I would try this and that, the normal bull crap. I never completed that sentence. He stopped me to say, "Oh, Keith, I'm signing with you and understand that I'll never leave you."

Twenty years later that is exactly the case. I can't get rid of him. If you actually finish reading this book, you will come to realize how unique an approach and result that is in this business. In a business as nasty and disloyal as this one, it was a display of loyalty that unfortunately is very rare.

Scott was actually ready to sign right there. He did, however, want to call his father to discuss it. He told his father that he had met a lawyer, and he was comfortable with him and wanted to sign. And his dad said, "Well look, Scottie, you know, you're a big boy, and it's your decision, but you met him last night; I'd hate to see you go off half-cocked like that—so quick."

Scott's response was, "Dad, Keith has kept Chuck Nevitt, Stuart Gray, and Greg Kite in the league for three or four years."

There was silence, and his dad said, "Well, maybe you ought to go ahead and sign."

SEND EVERY TAXICAB ON THE ISLAND

That trip to Hawaii included one of the funniest scenes I have ever witnessed. Marty Blake, the NBA guru of player procurement, and the people in Hawaii had decided for some unknown reason not to have all of the games in the same arena on the big island. We used to have all of the games at one location, the University of Hawaii. This year, to attract bigger crowds or more attention to all of the different islands of Hawaii, they scheduled one game in Kauai. This necessitated that all NBA personnel, scouts, general managers, head coaches, assistant coaches, even some owners, all the agents that were there, and, of course, the players themselves to fly small planes to the island of Kauai. We had another game scheduled the next night on the island of Maui.

All of us were packed into little planes. Jerry Reynolds from the Sacramento Kings, who has since been their coach and player personnel director and is currently their television color man, was sitting next to me. Bob Ferry from the Bullets, Wes Unseld, and Willis Reed were also on board. George Irvine, Elgin Baylor, and Lenny Wilkins were also with us. There had to be a hundred us. When we got to the airport in Kauai, it was like a scene from *It's a Mad, Mad, Mad, Mad World*. The entire management section of the NBA landed to find no ground transportation to the game waiting for them at all. And they proceeded to go running—and I'm talking literally running—Wayne Embry, Cotton Fitzsimmons, and so on—trying to get cabs, trying to get rental cars (which was not easy at that airport). It was, to say the least, a very surreal scene considering the people involved.

I remember Stan Kasten, then the general manager of the Atlanta Hawks, yelling on the phone to a taxi stand, "Send all your cabs immediately to the airport!" Some guys managed to get rental cars. Everybody took off in a different direction, with no plan. I had the good fortune to end up with the late Gary Wortman, a terrific NBA scout and person, and Lenny Wilkins, who has gone on to break Red Auerbach's record of total wins in the NBA. We went to dinner at a Hawaiian-type restaurant, where we had to take our shoes off, and our feet were in a well underneath us. I'm not saying this because he bought dinner, but Lenny Wilkins turned out to be one of the classiest people that I've met in this business. I've, therefore, been *very* thrilled for him and the success that he's had. He is the most down-to-earth and easy-going of guys, just a nice human being and another guy who coached the Knicks later on.

Even though all of us had taken different and circuitous routes, everyone actually ended up at the game site somehow. It was a high school gym, and it was packed. This was a big event for Kauai. It also was extremely hot in that gym. Scott was playing, and so was Maurice Martin (aka, Mo), another player that I had signed out of St. Josephs University in Pennsylvania. Mo would become the fifteenth pick in the first round of the NBA draft two months later.

I represented Mo throughout his short, injury-plagued career in spite of my son, Tyler. When I signed Mo, he came to stay with me at my house for a couple of weeks. Tyler was four years old, and Mo and Tyler became fast friends. They hung out all day together. They did everything together or so I guess Tyler thought. While I was on the phone, Mo was attempting to take a shower. His little friend, apparently, assumed there was an invitation for him as well. The following exchange occurred, Tyler yelling from the bathroom:

TYLER: Hey Dad, did you know that Mo is brown?

KG: Yes, Tyler, I did.

TYLER: *Everywhere?*

Back on the island of Kauai, everybody was falling; everybody was slipping on the floor. It was so hot that condensation started to form on the gym floor. They weren't used to having games, in April, in that part of the island and in that kind of heat. It got to the point where I reluctantly told Scott and Mo to stop playing. Somebody was going to get hurt. A quarter into the game, they had Larry, who was coaching one of the teams, get on the PA to apologize and say that they couldn't play anymore. Refunds were going to be given, which was not what these people had in mind when they bought their tickets and planned their evening. It was just one of the biggest fiascos that I've ever been involved in. I'll be honest: I thought we were going to have some trouble getting out of there. The fans were a little restless!

All of us made it safely off of Kauai, and Scott went on to play in the NBA predraft camp in Chicago. He played well enough there to be selected in the first round of the NBA draft a month later, number twenty-two to Milwaukee. It still bothers him that he went that "late." We were both flown in to Milwaukee for a press conference the day after the draft. After the press conference was over, two conversations stick out for me. The first involved a meeting with Don Nelson, who was both the coach and general manger of the Milwaukee Bucks at the time. It was my first time meeting "Nellie," and I have to say that I liked him and still do.

At this initial meeting for Scott's contract, I guess he wanted to show who was going to be the boss. He said basically "Keith, I'm going to show you an offer, and if you don't think it's a fair one, just get up and leave!" It was a three-year deal, and, to be honest, it was very fair as a starting offer. I left!

At the airport on the way home, Scott and I were sitting waiting for our flights. I told Scott about my meeting with Nellie. Again he demonstrated why representing him was going to be different. He said, "Keith, I know that you have to go about these negotiations in a certain way and that you probably enjoy it, but if we took what Nellie just offered, what would my checks look like?" I figured it out and broke down what he would be receiving twice a month. He started laughing out loud and noted, "That's more than people back home make in a year!" No sense of entitlement, just amazement and gratitude. It was refreshing to see a player, even in 1986, who realized that he was about to become rich for playing a kid's game he would have played free.

Scott allowed me to have my fun with Nellie, but in the end, we agreed to his first NBA contract. I remember going to the Spectrum in Philadelphia, to watch him play the 76ers his rookie year. Nellie obviously loved Scott. He didn't start the game, but he put him in when they were down by eight or nine points in the middle of the first quarter and never took him out the rest of the game. The Bucks came back and won. I saw Nellie in the lobby of the team's hotel. Nellie gave me this little grin and said, "You know what the trouble is with your boy, Keith? He has no balls."

Scott had a decent, but not spectacular, rookie season in Milwaukee, but he wanted to get out. He had injured his back during that initial season and had a feeling that there were some management people who didn't think he was hurt that badly. Not Nellie or the coaches, but others in the front office who had no clue how tough and proud a player he was. Indiana was home, and Scott asked almost casually if I could somehow get him traded to the Pacers. I don't remember how we did it, but George Irvine and another friend of mine, Donnie Walsh, were running the Pacers, and we got it done.

But there were more struggles with the Pacers. The problem with Scott was that he was the type of player who had to play major minutes. He was a natural leader, and from the point guard spot, he could really run a team and showcase his abilities. As a backup point guard playing twelve minutes a night, that was not going to happen. There was no opportunity to put his stamp on the team, and his leadership and intangibles were eliminated. The prevailing thought in the league was that he was a backup. He was, quite frankly, one of the worst backups in the league. Scott had to play! During his rookie summer league while with Milwaukee, I had to physically take him and play with him in a park in Los Angeles because he wasn't getting enough minutes with the Bucks.

The reason that Scott and other players have problems with these types of situations is rooted, in some ways, in a not-so-subtle form of prejudice— the prejudging of people based on size, shape, and obviously, color. Prejudice flows in all directions. If you are black, you're labeled. You're an athlete. The inference in this one is particularly disturbing. In that one observation, people seem to discount totally the effort that every player has to make to achieve a certain level of play. You get lumped into a category of players who are simply naturally gifted. They haven't worked at their game. They are therefore not great shooters because that takes practice—natural athletes like Reggie Miller and Michael Redd, who obviously have *never* worked on their jumper. Yeah, right. If you're white, you're labeled as well. You are probably a stand-still shooter. You can't create your own shot, etc.

I recall a conversation I had in the late 1980s with Jerry Krause, the general manager of the Chicago Bulls. We were talking about a client I had just signed named Steve Henson from Kansas State. I was trying to get Steve drafted. When Jerry told me matter-of-factly that Steve was not a very good athlete, I had heard enough and asked him if he was aware that Steve Henson had won the decathlon in high school? Did he realize that Steve Henson was a seven-foot high jumper? That was the end of that conversation. Steve was drafted by Milwaukee and spent eight years in the NBA. Yet Jerry Krause and the Chicago Bulls would win six NBA titles. Then again, it didn't hurt to have two guys on the roster named Michael Jordan and Scottie Pippen.

Meanwhile, Scott Skiles was a backup in Indiana, and not a happy one either. He did spend two seasons with them, but he never made the impact that we knew he could. In the middle of a Pacer practice one day, I got a call from Scott. He was whispering, and he was pissed off. "Keith, do you know what the coaches just told me to do? They told me to *swing* the freakin' ball! I don't *swing* the freakin' ball; I *shoot* the freakin' ball!"

Maybe it was time to get out Indiana. Thank goodness for NBA expansion. Sometimes greed is good, at least when the money flows in the direction of my clients. In 1989, a gentleman named Pat Williams brought NBA basketball to Orlando, Florida, as part of the NBA expansion. There were to be other franchises in Miami, Charlotte, and Minnesota. Each franchise cost the new owners about $36 million to buy. Today, they are worth north of $300 million or so. Pat actually wrote a book called *Making Magic*, which was an in-depth look at how an expansion franchise is obtained.

An expansion team gets its initial roster of players through a separate draft—the expansion draft. Basically, players that existing teams either don't want or who make a lot of money compared to their contributions are exposed to the expansion teams. The new teams then have the right to select from this list of exposed players. The existing teams in the league get to protect eight players. If a player is overpaid, then their team won't put them on the protected list, hoping that they can get relief from the mistake that they already made. Professional sports is a beautiful thing. In what other industry can you make multimillion dollar mistakes and simply ignore or trade them away to somebody who is more than happy to give you his multimillion dollar mistake in return?

Due to his mediocre performance and limited opportunities with the Pacers, Scott was indeed exposed to the expansion draft. It was something that we both wanted to happen. I felt that with a brand new franchise with no encumbrances toward existing players, Scott would at least get an opportunity to be the go-to guy. If he didn't cash in that chance, then he and I could live with it, but we wanted that new lease on his basketball life.

He was indeed selected, and he attacked his opportunity like he does most things. However, even in Orlando, they had players in front of him. Nobody believed he could do it. Nobody thought that he was a starting point guard in the NBA.

It wasn't immediate, but Scott slowly started to assert himself into an actual career with this original Orlando Magic entry. He played about the same amount of minutes as he had in Indiana the previous year, but he knew that he could take over the following season. He had an extraordinary second half of the 1989–1990 season, and in fact, he was named the Magic's MVP.

On top of these accomplishments, it became almost embarrassingly apparent that Scott Skiles was the most popular player on the team. I think if you did a survey today, sixteen years later, Scott Skiles would still rank as the most popular player in the history of the franchise. Keep in mind that this is the team that drafted Shaquille O'Neal, who led them to the NBA Finals.

When I began to write this chapter, I realized that I would never be able to fully capture the essence of Scott Skiles. The general public knew him as a tough competitor, which was all too obvious. They also were always drawn to something more. There was a joy in watching him play. You knew he was enjoying the experience, and he never cheated the fans. He said many times, "I hate losing so much; I'd even cheat to win." I personally never believed that. Fans also seemed to respond to the fact that he worked as hard as they did. There was a certain simple honesty there.

After twenty years of being much more to each other than an agent and a client, there are literally a hundred stories I could tell about Scott. One in particular I think shows what he is all about. During the mid 1990s, my family was acquainted with another family who suffered an immeasurable loss. Their four-year-old daughter was stricken with cancer and ultimately succumbed to the disease. When all of us realized that not only were they faced with this nightmare but they also had huge medical bills to pay, a group of us decided to try and use my players and their notoriety to raise some funds to help them.

Thus began "The Follow Thru Fund," aptly named by my eight-year-old son, Alex. I contacted all of my players from around the NBA, and over the next six years, all of them came except for one. Many of them came over and over. Scott came all six years. During our first fund-raising weekend, we had an all-star basketball game, which I coached, and the following day we had a golf tournament. The golf was followed by a dinner and an auction at which I was the auctioneer. I had informed every NBA team of what had happened to this family on the Jersey Shore, and I asked them if they could send me anything that they could have signed for me to auction off. The response from the league was extraordinary. Almost every team in the league sent us something autographed. It really made the auction special. As amazed as I was by the league's generosity, I didn't just want to rely on it, so I gathered anything of value that I thought people would bid on.

I was, admittedly, becoming overwhelmed by the effort, and on the way in to coach the game, my ten-year-old son, Tyler, could sense that I had had enough. He asked, "Dad, why are you doing this?" It made me stop and think. I told him that I thought it was important to give to something that really mattered to me. My time really mattered. He thought that through and told me that he wanted to give something that really mattered to him for me to auction off the following night. He made some pretty lame offers. He had a T-shirt he could clearly spare. A used basketball or two. I informed him that those were not going to get it done. I also added that he didn't have to give anything; I was just trying to answer his question.

During that time period, Larry Brown was the coach of the Indiana Pacers. Therefore, Tyler's favorite player was, by far, Reggie Miller. My parents had gotten Reggie to autograph a jersey for Tyler for his birthday six weeks before our fund-raiser. Suddenly a look of panic crossed Tyler's face. He suddenly understood, and he didn't like the revelation. "Oh no, Dad, not my Reggie Miller jersey!" I explained that he didn't need to give anything, but if he ever gave that up, then that would really be something.

The next night, the dinner and auction was about to begin, and here came Ty hiding something under his little sports jacket. Why, it's the Reggie Miller autographed jersey! It was very emotional for the both of us. I was very proud of him, and he was just plain emotional, on a purely practical level. He was really going to miss that jersey!

The dinner went great, and the auction was generating more money than we had dreamed of. Now it was time for a late added item: a Reggie Miller signed jersey. I took the time to explain how the jersey made its way into the auction, and I then called Tyler up to the podium to help me sell it.

Normally, the first bid at all six of these auctions would be made by my mother. It seemed that her limit of seeing me standing there without a bid was three seconds. Not only would she be quick, but also she would be high. Reggie's jersey, I figured, coupled with Tyler's story, might get us $500. My mom started at $400, and it went up to about $600. I was thrilled. Going once, going twice . . . $700. A new bidder: Scott Skiles. Now I know Scott doesn't particularly like Reggie Miller. The thought of him spending $700 for his jersey, and then it hanging in his den didn't seem to add up. Someone else went to $800. Scott went to $900. From the back of the room, $1,000, which Tyler declared "ten hundred." The winning bid was for $1,100. The bidder was Scott, who bounded up to the podium, handed me a check, and promptly gave the jersey back to Tyler. On his way down the steps, he turned to me and angrily said, "He shouldn't have to give that up, Keith."

The conclusion of the 1989–1990 season also happened to coincide with Scott becoming a free agent that summer. It should have been incredible timing for us. You have the MVP of an NBA team, and he is not under contract. Gold mine! That would have been the case if not for one word preceding the phrase "free agent"—*restricted*. A player in the NBA is labeled a "restricted free agent" based on the number of years he had played in the league. The definition of a restricted free agent changes from time to time, but at this point, Scott did not have enough years of service to qualify him as an unrestricted free agent. This enabled the Magic to match any offer that we were able to procure. This right has a serious dampening effect on the interest of other clubs. The teams in the league figure, *why bother to sign a restricted free agent when his previous team will simply match the offer?* The chilling effect is enormous.

To my way of thinking and in an obvious self-serving way, I never understood why a team wouldn't simply sign restrictive free agents to above fair market levels, to increase the cost to the player's existing team. In other words, put pressure on your competitor to sign their own guy. In reality, however, the way it works in the NBA is that teams are reluctant to piss off another team because when their own free agents hit the market, turn-around will be more than fair play. Suffice it to say that it didn't merely lower the interest in signing Scott to other teams, it eliminated it. I spent the entire summer trying to get anyone to offer us anything. With the type of season Scott just had, there should have been several. There were none.

Since Scott's contract that we had signed followed us from Indiana to Orlando, he was on the books for approximately $360,000. The rule in effect at the time of his impending free agency only required a team to extend an offer to its restricted free agents for 125 percent of the previous year's salary. A team *could* offer more if it wanted to. In other words, to keep their MVP for another year, all the Magic was required to do was offer us $450,000. I understand that is a lot of money in the real world, but the NBA, as you have seen, is not in the neighborhood of the real world. It's not even in the same solar system. For an MVP of any franchise, that was a very low number. I wasn't looking to break the bank on this deal either. I wanted to get Scott a three-year contract for about $600,000 per year. If Orlando offered a total of $1.8 million Scott would have signed it, and we both would have been thrilled.

As general manager and founder of the Orlando Magic, Pat Williams had other ideas. Pat obviously knew the rules, and he was determined to live up to the letter of them. In a case like this, it greatly benefited the team to have all of the power over their best and most popular player. I disagreed with that approach then, as I do now. If a guy performs and you think he is going to continue to perform for you, then pay him. You don't have to go crazy, but be fair. I know that sounds trite, but I have always believed in that approach. So although Pat may have lived up to the letter of the rule, he sure didn't live up to the spirit of the rule.

Pat, armed with the knowledge that I had nothing else in my hands, made it clear that he wasn't going to budge off the minimum number he was required to offer. Scott, however was incensed. He just could not understand why his team wouldn't at least negotiate after he had played so hard and so well. Why would they not even acknowledge that he deserved some kind, any kind, of reward for what he meant to the franchise and the city? Scott was looking for something above what they were required to give him.

I know that when a player or agent says, "it's not about the money," that's what it's usually exactly about. In the case of Scott Skiles, it wasn't. It never was, and it still isn't. The reward for Scott has always been in the actual performing of his job. He just wanted to feel appreciated. He was really struggling with the process.

Just before training camp was to open, I had to tell Scott that I couldn't get anything done from any other team in the NBA. I also had to tell him that the Magic would not move off what they were required to offer. I told him to go to camp and kick everyone in the ass every night. He agreed and started to drive from his home in Indiana back to Florida. Somewhere outside of Savannah, Georgia, he just couldn't swallow it anymore.

He called me from the road and said he was turning around. He would rather not play than accept the manner in which this was being handled. After convincing him to let me call Pat one more time, I did just that. As always, Pat was pleasant and said he was looking forward to having Scott in camp. He also explained the following:

WILLIAMS: I know what you guys want. You want a three-year deal for about $700,000 a year.

KG: That's about right.

WILLIAMS: You know he's worth it, Keith, but I'm not going to give it to you. You want to know why? Because *I don't have to!*

Pat didn't know it at that moment, but he actually had just given me more than I needed. Repeating my exchange word for word to Scott, he got back in his car and sped the rest of the way to Orlando determined to make the Magic and everyone else in the league who doubted him sorry for their snubs.

Scott proceeded to basically terrorize the league that year. He played like he was possessed. The way the summer had progressed (or actually hadn't progressed) fueled him to establish himself as a legit point guard in the league. As with all players, the first step to accomplishing this is the most obvious; you have to get or earn the opportunity. The agent in me has never quite understood the modus operandi of professional teams in this area. In many instances, the difference between one player and the next is merely the chance to play or minutes. I am not talking about the truly great or impact player. I am not talking about Shaq, Michael, or Magic, not the one-name guys. I'm talking about the majority of the players. They have value, but they need a chance. Once given this opportunity, the league treats them as if they can never find another one like them again. This is why you have the Brian Cardinals and Adonal Foyles of the world, "earning" $36 million for six years, and others who are virtually the same players sitting on the bench, in the minor leagues, or playing overseas.

Scott set about grabbing this opportunity early in training camp for the 1990–1991 season. He became the starter and never looked back. Even though a look at his sheer numbers is impressive enough, it does not tell the full story of what he accomplished that season. The year before, when he became the MVP of the team, he averaged 7.7 points per game and 4.8 assists. He played 1,460 minutes—not bad, but not great.

In the 1990–1991 season, Scott played 2,714 minutes. He got his chance, and he cashed it. He averaged 17.2 points per game and 8.4 assists. He shot 377 foul shots and made 340. That's 90.2 percent. He even had a career high for rebounds. Good things can happen when you're actually in the game. It's a tough angle to shoot or pass from when you're sitting on your ass on somebody's bench. In short, Scott had career highs that season for points, assists, free throw percentage, and rebounds. Coincidentally, he also had a career high for minutes played.

Scott was named the NBA's Most Improved Player for that season. Even at the time, I looked on that award as an insult. It was just another way for the league to celebrate one of its mistakes. Instead of just admitting that they never gave the "winner" a chance before that particular year, they spin the error in judgment into a reason for another ceremony. It wasn't that the recipient was previously unjustly ignored; it was that he had "improved" over the year before. Even better, how about if the league actually could claim some credit for this improvement. Yeah, that's it! We taught him how to become an improved player!

This sleight of hand ritual continues and probably will as long as the public buys into it. After all, there's a sucker born every minute as my man Barnum liked to say. In 2006, the league wants us to believe that Boris Diaw of the Phoenix Suns suddenly improved so dramatically that he went from bust to the most improved player over the summer. It's odd since he was six feet eight inches tall the season before with the identical set of skills. Again, the only change was that he was actually on the court consistently and was playing with Steve Nash, who has a tendency to make everybody he plays with better. Why don't we just rename the award the NBA Schmuck-Who-Wouldn't-Listen-to-the-Negative-Bullcrap-About-Him-Last-Year Award? I guess the problem is they can't fit that on a trophy. Enough of my free constructive suggestions. I don't work for nothing!

It is an interesting footnote that Boris Diaw was part of a controversial trade involving Joe Johnson the summer before this miraculous transformation. When Johnson made it plain that he no longer wanted to play third or fourth fiddle to Nash, Amare Stoudamire, and Shawn Marion in Phoenix, the Atlanta Hawks were more than willing not only to pay him the sum of $72 million, but also to actually compensate Phoenix for the privilege. In addition to draft picks being sent, they threw in Boris Diaw, who was deemed totally expendable and an abject flop in Atlanta.

You can now get into an argument not only over whether $72 million was a tad high, but also as to who is the better player, Joe Johnson or Boris Diaw. This will only get more interesting as we will now be treated to Boris Diaw's impending free agency. I can't wait to see those numbers!

Back to Scott Skiles. Since Scott was having a terrific year and now was going to be a free agent again in July, I was becoming much more popular with Pat Williams as well as the other GMs around the league. The difference this time around, however, was the removal of the word restricted. We could go anywhere we wanted with no restrictions and no matching.

In other words, Pat was faced with the very real possibility of losing his best and most popular player and getting nothing back. I never mentioned this fact to Pat, but I thought enough of him to know that he understood.

Pat began to negotiate during that season. At one point, he actually offered me $1 million per year for three years. I rejected it after discussing it for thirty seconds with Scott. We were clearly having too much fun. In addition, every single night Scott was doing something more to elevate his standing and value in the league.

News of this offer and my rejection of it made the papers in Orlando as this negotiation was beginning to draw a ridiculous amount of public attention. It obviously also made some news in East Lansing, Michigan, the home of Michigan State. I discovered this fact when I received a rather irate phone call from Jud:

JUD: You turned down a million dollars a year for three years for that little pissant?!

KG: Yes I did.

JUD: You guys are all alike. You screwed Gregory Kelser (one of Jud's former players) and a lot of other guys, too. You're screwing my kid!

KG: Hey Jud, why don't you try and coach your freakin' team and let me negotiate my freakin' contracts?!

This time it was my turn to hang up. Rather than having the obvious negative effect, this conversation cemented my relationship with Jud. He admired me for standing my ground. I ended up signing many of Jud's players over the next several years. Suffice it to say that every single negative comment I have or will make regarding the trend in today's coaching and teaching do not apply to Jud Heathcote. He gets the Keith Glass exemption. To me, he is the model for how you're supposed to do it. I am not referring to the actual coaching part, of which he was obviously one of the best in the country. I'm referring to the caring part, to the following through part. Jud really cared about what happened to his players, not only when they were actually playing for him at Michigan State, but also long after they had left and they could no longer directly help him win games. Every time at the beginning of our relationship when we had any kind of words or strain, it was because he was looking out for his kid. He was testing me to see if I was just another one of these scumbag agents who didn't share the same feeling that he had regarding the welfare of the kids who had played so hard for him. The fact that I eventually passed that test with Jud and became a trusted part of his world meant a lot to me.

One particular night during Scott's fabulous season will always stand out to me, not only as far as achievement is concerned, but also as an insight into Scott as a person. In January, Scott broke the NBA record for assists in a single game, previously held by Kevin Porter of the Washington Bullets. For those viewers of current NBA games who may be unfamiliar with what an assist actually is, it is the art of actually passing the ball to a teammate who has a better percentage shot than you. Of course, he actually has to convert the shot. It is the unselfish and beautiful part of the game that players like Bob Cousy, Oscar Robertson, Magic Johnson, and John Stockton mastered. Scott entered this elite company that night by dishing out thirty assists! His last one was on a jumper by Jerry "Ice" Reynolds, who was another one of my players along with Greg Kite on the Magic. That alone was memorable because Ice didn't make a lot of jumpers.

The real memorable part came after the game. Since this was 1991 and therefore the prehistoric days before NBA League Pass was mercifully born, I didn't see the game on TV. Scott would call after every game, and we would discuss how he played and what it might mean to him in free agency. Luckily for me, he had set the record against Denver. Marcus Liberty, another of my players, was playing for them. I got a call from Marcus's wife, who was watching her husband, on local TV in Denver. She called and said, "Your boy was dealing tonight!" After getting the details from her, I was prepared for my call from Scott. It didn't take long.

SCOTT: Hey.

KG: (faking sleeping) Hey.

SCOTT: Are you sleeping?

KG: Oh, did you have a game?

SCOTT: You heard, you asshole!

We talked about the game, and he was obviously thrilled. He was also whispering since he was in the locker room, and the media was waiting to talk with him. Then he said the following: "Keith, they just came in and took my shoes. They're putting them in Springfield. I don't care about the money anymore—they're putting my shoes in the Hall of Fame!"

After all of that time and perseverance, this is what it was always about. Scott Skiles, like all of us, just wanted to belong, to be appreciated, to be respected. He didn't care about the money anymore. . . . But thank God, I did!

THE RISING COST OF A BAG OF PEANUTS

The process was certainly heating up as Scott continued his assault. The media was also very much aware of the situation. This negotiation really became the first pro sports contract controversy that the city of Orlando had ever witnessed. With no other professional team in town, this was it. I found this press coverage to be of tremendous benefit to us. A player as popular as Scott and having such a good season generated a lot pressure on the Magic. And the story of how all of us got to this point helped ingratiate Scott to the public. Scott's blue collar work ethic didn't hurt either.

Finally, Pat got the idea that this was not going to be so easy. He asked me to come down to Orlando at the end of March to try and work this out face to face. By this time, the media spotlight was getting so glaring that Pat told me the press would be waiting for me when I landed. To avoid them, he said I should switch from the A side of my terminal to the B side.

He would be waiting for me in his car. I did what he asked, though I thought it was a little dramatic. I can still visualize Pat waiting for me, slumped down in the front seat of his car, hiding behind a newspaper.

Pat's plan, for some reason, was to take me to a spring training baseball game. The Dodgers and Astros were playing that afternoon in Orlando. It seemed like an odd move. Why go to the trouble of clandestinely having me switch terminals at the airport to avoid detection only to show up in the stands of a baseball game with 5,000 other people? But I also knew that Pat was a character, and he was either trying to throw me off somehow or get me to relax enough to make a deal in his favor. It didn't matter to me. I love baseball, and Pat was always good company.

His first move on entering the ballpark was to take me down to the locker room where he introduced me to Tommy Lasorda, the Dodger manager. Pat was old friends with Lasorda, and he jokingly said, "Hey, Tommy, help me out with this kid, will ya! He's trying to hold me up!" Before Tommy could respond, I replied, "Mr. Lasorda, with all due respect, unless you happen to have a bunch of extra money with you, I don't think you're going to be of much help."

Pat understood full well that the previous summer's dictated extension of Scott's contract coupled with Scott's season was conspiring to create a huge problem for him and his young franchise. I was in the process of letting him know that I totally understood the dilemma.

Once in our seats, I found myself in the middle of a sold-out ballpark. It seemed to me that everyone knew what we were doing there. Pat was, after all, a major celebrity in the city of Orlando, having brought major league sports to the city and central Florida when nobody thought that was possible.

Now that it's fifteen years later, I can make a slight confession myself. I liked and respected Pat as well. In spite of my anger from the summer before, I always enjoyed any conversation I have had with Pat. He is different from some of the other people I have crossed paths with in this business. Mainly he has a personality and a terrific sense of humor. How mad can I get at a guy who makes me laugh? It was Pat who said the following about his seven-two, 385-pound draft choice, Stanley Roberts: "Anyone who says 'No man is an island' has never seen Stanley in a swimming pool."

I had to remind myself very often that I had to hold Pat's feet to the fire. In the end, it wasn't that difficult since my own feet were still scalded from six months earlier.

A minute or so after sitting down, the fun began. Pat took out a paper napkin from his pocket, wrote something on it, and put it in my lap. It basically read $1.2 million per year for three years, for a total of $3.6 million.

"Pat," I said, "I just got off the plane, and I'm at a baseball game; I gotta get a hot dog. Do you want anything?" Pat said to get him a bag of peanuts. While I was at the refreshment stand with my hot dog and Pat's peanuts, I grabbed a four-inch thick stack of napkins. When I returned to my seat, I gave Pat the peanuts put the napkins in his lap and said simply, "You're going to need all of these!"

I meant it, too, and Pat understood. He kept writing on those napkins. I told him I could get more if he ran out. The availability of paper napkins was not going to be the issue. Money and security were. By the time we left the ballgame around the fifth inning, Pat had committed, by napkin, to pay Scott $4.5 for three years. I rejected that one along with the other offers from the earlier innings.

I now had to return to the airport to fly back to Jersey. Pat was driving. After he made one last pass at making a deal for $4.8 million for three years, he angrily pulled the car onto the shoulder on the road, and the following conversation took place:

WILLIAMS: Let me get this straight, Keith. You're not going to accept almost $5 million for that little. . . . . ! I want to know why?!

KG: *Because I don't have to!*

I waited six months to say those five words, but man, it felt good! I could see in Pat's eyes that he now truly had the total picture. He got the full force of the depths of our frustration and anger from last summer.

WILLIAMS: Okay, Keith, but you know I have to sign him! What is it ultimately going to take?

KG: $9 million for four years.

We got it, too! I always found it interesting that over those six months between Scott reporting to late summer camp and April of the same season, the Magic had been forced to pay an additional $7.2 million over what Scott and I had originally wanted.

When you're scratching your head over the cost of your own hot dog at your next visit to an NBA game, make sure to take plenty of napkins.

agencies with t...
and no rest...
sociatio...
shop...
ar...

EIGHT

RUNNING FOR YOUR LIFE

Believe me when I tell you that the way I began in this business was and is not the norm. I don't recommend as an entrée into the field of representing players that you get yourself an assistant coaching job at UCLA, become a lawyer, and hope for the players you are coaching to become NBA players. You are going to be waiting a long time. I was just lucky. I found myself in the right spot at the right time. I also was lucky to have an actual family connection with Larry. My only role in all of this was realizing the opportunity I was given and cashing it in.

Much of the book up to this point has dealt with my overview of the business. My disdain for the recruiting part and, therefore, the seeming irrelevance of the actual representing of clients. I am also detecting in my own writing a hint of my own purity in these matters. This is hardly the case. I don't believe there is a successful agent existing in this industry today that hasn't engaged in some form of recruitment that they either are not proud of or are merely silent about. I am no exception.

My brushes with the seedier side of the business have always centered around one person, Greg. If there was any hint of corruption involved, Greg was somewhere in the neighborhood. Sometimes I didn't even know he was involved. It might have taken me awhile to realize who was at work. But whenever things got really crazy, it was Greg.

To call him a *runner* would be too easy and inaccurate. Firstly, runners are everywhere. They are guys who are employed by certain agents or he express purpose of procuring clients. There are no rules ctions since these runners are not licensed by the Players As- . They show up in every imaginable venue: at gyms, at barber , at clubs, you name it. Some (if not the majority) of the people who considered to be the big-time agents have these runners to thank for the bulk of their client list. Greg never considered himself a runner. He truly thought of himself as a guy who was helping kids. The fact that every kid he was helping was a star basketball player and that he was receiving money for his efforts was just a coincidence to Greg.

Understand the following, however: For all his faults, his heart was usually in the right place. The only time it wasn't was when his judgment became clouded. When this clouding occurred, Greg was capable of concocting any scheme that you have ever heard of and more. Greg has sent me on trips to nowhere. I remember one where he devised an elaborate scheme to get me to send him $500. The hook in this case was that I was going to get to meet Glenn Robinson of Purdue University, who would become the number one draft pick in the NBA draft that June.

Greg told me that we would meet with Glenn and his father after the Purdue game at home against Michigan State. I needed to send him the $500 so that he could get to Purdue from Chicago. Always being skeptical of Greg, I even told him that I needed at least to speak with Glenn and/or his father before I would send Greg's travel expenses and book my own trip. This was no problem according to Greg, and I did speak with two people, but I later discovered that they were just two guys Greg grabbed off the street and passed off as Glenn and his father to me on the phone.

After sending the money to Greg, flying to Indiana, renting my car, and checking into my hotel, I quickly discovered that I was alone in Indiana. No Glenn Robinson, no Mr. Robinson, and obviously, no Greg. All this for $500. If he had leveled with me, I would have preferred just sending him the travel costs and at least staying home.

To most people, after this fiasco there would be no way that they would ever have anything to do with Greg again. Most people never met Greg.

He had a gift. He was a charmer. I told him hundreds of times; if he would just cut the crap, he would make a fortune. We would argue for hours about him just coming clean. Every time I thought I had him, something would occur that would revert him back into a street hustler. He could have been so much more.

THE THOMAS HAMILTON AFFAIR

As awards ceremonies go, this was about as impromptu as it gets. But there I was, standing in the lobby of the Ritz-Carlton Hotel in Phoenix, Arizona, in the middle of the night, with a lamp in my hand and a half-puzzled smile on my face. John Nash, the general manager of the Washington Bullets at the time, had just presented me with this trophy and announced to everyone in the lobby that this was my award: "Scam of the Year 1994." And all of the NBA people assembled there that night thought this was pretty funny. Now the question that needs to be addressed is how I came to receive such a high honor.

The first time I ever heard of Tommy Hamilton, I received a phone call—a collect phone call. It turns out it was Tommy's brother, but I didn't know that at the time. I didn't know that Greg was lurking in the background, orchestrating his finest work to date.

I have met Greg three times in my life, face to face. Yet, in some ways he became part of my family. He knew all about my kids. He referred to my wife, Aylin, as the Queen. She never met him. They only talked on the phone. Yet Aylin loved Greg. I did, too.

I met Greg out in Hawaii. He was walking down the street in Honolulu with one of my players from UCLA, "Rocket" Rod Foster, who I had coached for two years at UCLA and then represented during his NBA career. Greg was just one of these guys on the periphery of the league. He would try to get close to the players and then, I imagined, peddle them to someone. I gave him my card and figured that would be that. It wasn't. For the next couple of years, Greg would call me—collect. It was interesting in that he never really asked me for or about anything specific. I figured he was a street agent and eventually would get around to what he really wanted from me.

One day while sitting in my office, the phone rang.

"Mr. Glass, this is John from the Sunoco station in Fort Wayne, Indiana."

I replied, "Yeah, John, I was expecting your call." I had no idea who this guy was.

"I'm calling about a gentleman by the name of Greg," he says. "Sir, I don't know quite how to explain this to you, but he comes here on his bicycle every day, and he makes calls from my pay phone. Well, sir, he was in the phone booth about twenty minutes ago. Somebody who came in to buy the paper parked out front, and the gears must've slipped or something. And, well, to make a long story short, tragically the car rolled back into the pay phone with your friend in it, and it knocked the pay phone down an embankment and into a gully. And, well, your friend has suffered severe injuries."

Another phone booth–related injury, I thought. "He had your card in his hand," the guy told me. This could only happen to me. "And they took him away in the ambulance," Sunoco John said.

"What hospital?" I asked him. He gave me the name, and I thanked him. As I was getting off the phone, I could hear him yelling, "But we still have his bike!"

All I could think about at that point was, *Here's this guy who could've been killed, and he's clutching my card. I ought to call the hospital to see how he's doing. I'm really not up on the etiquette regarding this type of injury.* So I call, and I tell them I'm a lawyer from New Jersey, and that one of my clients—one of my friends—was just taken to the emergency room, and his name is Greg. They had no record of him. Then after a couple of minutes as I tried to describe what Greg looked like, the guy on the phone said "Oh, you mean the guy in the phone booth?"

"Yeah, that's him."

Now the hospital guy's hysterical—he couldn't stop laughing! So at least now I know Greg wasn't killed.

Greg asked me to handle the case for him. It's obviously a case of negligence. Being the brilliant lawyer I am, I almost immediately realized that you shouldn't be pushed into a ravine while in a phone booth. I told Greg I would take a third of whatever he got, which is standard, and I went to the insurance company, and I settled the case. I got him $30,000, and it was all sent to me. That's how he wanted it. I kept $10,000, and I sent him $20,000. He was flabbergasted—couldn't believe it that I had actually done what I said I was going to do. He was so shocked that he actually sent me back his share of the money to hold for him. He explained that he would just blow it. So I opened a trust account for Greg and tried as best I could to control his expenditures. It wasn't easy. I managed at least to have that money last him as long as I could.

According to Greg, I was now "The Godfather." While I was certainly flattered with this new title I had been given, it didn't change my lifestyle much. It's not like I started wearing double-breasted suits, but from that moment on, he would call me constantly with different players. He would say, "I got this guy. I got that guy."

The truth is Greg didn't have any guys. He had phone numbers. He was a human Yellow Pages. Somehow, what he had done over the years was invoke the name of Jesse Jackson. He claimed that he was running a charity game for Jesse Jackson's Operation Push. That was his hook. That was how he was getting his name out there all of those years. Greg had a plan. He had a lot of them. As I said before, if he had done this the right way, then he would have been a wealthy guy. But there were always problems with him. He always seemed to need money, and he needed it now; he needed it within a half-hour.

Since our relationship always seemed to be fluctuating between amusement and anger on my part, there were many times during the twenty years I knew Greg where I simply wanted nothing to do with him. I would swear him out of my life, but somehow he would worm his way back in. Some of the ways he did this were remarkable. His masterpiece was the way he put me and Mr. Thomas Hamilton together.

Tommy Hamilton was, and I assume still is, a seven-four giant from the south side of Chicago. Somehow during one of our falling-out periods, Greg decided that Tommy needed to be with the Godfather. Since I wasn't talking to Greg and Tommy apparently wanted nothing to do with him either, Greg concocted a scheme involving Tommy's sixteen-year-old brother. It could also have been Glenn Robinson or his father, for all I know.

That's who called me first, the little brother, a sixteen-year-old kid. I'm not sure exactly how Greg did it, but I think Greg might have called Tommy's house, got the brother on the phone, and told him he was Keith Glass, the agent. Then Greg talked to the brother for awhile—a good long while I believe—and finally he said, "Look, I've gotta go do something right now. Do me a favor, call me back—collect." And he gave the kid the number at my office in New Jersey!

That's how Greg operates; that's his genius. He knew Tommy didn't want anything to do with him, and he knew I didn't want anything to do with him, so he concocted this scheme and somehow got us talking to each other with neither one of us knowing how he was involved.

Once you piece it together, it's a thing of beauty. After I explained to the kid brother that I wasn't going to call Tommy because I didn't even know who Tommy was, I got another call. This time it was Tommy. He said to me, "I wanna leave school. I wanna leave school and declare for the draft." This was interesting because he wasn't in school. He was supposed be enrolled at the University of Pittsburgh, but I found out later that he wasn't. I guess he viewed the idea of attending classes as a mere suggestion rather than a requirement.

So I asked Tommy, "How big are you?" He replied "Seven foot four." *Hmmm.* "Uh, whattaya weigh, Tommy?"

"Uh, well, that's a problem. I weigh about 380."

And I was thinking, *My car doesn't weigh 380.* "Whattaya mean, 380?"

He replied, "Well, I'm a little overweight."

My next call was to David Kaplan, the Chicago hoops guru. He started laughing. "Big Tommy? Yeah, I know Big Tommy. I would say that Tommy Hamilton is the best big prospect I've ever seen." Huh? "Keith, he's the most gifted big man I've ever seen in the Midwest. Soft hands, shoots twenty-foot jumpers. He can dribble the ball; he can pass the ball; he has courage. . . . he's the best."

"So what's the problem?" I asked.

"He won't make it 'cause he has no discipline at all. None. He has no control of himself. He's 400 pounds from what I'm hearing." Obviously, that's the problem. Now I'm a little interested. Now I'm figuring I can make a project out of this.

The next call I got was from a guy named Jim Williams. He was in Orlando, but he's originally from Chicago, which was how he knew about Thomas Hamilton. He's a personal trainer, a holistic trainer. Williams started giving me this rap about how he could get Big Tommy in shape, talking about stuff I couldn't even begin to understand. Then he mentioned a name that I did understand, Greg. Now I was starting to get the picture. This guy was a buddy of Greg's.

Once I realized this, I was on the phone with Greg again, and he was telling me how I had to bring both Tommy and this holistic guy to New Jersey because Tommy was as good as Shaquille as long as he didn't weigh 400 pounds. I was more than a little intrigued at this point, even though I should've known better with Greg at the controls.

I flew both Tommy Hamilton and Jim Williams to New Jersey, and I put them up. I put Tommy up with my friend Bob Susser, who had a relatively small house in Rumson. Suddenly, the house got appreciably smaller. Bob has since moved into a mansion there, merely on the off chance that Tommy may one day return. Bob used to tell me about how he'd come downstairs in the morning, and there'd be all these empty orange juice cartons strewn all over the kitchen. Tommy was foraging through Rumson! He was there at Bob's for two weeks.

I put up Jim Williams at a local hotel. We became a little family for a while. We'd go out together in Middletown, go shopping, and go to my son Tyler's baseball games, and we were probably quite a sight for the people who saw us running around together. Then again, folks were probably used to seeing me show up with large people.

We quickly realized that Jim Williams was a problem. He was trying to manipulate Tommy to make a reputation for himself, most likely. To make a long story short, I enrolled Tommy in the YMCA in Red Bank, so Jim could work him out. Meanwhile, Tommy was clearly homesick. He missed his girlfriend.

So here I was, I was Tommy's lawyer, I was trying to make him a millionaire, and Tommy was telling me about how he needed some shoes so he could take his girlfriend to the prom back in Chicago. He had to go home for the prom; that was what was important to him. This was a real adolescent-type situation, and I wasn't enjoying dealing with it. Nor did I much care for the lack of motivation I was beginning to see on Tommy's part. There was something missing with him—he didn't like to work, he was late all of the time, and it seemed like he was content just sitting around Bob's house all day watching TV. But it wasn't just because he was in New Jersey and homesick for Chicago. He did the same thing at home—just sat around the house all day.

People have since told me that he showed all of the signs of being manic-depressive. I don't know anything about that. I just went to the Y and worked out with him. I knew what he could do, and I knew that he was an ultra-talented kid; right or wrong, that was enough for me. I admit I was willing to look the other way, the same way everyone else who ever came into contact with him had. I'm sure his fourth-grade teacher let him get by simply because he was big and he could play basketball. Fourth grade, fifth grade, all the way up the line, they just passed him along. Tommy's type of situation is a running theme throughout this book and is symptomatic of the current culture of entitlement that we have created in the all-out drive to win.

By the time he got to me, I rationalized the whole thing. *This is my job,* I thought. I was trying to help him. But why was I trying to help him? For gain, of course. *My* gain. If it so happened that I actually did help Tommy Hamilton and that I actually did give him a future, great. But that wasn't my primary motivation. Let's be honest about it. If this kid was not seven feet four inches tall, I wouldn't fly him to New Jersey in the first place, I wouldn't hire a trainer, and I sure as hell wouldn't put him up at my friend's house.

So Tommy returned to Chicago for the prom. Jim Williams was another matter entirely. This was a guy I put up in a hotel and paid to come here to help Tommy, to be his trainer. After I discovered that he was a problem—I mean, the guy really had some whacked-out ideas, training and nutritional—I paid him a couple thousand dollars and sent him on his way back to Florida. Or so I thought. The next day, Tommy called me from Chicago. Jim was there at Tommy's house, and he was with a local agent named Eloise Saperstein. Eloise happens to be the daughter of Abe Saperstein, the man who came up with the idea for the Harlem Globetrotters. Jim Williams wanted Tommy to switch agents, to go over to Eloise—after I paid him! He saw Tommy as his meal-ticket, and now he was going to get the big kid involved with Eloise. So I stopped payment on the check I sent Jim. That got his attention *real* quick. We kind of had a meeting of the minds after that, and everything was fine between me and Jim.

Tommy was another story. He was obviously back in Chicago at this point because he had to take his girlfriend to the prom. He was out of sight, if not out of mind.

When Tommy was in New Jersey, he lost fifteen or twenty pounds. I was trying to get him down to 340–350, where it was healthy for him to play. He couldn't play weighing 400 pounds, he would get hurt carrying that kind of weight around. I would worry about somebody that heavy, about his heart, every time he'd go up and down the floor. His ideal playing weight was probably 315–320. We'd been making progress while he was in New Jersey. But now he was in Chicago, and I couldn't see him through the telephone. I told him, "Look, can you get ready? It's like a month until the Chicago pre-draft camp. Will you be ready?"

And he said, "Sure I can, Keith. Yeah."

At this point, I tell the NBA league office that he was in the draft. In fact, they were trying to find special shorts to fit him. A couple of weeks went by, and I talked to him on the phone every day. He was telling me everything was fine, that he'd be ready and not to worry about a thing. But in the meantime, when I talked to Marcus Liberty and Byron Irvin, two of my other players from Chicago, they were telling me that there was no way Tommy was in shape for the pre-draft camp. After hearing this, I flew to Chicago, and sure enough he was not in shape, and so I had to back out of the pre-draft camp. In fact, stories were circulating at the time that Tommy was now 450 pounds.

In those days, the NBA pre-draft was the most competitive setting for players trying to get drafted that there was. The draft was only weeks away when the pre-draft camp was held. You had some of the best athletes in the country ready and eager to attack. They were focused on their immediate goal. They were hungry and had been training. None of them were 406 pounds. None of their principle concerns was being at the prom and what shoes they were going to wear. If I left Tommy in that setting, they would have eaten him up with a knife and fork.

But he was so skilled; I still wanted some people to at least see him. So I came up with a plan: the entire NBA, from general managers and coaches to player personnel directors and scouts was already in Chicago for the pre-draft camp. So I would hold my own pre-draft camp. The NBA had theirs, so I'd have mine. And the NBA was kind enough to fly everyone to Chicago for me.

Now that everybody was there, all I needed was a gym. I called Mac Irvin, who ran a recreation league out at Fernwood Park, on the South Side. Mac's got five sons and a daughter, and all of them play basketball. I represented one of them—Byron. Mac could get me the gym, no problem. Now all I had to do was advertise this thing, and we were in business. So every time I met somebody I knew in the lobby of the hotel or in the elevator, I told them, "Look, I'm having this private workout for Tommy Hamilton. Marcus Liberty will be there, along with Byron Irvin, J. J. Anderson, Donald Reese, Antoine Walker, and Rashard Griffith." That got many people interested, among them Jimmy Lynam and John Nash from Washington, Dave Twardzik and Don Nelson from Golden State, Ernie Grunfeld from the Knicks, and George Irvine from Indiana. Isiah

Thomas didn't show, but he was about the only one I expected to see who didn't. It was on purpose, I found out later.

If you schedule it, they will come. That was the gist of the reaction. So I scheduled the Thomas Hamilton Pre-draft Camp and Traveling Sideshow for Saturday afternoon at Fernwood Park, between sessions of the regular pre-draft camp—2:00 p.m. sharp. Of course, I got lost. I was the one who gave everybody directions on how to get there, and I got lost. I was ten minutes late to my own damned thing. But when I got there, it hit me. Here was this tiny little gym in a fairly tough neighborhood on the South Side of Chicago, and as you drove up to it, there were all of these big cars parked everywhere, shiny brand-new cars from Hertz and Avis.

I walked inside, and all of these NBA people were standing around waiting for something to happen. Meanwhile, outside the door to the gym, there were about a hundred people milling around just looking to get a glimpse of the NBA celebrities inside. When you think about it, how often do they get to see people like that at Fernwood Park? It was like the circus came to town.

I walked in, and instead of thinking things through, I gathered the players together and I told them, "Go ahead and just run full-court." That's where I screwed up. Tommy went up and down the floor twice, and the next thing, he was grabbing his hamstring. Play stopped. He went into the bathroom. Now the other guys were still out there playing. It was not their audition, but that was okay. Rashard Griffith, and a high school kid named Antoine Walker were still going up and down the floor, and it was still a good opportunity for the NBA guys who might have been interested in them. But that was not what they were there for. They were all there to see Tommy.

Ten full minutes went by. No Tommy. He still hadn't come out of the bathroom. I was sitting with Ernie Grunfeld, and I said, "Ernie, let me go check on him." By then Don Nelson, Jimmy Lynam, Don Chaney were all going, "Hey Keith, where is he?"

Anyway, I went into the bathroom, and there were J. J. Anderson and

Marcus Liberty, two of my other players, standing over Tommy, trying to talk him into coming back out. Try to picture this scene: Tommy was wearing this gray T-shirt—that I bought him incidentally—and he had it stretched up over his head to hide his face. Why? He was crying. He was lying there on the floor crying. You don't cry from a pulled hamstring. You cry from something else, something that hurts a lot worse than a pulled hamstring. You cry from being completely overwhelmed by a situation. And that was what happened to Tommy. He completely broke down emotionally. He kept holding his hamstring, saying, "It hurts Keith; it hurts." But I didn't think physical pain had anything to do with this. He was just laying there crying.

At that moment, I snapped. I just went off to the point where J. J. and Marcus had to grab me and pull me off of him. I was all over him; I was crazed. "You big mother blankety-blank; you get your big ass out there on the floor. I got the whole league waiting out there for you!" It was one of my more inspirational speeches.

I mean, the guy could have crushed me. He's seven feet four inches tall, 400 pounds; I'm five feet ten inches tall, 180 pounds. He could've killed me. Instead, I got him to get up off his ass and come back out with me. At which point, he went up and down the floor four times, broke down again, and went to hide behind a big curtain they had behind the basket. He was crying again.

At this point more than half the NBA people got up and left the building. Not necessarily quietly either. Most of them had a parting shot for me, which I was less than thrilled about. After all, my credibility was at stake. But the Knicks, the Celtics, and Don Nelson stayed. Nellie was the last one to leave.

By then I had calmed down and gathered my wits, and I did what I should have done in the first place. I put Tommy in a half court-situation, so he wouldn't have to run up and down the floor. In a half-court situation, you could start to see some of the skills you couldn't see in the full-court situation simply because in full-court he was always trailing everybody. So he started making a couple of shots. And he got a rebound, and he made a pass. A couple of the NBA guys were leaning forward in their seats a little bit. I remember Ernie Grunfeld called me over at one point and said, "Keith, get him in a one-on-one for me, will ya?" The guys who did their homework stuck around because they saw the talent.

As much of a fiasco as The Tommy Hamilton Pre-draft Camp and Traveling Sideshow was, that kind of size and that kind of talent will always hold somebody's attention. It'll always hold the ones who dream, the ones who have a little vision. Those are the guys who don't feel they absolutely have to play the cards they are dealt. They can develop something.

So Don Nelson, Ernie Grunfeld, Don Chaney stayed strangely enough; both Nellie and Cheney would later coach the Knicks. That says something . . . what, I don't know. I remember Nellie coming down from the bleachers when he saw Tommy was in distress at the end. He went out on the court to show Tommy a drop step, show him a move on the low block, and to check to see how he was doing, that type of thing. I will always be grateful to Nellie for this. You could look at what he did in two ways. You could look at it like he was simply trying to see if the kid could learn. Or, you could look at it like Nellie just felt bad for the kid and wanted him to know that everything wasn't lost. I choose to think that Nellie wanted to leave the kid with something positive.

When I got back to the hotel later that afternoon, I took my share of abuse. But it was still the talk of the pre-draft camp. Of all the things that happened that day, the thing that stuck with me was Marcus Liberty standing over Tommy in the bathroom trying to get him to go back out there saying, "You know Tommy, I wish someone would've done this for me, man. . . . You're crazy." Marcus is a kid from Chicago, a kid who grew up playing ball on the same playgrounds, who went to the same high school, who played for the same coach. He realized what an opportunity this was. But Tommy Hamilton didn't get it.

When I got back from Chicago, I was still working on getting him drafted by somebody. Boston wanted him to fly in; he missed the flight. Cleveland wanted to fly him in; he fell asleep at the airport and missed that one, too. Milwaukee had him drive up, they interviewed him, and apparently, they didn't think much of him because they had two second-round picks that year and he went undrafted.

The night of the draft, I was actually thinking someone would take him with the fiftieth pick or something. But it wasn't like I was holding my breath. At twelve-fifteen on the night of the draft, my phone rang at home. There was a very soft-spoken voice at the other end. "Keith, this is Isiah Thomas."

I had never spoken to Isiah Thomas before in my life. You could say I was expecting a call from him less than I was expecting the call I got from Sunoco John of Fort Wayne telling me somebody ran over his phone booth with Greg in it. Isiah says, "Keith, I have interest in your big kid. I know the kid. I've got interest in him." That started my relationship with Isiah, which I have come to value, even today.

Anyway, this is what Isiah wanted to do for Tommy; he would pay him a salary, train him, get him to a nutritionist, find him a place to stay in Toronto, get him a car, and pay for all this—in short, do everything he could. Think about it: You're a nineteen-year-old kid who weighs 400 pounds, and Isiah Thomas wants to do all this for *you*. The idea being that two or three years down the road, Toronto would have a center. Great plan, great idea, especially when you consider the money that's being spent on big people today.

Isiah wasn't alone in his interest, either. The Denver Nuggets contacted me about Tommy and so did the Celtics, again. But we wanted to go to Toronto because Isiah was from Chicago and he knew Tommy's background. I thought that would be the best thing for him. Isiah was going to get Tommy enrolled him in classes up in Toronto: some college classes and some classes that would help him in terms of everyday living skills, teach him how to balance a checkbook, and so on. It wasn't like the Raptors were just going to take him up there and make him a basketball player.

Basically, we didn't want to throw him out there in the world and not give him any education or any skills that he would need in order to survive. Yes, Isiah and I were doing all of this because we thought we had something there in terms of a talent. However, we were all trying to do the right thing by this kid.

Tommy was also getting an opportunity out of this, of course. Isiah was trying to teach him something. He was trying to make Tommy part of a new family up there. This proved to be a very difficult thing to do. But first, before they could even get to that part of the procedure, the Raptors had to sign Tommy, which technically they couldn't do because they were an expansion team. So Isiah said to me, "Keith, you're a fairly creative guy; maybe you can figure this out."

I thought about it for awhile and called him back. I said, "You know Isiah, it might surprise you to know that in addition to Tommy's obvious gifts, he is also a fantastic judge of talent." That's how Tommy Hamilton became a scout for the Toronto Raptors.

The deal was that he would make the minimum salary, which was $150,000 at the time, plus they paid for everything—his flights, his apartment, *everything*. I couldn't envision a better scenario for a kid like this. So off Tommy went with a personal trainer by the name of Jim Williams, who happened to be a friend of Isiah's from Chicago as it turned out. Unbelievable!

Big Tommy invaded Canada. He was in Toronto, he was working, he was losing weight, and he was getting in shape. Not being drafted must have been a cold slap in the face for him. Pretty soon he was down to 328. Three hundred and twenty-eight pounds! I'm thinking, *Man, this is working. This is great!*

Five weeks later, he was 401. In five weeks, he gained seventy-three pounds. Five weeks! They let him go home to Chicago. I was devastated. They should've kept him there in Toronto and weighed him every hour. Only God knows what he did to get back up to that weight. I didn't know if he was eating ice cream around the clock or what, but seventy-three pounds in five weeks? *That's* not easy to do. That takes talent.

I had at least to get him to the Raptors camp, though. I promised Isiah that I would get him to one camp. I had to, especially after they spent all of that time and money on the kid. So I had him go to their rookie camp that summer. They released him. He was out of shape, and supposedly he wasn't taking it seriously, which, sadly, wasn't all that hard for me to believe.

WHY AM I DOING LAUNDRY WITH ISIAH THOMAS?

Isiah and I must have had fifty phone conversations about Tommy. We had never met face-to-face though we had laughed a lot over the telephone. We finally met in April of 1995, when we were both checking in at the Holiday Inn in Portsmouth, Virginia. We were both there for the Portsmouth Invitational Tournament, which was the first big post-season audition for college seniors who were looking to get noticed by professional teams.

I saw him checking in, and there were people all over him—kids trying to get his autograph, media, everyone and I walked over to him, and I said, "Hi Isiah, I'm Keith Glass." We both just cracked up. We couldn't stop laughing. So we decided this was neither the time nor the place to talk about Tommy Hamilton since neither one of us could keep a straight face and that we would meet up later over at the gym.

The gym used in Portsmouth is the Churchland High School gym, which is the biggest high school gym I've ever seen. It has to seat 4,000 to 5,000 people, easily. And of course, all 4,000 to 5,000 of the people there are going to want to meet Isiah Thomas.

Isiah couldn't go anywhere. He couldn't sit out in the bleachers, he couldn't walk around, and he couldn't go into the hospitality room to eat. Otherwise, 500 kids would come rushing out of the stands at him. This was why Isiah wanted to meet me in the laundry room that was located under the bleachers behind the locker rooms.

I've done business in some strange places before, but this? I walked into the laundry room, and Isiah was eating a sandwich as he sat on top of one of the washing machines. And I thought, *This is Isiah Thomas here in this tiny laundry room.* As I looked at him, I couldn't help but say, "You know if somebody had told me a year ago that I would be meeting you surreptitiously in a laundry room in Portsmouth, Virginia . . ." Then again this whole Tommy Hamilton thing began with a guy in a phone booth in Fort Wayne, Indiana, so I suppose it was only fitting that we would end up in a laundry room.

Anyway, the purpose of the meeting was to straighten out what was going on between the Raptors and Tommy. I told Tommy that I would see Isiah in Portsmouth and talk to him.

Meanwhile, unbeknownst to me, one of Isiah's people had called Tommy and told him to fly back to Toronto. Tommy's response to that was, "Oh no, Keith said unless he got a contract from Isiah in Virginia, I'm not going anywhere." The only discrepancy in Tommy's statement was the fact that I had never said anything like that. Toronto and Isiah owed Tommy and me nothing. They had done everything they said they would do and more. It was Tommy who hadn't held up his part of the bargain. To think that we were in a position to ask for anything else was ridiculous. That's what this laundry room meeting was all about.

Isiah Thomas, NBA legend turned NBA executive, had a head start on everyone else in the league when it came to Thomas Hamilton. "His uncle was a good friend of our family's," Isiah said at the time. "I followed his progress all through high school, and I heard about some of his hardships in college." That was when he was briefly enrolled at the University of Pittsburgh, where he never played basketball, never practiced, and never attended classes. "I actually saw Tommy play once his senior year," Isiah recalled. "That was the year (Martin Luther King High School) won it all. He and Rashard Griffith were on that team. They were probably the two biggest centers playing on a high school team that I had ever seen. Once I got the job in Toronto, with us being an expansion team, you more or less have nothing to lose in taking a shot with a kid like Tommy. Because of his size, but also because he possesses some skills with that size.

"He was a pretty good kid. He probably had some tough breaks in life, and if given the opportunity, maybe he could see the light. He needed to lose a lot of weight; he needed to try to get acclimated to what the NBA and entertainment life would be about, and we figured we had a good six to eight months to try to do that," Isiah said.

When I would ask how Tommy was progressing once they got him to Toronto, Isiah had to think about how best to phrase his response to that question. "They were interesting times," he said and left it at that. "Tommy had it tough growing up, tough as anyone can have it. He lived in the projects on the west side of Chicago, and that's all you need to know."

Isiah continued, "When we got him, he lost some weight at first. Then he went home and gained it back. But I expect those things to happen. I knew it wasn't going to be any easy thing. I understood the history coming in. You would have hoped, seeing that he had a legitimate opportunity to make it in the NBA, that he would see the light. However, we had some ups and downs. Then we ran into a situation where we just didn't have enough time to spend with him. Had the lockout in 1995 not occurred, we felt he could've played in the summer and gone to training camp. The problem was that while the lockout didn't last much past the summer, and therefore did not affect the NBA season in any significant way, it did end up canceling all of the summer leagues. Those summer leagues are the best opportunity for young players to develop and make an impression. This was lost for Tommy and many others. He ended up missing the summer of playing, went right into training camp, and, therefore, was behind. When you have guaranteed contracts and everything else you just could no longer take the risk.

"He came into training camp, and we had fourteen guaranteed contracts on our roster. Without having a chance to evaluate anybody over the summer, we were put in a situation where we couldn't give a long enough look to the kid because of what just happened with the collective bargaining agreement. So we ended up having to make a tough choice, and let him go."

THE ODYSSEY CONTINUES

Tommy sat for a month or so after that. Sat in Chicago doing who knows what, telling me he was working out every day. Maybe he was bench-pressing Big Macs. I then received a call from the Boston Celtics. They had interest in the big fella. The Celtics kept coming back for more throughout this whole thing. They wanted to know what I thought. I told them the truth. I told them about the Toronto experience. Because of his kindness, Isiah was too easy on Tommy, I said. If the Celtics were planning on doing the same thing with Tommy, it probably wasn't going to work there either.

My discussions were with the then general manager M. L. Carr and an assistant who was a friend of mine, John Jennings. John had taken a particular interest in Tommy. John recently lost a close election for the United States congressional seat from Indiana. He is currently a campaign manager for John Kerry, assessing a possible run for president in 2008. Tommy was not consulted on either of these races.

I leveled with the Celtics. I also mentioned the fact that if we didn't stick with this kid, we would probably be living in fear of the day the light went on in this kid's head, and he decided he was not going to waste his life and our time anymore. He was twenty years old then. If the light went on in his head when he was twenty-three, everybody would want to be in the room. That's what this was all about.

The Boston Celtics signed him. And they hated him. And they bitched and moaned to me about it every chance they got. The Celtics, who came into this project with the greatest of intentions, wanted to kill Tommy. Eric Montross, a fellow center on the Celtics, tried to befriend him. Dino Radja, another teammate, tried to befriend him. You know what Tommy said to me about these attempts at friendship? "It's not in my contract; I don't have to be friends with people." He just didn't get it.

But in spite of everything, the Boston Celtics activated Thomas Hamilton. The team of Cousy, Russell, Bird, McHale, and Havilcek put a uniform on a guy who could barely get into it. In actuality, Tommy did pretty well. In one game, he scored thirteen points on six-for-nine shooting. Besides his appearance, he really did very little to embarrass himself on the floor. The Celtics and I had many discussions. The people in the organization still couldn't stand him, but all of them clearly realized that he had the potential to be a player in this league. Centers are hard to find, and teams will go the extra mile and beyond if they think they have one.

Our discussions centered on the summer and what Tommy needed to do to reach that elusive potential. We agreed that he would stay in Boston and work out daily with their trainer after a visit back to Chicago after the season. The club had an option for $275,000 on Tommy, and they were very specific with him. All he had to do was show up at the rookie summer league at 330 pounds, and the job would be his. Simple. Easy.

Tommy went home to Chicago and never went back to Boston again. I began receiving phone calls from his apartment complex complaining that he wasn't paying rent. They instituted legal action against Tommy and ended up taking all of his possessions that he abandoned inside the apartment. He never responded to those proceedings.

M. L. Carr was getting angrier and angrier with this situation, and I didn't blame him. Normally, I would have felt some kind of responsibility for this behavior, but in this case, I did not. They had been warned. I tried in vain to get the seriousness of his lack of cooperation across to Tommy, but it didn't get through. In July of 1996, M. L. said it very simply. If Tommy didn't show up at 330 pounds, they would release him.

Up to this point, I was really on the Celtics side. Then they started to get a little cute. They were worried that there was going to be another lockout in the NBA. They were therefore concerned that they would in essence be stuck during a lockout with Tommy's option. With the league potentially shut down, they would not be able to waive him and would therefore owe him the $275,000. I think it was a combination of that plus the fact that they were hearing negative reports about Tommy and his conditioning in Chicago. This, coupled with the obvious fact that Tommy had virtually vanished, was cause enough for them to waive him. The lockout never occurred, but the waiver did. They were quick to say, however, that if Tommy were at 330 they would still have him to camp and would in fact sign us again.

Tommy continued to miss the boat with Boston. He still insisted on staying in Chicago even after these developments. I know it seems incredible to some that a young man with nothing would simply turn his back on one lucrative opportunity after another. It is hard for me to express the frustration I was feeling during this time. Here I was, a guy who had worked for years trying to get teams to show this much interest in my players, and this kid didn't return the interest when it was given. What some of my players, past and present, would have given for just one of these situations made me feel empty. I kept thinking about the work and time they had all put in, and instead of just feeling frustrated by Tommy, I started to get angry.

Boston turned a little bizarre themselves during the days leading up to the camp. Anticipating that Tommy would in fact amble in at considerably more that the prescribed 330, they insisted that Tommy pay his own way to camp, and that if he was indeed 330, they would reimburse us. No deal. I hadn't seen him for awhile either. We turned them down on that offer, and that was the end of the Celtics.

However, when you're seven feet four inches tall, your chances just don't seem to end. The Denver Nuggets were next in line to get their asses kicked. They asked what I thought and what went wrong in Toronto and Boston. I told them the truth. They invited Big Tommy anyway. We made all the arrangements. This time just to vary up his modus operandi, Tommy never went to Denver at all. He just blew them off completely. A variation on a familiar theme.

This was it, even for me. It was getting ridiculous and embarrassing, and I didn't want to be part of it anymore. I let Tommy know my true feelings, and we parted company. Even though I was glad to be rid of him, I still never have thought of Thomas Hamilton as a bad guy. I still can see him playing on the floor of my house with my two-year-old son, Lucas, who Tommy got along with particularly well. Tommy's story is a complex one. It does in fact seem like a cross-section of what is wrong with much of the basketball community and much of our society as well. This cross-section could include a section on dreams, but unfortunately, the only dreamers were me and the teams involved, not Tommy.

Later in the summer of 1996, I had placed Matt Steigenga from Michigan State on the roster of the World Champion Chicago Bulls. Matt had been drafted in 1992 in the second round by the Bulls, and under NBA rules, he remained their property since Matt had played professionally in Japan for those intervening four years. Until you are either released or make the roster, you are the property of the team that drafted you.

Matt played his ass off. He went with the Bulls to the Rocky Mountain Revue in Salt Lake City. He was asked back to camp. He did everything they asked him to do and more. The Bulls loved him, and he was playing his way at least onto the injured reserve list, a place where many teams hide extra guys who they like but don't have room for on the regular twelve-man roster. Michael Jordan was singing his praises along with Coach Phil Jackson.

During this time, Thomas Hamilton was sitting at home in Chicago gaining a little more weight for the winter. Steigenga called me ten days before the rosters were to be set to ask me if I had ever heard of a Tommy Hamilton. The Bulls had signed him that day, and Matt didn't understand what was going on. I unfortunately did. Jerry Krause of the Bulls had called me some time before to get the story on Tommy. I told him just like I told the others. As the creator of this cheap takeoff of *The Twilight Zone*, I guess the final irony was that the Bulls would choose Tommy to go on the injured list while waiving Matt Steigenga. Thomas Hamilton became of member of the World Champions, which seemed about as appropriate as him squeezing into that Celtic uniform.

For those who might be wondering, during the time of the writing of this book, I invited Tommy to speak on these issues. He accepted, but only on the condition that I pay him. Of all the people I talked to about this project, he remains the only person to ask for compensation. As far as my compensation is concerned, I have no complaints. Over the course of two years I represented Tommy, I received all of $1,200 . . . and a chapter for my book.

NINE

STAR-SPANGLED DISASTER

"Keith, it's Ted Koppel from *Nightline* on line eight."

"I can't talk to him!"

"Keith, Reverend Al Sharpton is on seven."

"Not now!"

What the hell is going on here?

The first time I met Mahmoud Abdul-Rauf, it wasn't even him. His name was Chris Jackson. While I had seen him on TV and marveled at his sometimes amazing ability, I met him outside Madison Square Garden with one of my clients, Marcus Liberty. They were rookies together on the Denver Nuggets but not exactly friends. Marcus pointed to Chris, who was standing apart from us on Thirty-third Street and said, "I'm going to knock that sucker out!" After I asked why, Marcus explained that the next time Jackson shouted some expletive at him, it would, in essence, be the last time.

It struck me at that moment that Marcus and his teammates had not been educated, not to mention even informed, that Jackson had an affliction called Tourette's Syndrome, a disease that causes one to have uncontrollable outbursts in sometimes unusual surroundings. Marcus had apparently been in some of those surroundings.

After dinner with Marcus, where we discussed Chris's disease in greater detail, they slowly started to become good friends and teammates. Interestingly, Chris was supposed to be a star, having been the third overall pick in the NBA draft of right behind Derrick Coleman and Gary Payton, but Marcus having also left school early for the NBA draft, was disappointed being taken forty-second overall in the second round. As the season unfolded, however, Marcus was beginning to thrive while Chris, who should have been a junior at LSU, was struggling. The word "bust" started to circulate after the all-star break. Chris was gaining weight and, to my view, looked a little spaced out or lost on the court. Theories were abounding blaming his medication for his troubles on the floor.

Luckily for me, Chris's agent at the time was a local lawyer from Chris's hometown of Gulfport, Mississippi. I say luckily because in my business you always have people who think my job is a snap. No problem. This guy managed to get Chris a little less than half the guaranteed money than the guy selected after him. This led to some obvious disenchantment with his agent, and Chris terminated their relationship in their first year.

My first real contact with Chris occurred after that rookie year. Each summer, many of the NBA teams hold rookie/free agent camps. Before the advent of the current Las Vegas Summer League, between ten to fourteen NBA teams sent squads to Salt Lake City where the Utah Jazz hosted the Rocky Mountain Revue. In the summer of 1991, there was the Seattle Supersonics, Golden State Warriors, Houston Rockets, and others. The Nuggets also fielded their team. The star of the Nugget's summer league was Marcus Liberty, while an overweight Chris Jackson was being looked on as a waste of a very high draft choice.

My first night in Salt Lake City, I waited for Marcus after his game, so we could go out. Chris came out of the locker room with him, and he actually introduced himself to me.

This is a good time to shed a little light on the business of getting players to represent in the first place. Every agent I had ever listened to or read in the paper has one peculiar thing in common. They are always contacted by the players. They never have to make even one phone call to get clients. So they say. This is bull, as so many others things that agents put out there are. The reality, of course, is that it hardly ever happens that way. In fact, unless one of my existing clients recommends me to a player, it never happens that way.

For example, for me to have ever had an opportunity to sit down with the third pick in the NBA draft would have required about a year and a half of effort. At least that would have been the case in 1990. Today, I would have to track him down somewhere in junior high school and adopt his AAU coach. Even in 1990, I would have had to find some connection to Chris—maybe through LSU, his high school coach, his family, or his gardener. As I'd mentioned before, the current way in for even reputable representatives is to employ runners like my old buddy Greg, whose sole job is to recruit and then babysit those prospects.

I bring this up here because I want to stress how unusual it was for Chris Jackson to be introducing himself to me one year after I couldn't have gotten near him. It became even more unusual when he asked if he could join us for dinner. Marcus said okay, if Chris was buying. I almost smacked Lib right in the head.

Our dinner meeting was more educational than business-related. At least for me it was. It was my first glimpse into Chris's world of Tourette's. What I immediately noticed was that periodically throughout the meal, Chris would shout out a word or just a sound that would resonate throughout the entire restaurant. It was, to say the least, disconcerting. The other patrons would look up in surprise and stare at our table. What struck me was how well Marcus had apparently learned to deal with this— he had come a long way from Thirty-third Street. As for me, it was also very enlightening to see what Chris had to endure on a daily basis.

Our meeting went well enough that Chris asked if I would come to Denver later on to meet with him. Being the genius that I am, I accepted and traveled to Denver for another dinner. After dinner, I was invited back to his house to talk further. It was here that I got more insight into what the Tourette's situation actually meant. Everything that Chris did was controlled to some degree by the disease. For him to make me hot tea, for example, the water had to be just right. Thirty-five minutes later, I was actually drinking the tea. In short, the problem with Chris was that everything had to be perfect—the temperature of the water, how he tied his sneakers; how he shot his shots, and so on.

It took Chris about ten minutes just to tie his shoe laces because the knot had to be perfect. I also was told of the story of how a ten-year-old Chris Jackson was found crying in the playground, while shooting foul shots. When a neighbor asked what was wrong, he said that he just wanted to go home. The neighbor replied, "Well Chris, I can take you home." But Jackson said that he couldn't leave until his shot felt perfect. Even though they were all going in, it wasn't quite right for him. It wasn't perfect.

I tried to imagine the pressure that this disease put on him, but I realized that I really couldn't imagine. I did, however, begin to feel a fondness for this kid with the obvious gifts on the one hand and the burdens on the other. I signed him right there before the tea even cooled down.

I realized right away that my first real job with Chris was to reestablish his confidence in himself and his career. There are different ways to represent a player. There are different stages that an athlete goes through. My niche has always seemed to be with guys who have had to struggle some. It's probably the coach in me that draws me to those kinds of cases and them to me.

I have found it more rewarding than say representing the top pick in the draft. Don't get me wrong. I'd love to, mainly because it's easier. But the real trick about getting those kinds of guys is the recruiting of them. It's in the marketing of yourself as an agent. This clearly is not one of my strengths. It's not easy to recruit them, but it's pretty easy to get them their contract. I have always been known throughout the industry as the guy who will work harder for his guys even if they don't have the same reputation or abilities. I'm proud of that. For me, to end up with the third pick in the previous year's draft meant something had to be wrong. I actually was surprised that it was legal. I'm sure several of my colleagues were ready to launch an investigation. But I guess it's hard to mobilize such an inquiry when your own conduct is likely to land you in jail.

So Chris had some warts on him. Big deal. The overriding question I always ask myself about a prospective client is the seemingly obvious one—and the one that's at the root of a lot of the league's problems—can he play? The answer in this case didn't take me long. Chris had gained about twenty-five pounds since leaving college, and whatever was causing that had to go. His diet was a key factor, but his medication was also a problem. Once I became Chris's agent, the Nuggets, specifically general manager Bernie Bickerstaff, constantly called to voice their concern over Chris's medication. Bernie really felt like I was in control somehow. The truth was I had no idea what was going on with his medication.

Teams have a tendency of giving agents too much credit for their influence over their players in certain matters and not enough in others. This was one area in which I had very little influence. When I was together with Chris, after a while, I could tell if he wasn't taking his medication because the ticks would be much more pronounced. I always felt that the ticks were nerve-based because they would arise more prevalently during certain discussions. The worst occasions were always when we discussed money. Whenever we talked specifically about his contract situations, the ticks would come out.

It was the summer of 1992 that he really started to get serious about his weight and his conditioning. He went on an unbelievable regimen that included a strict diet as well as playing ball roughly six to eight hours every day. The results were astonishing. He lost thirty-two pounds, and together with a new found mental approach that was at least partially due to his pending conversion to the Muslim religion, Chris went to training camp for his third NBA season in the best shape of his life.

It might be interesting at this point to examine some of the business side of my relationship with Chris at this beginning stage. Since Chris already had a contract in existence when I signed on to be his agent, I realize that most of you must be very concerned about how his poor agent is actually going to earn a living. I can only speak of my own policy in situations like this. My view is that I don't want to be paid for anything that I didn't do, and conversely, I would appreciate being paid for something I did negotiate, though there are probably some players who would strenuously argue against the latter. There have been several situations where I have charged either nothing or a very nominal percentage when I have taken over during an existing contract. It really depends on what the player is looking for me to accomplish.

In the case of Chris Jackson, I didn't want to be remotely associated with the deal that had been negotiated by the original agent. And the guy who did the deal shouldn't have wanted to either. What I did work out, however, was an arrangement with Chris whereby I would negotiate a settlement between him and his former agent. Anything I saved Chris we would split. This really was an afterthought on my part, but it netted me about $40,000. It didn't cost Chris a dime, and in fact, he saved $40,000.

From a purely business point of view, what concerned me the most was that Chris was failing as an NBA player. Entering the third season of his career, we were faced with the fact that this 1992–1993 season was the last guaranteed year of his contract, for which he would be paid $2.35 million. Not bad for a bust, but my real dilemma was that the last year of this existing deal for 1993–1994 wasn't guaranteed at all. He had a $4 million option, which naturally was the Nuggets' to exercise. Due to the way he played his first two seasons, there was as much of a chance of that happening as there was for me to be named pope. Unless we turned this thing around quick, Chris Jackson was about to enter the land of Chris Washburn—the third pick drafted the year before Chris Jackson who ended up never playing in the league again. Cue the ominous music here.

The 1992–1993 season saw Chris Jackson go back to the promise that everyone throughout the basketball world envisioned when he left college as a sophomore. He basically exploded. His conditioning and new approach to his job and career were obvious from the outset of the season. Chris ended up leading the Nuggets in both scoring and assists, a very rare double combination in the NBA, though this was a little misleading being that the Nuggets were really a horrible passing team and Chris led them with about four assists per game, hardly anything to get excited about.

Any honest discussion of Chris Jackson as a basketball player leads me to a classic scenario. Chris is what is called "a tiny two guard." This is not a compliment in NBA circles. What it refers to is the fact that many very talented guards are really not point guards but rather scoring guards. The fact that they are small does not classify them as points. I have had this argument for twenty-five years with general managers and coaches throughout the league.

To me, a point guard begins with a player's state of mind. He must be someone whose main objective is getting his teammates involved. He can be a scorer as well, but his primary role is to get the ball where it has to go. Although historically, point guards have been shorter than shooting guards, that is not the prerequisite. Years ago Oscar Robertson, who was six feet five inches tall and stronger than most power forwards, broke the mold for point guards. Magic Johnson was a legit six feet nine inches tall when he ran "Showtime" for the Lakers. It's the head that matters.

Conversely, a shooting guard's job is to score. He must obviously be able to do many other things as well, but his function is to fill it up. The best story I recall regarding shooting guards actually concerned a college basketball coach. In the 1970s and 1980s, Joe B. Hall was the coach at the University of Kentucky. Joe was notorious for not allowing his guards to shoot. He wanted the ball inside to his big guys. Coach Hall also owned a bank in Lexington. One day the bank was robbed. The robbers got away with everything. Joe B. wouldn't let the guards shoot!

In short, the Glass Theory concerning guards is very simple: Just because a player is small does not mean you can make him a point. The NBA is littered with "tiny two guards," who are tremendous scorers, but are simply not point guards. Some make the transition to the point, but most do not. It really is a state of mind. The ones who do make it in the league are the ones that get to a team that doesn't play in a system with a true point guard. They play guards, period. In that type of setting, a tiny two guard has a chance.

Chris was a good one, but at five feet eleven inches tall, he was a "tiny two guard." The fact that I was representing him excused a lot of those problems in my mind, but I knew that the man I would have to go up against to secure a new deal, Bernie Bickerstaff, was at least as clever as I was, and I knew, from having dealt with him in the past, probably more so.

In spite of all of those concerns, Bernie came calling sometime in December 1992. He was basically feeling me out and really spent the entire month trying to get me to come up with some numbers for a new deal for Chris. He knew I wouldn't do that because I don't like to go first, but what the hell, he gave it a shot. On January 22, 1993, Bernie called again, and I explained that I wasn't trying to avoid him, but I wanted numbers from him. He said okay. Another reason for not tipping our hand was that Chris was cookin'. My thought process was that he had failed for two years, and now he was having success for two months, so let's let him go for as long as he can.

At this point we should ask the question why the Nuggets even approached me at all since they had an option for another year. The answer to that is twofold:

1. At $4 million, the option was extremely high for that place and time. I know that today, it's a relative bargain, but it was not in 1993.
2. On a more complicated note, the rules in the league at that time actually had the same effect as the rules today. There were and are two classes of free agents: unrestricted and restricted. As I previously explained, an unrestricted free agent could sign with any team with no compensation or recourse to his former team. A restricted free agent could negotiate with any team in the League, but if they were to sign an offer sheet form with another team, their existing club would have the right of first refusal, which, in essence, gives them the right for seven days to match the offer and retain their player.

Chris was a restricted free agent. On the surface, this would appear to be a negative as it was for Scott Skiles, but I never viewed it as such in this case. The catch here was that the Nuggets, to maintain their right of first refusal on Chris had to, under the rules of the collective bargaining agreement in effect at the time, qualify Chris. Just like with Skiles, this meant in short that the club had to offer their player $250,000 or 125 percent of the players last years compensation, whichever amount was greater. In our case, that meant 125 percent of $2.35 million, or $2,937,500.

So much for Agenting 101. On January 25, 1993, Bernie made me his first offer. Bernie was the GM, with Dan Issel, the former great Denver Nugget and future Hall of Famer, as the head coach. Just as an aside, Dan had been a friend of our family for years and, in fact, had worked together with my father and Louis Dampier on a basketball camp back in Kentucky. This made me very comfortable with Dan, and I always felt like I could talk to him fairly freely regarding Chris.

The offer from Bernie was as follows:

- A four-year contract for $7.2 million.
- $400,000 weight bonus—$100,000 per year if Chris stayed at a given weight. (I had Chuck Nevitt negotiate the details on that one!)
- $400,000 minutes bonus—Chris had to play an average of twenty-eight to thirty minutes per game.

The offer told me a number of things. The total of $8 million over four years said that even though they were disguising the money in some makeable bonuses, they still were willing to pay us about $2 million per year. Coming from where we were just three months earlier, this was encouraging. I also had to factor in that this was where Bernie was starting, not where we would be finishing.

However, the offer also concerned me from a basketball point of view, and I told Chris my concern. There had been a lot of talk in the media that Chris was the perfect sixth man to come and change the tempo of the game, to give a club an offensive lift off the bench. Neither Chris nor I liked that characterization very much. The minutes bonus was a clear indication to me and Chris that this was the plan. Simply, starters don't average twenty-eight to thirty minutes a game, but rather thirty-five to forty.

After a follow-up conversation with Chris, he indicated to me very clearly that his goal was to get $2.4 million per year for four years. When negotiating contracts of this size, the obvious factor that the public looks at is the money. I have always realized, however, that the guaranteed aspect of a contract is of equal if not more significance. It is the guarantee that gives a player his security, possibly for life, if he does the right things with his money.

I have always looked in amusement at the contracts in the NFL. One day you read how an NFL player has signed for millions and millions of dollars. The next month he injures his neck, and that money vanishes. These deals are illusions, not real dollars. They are good only year to year. The only guaranteed money in the NFL is a player's signing bonus and first year contract. In the NBA, if you sign a six-year guaranteed deal, then it is just that.

Now it was February 3, and Chris was still rolling. I called him to tell him that I thought his desired $2.4 million might be too low. He didn't argue. On February 22, Bernie called again, and we had our longest negotiating session. He made some indications that he would not qualify Chris at the $2.9 million figure, but I knew then that he really wanted Chris. I also remember that it was in this session that I felt they would consider a fifth year. I was asked to make a counterproposal, and I did on March 16.

I countered at $14.5 million guaranteed for five years, an average salary of $2.9 million. I also asked for the right to terminate the contract after three years if we wanted. I also insisted that the deal be all cash with nothing deferred. Bernie's response was that "we have major problems." He also indicated that he wouldn't do that to Reggie Williams. Bernie, in my opinion, had just snookered Williams into signing for too little at $1.5 million per for four years. Bernie was in essence asking me to get on line and be next. I respectfully declined.

My problem with Bernie is that I like him. When he invokes the line about not wanting to upset another player with my deal, I really believe that he means it. It is the coach in him talking from the point of view of team chemistry. Of course, he's right in a lot of ways. The coach part of me agrees with that philosophy. But this is where the coaching stops for me, and business begins.

It was always a very unusual feeling to turn down $12.5 million for a basketball player, get in my car, drive to Mater Dei High School in New Jersey, and start teaching sixteen-year-olds about the importance of athletics and the value of teammates and working together for one another. I had been doing just that for the past twelve years, somehow juggling these emotions and motivations to the point where I have literally felt like two separate people. The combination of these disparate philosophies gives me a tremendous insight into all of the different layers of the game, but there is no denying that it was additionally turning me into a basketball schizophrenic. No matter how hard I tried, I just couldn't reconcile the fact that the NBA is much more about selling and marketing than about basketball.

Well, back to the negotiations. (If some of you aren't into negotiations, you have my permission to skip the next two pages.) For those sticking with me, I remember the March 16 phone call was short and ended abruptly, usually a sign that someone is pissed off. I was fine, so I figured it was Bernie. But he called back the next day so my assessment that they really wanted to make a deal appeared to still be the case.

The Nuggets countered my counter with the following two options for my approval:

1. A four year deal at $8.4 million, or
2. A three year offer at $6.3 million

In either case, they were offering us $2.1 million a year, and obviously, I was less interested in the three-year option because of the security issues. My response was, "No way!" But I also indicated that as usual I would relay their offer to Chris for him to reject officially. It may surprise some that an agent only negotiates; the final yea or nay belongs to the player. In most cases until the very end, the agent and player are in complete agreement on accepting or rejecting an offer, and they both understand that it is a good strategic move to have the real rejection come from the player. The reason is that a general manager doesn't give a rat's ass if I'm mad—I don't play for his franchise. However, he really doesn't want one of his top performers angry with the franchise, especially when I'm negotiating during the season.

We officially rejected the offer the next day. You don't want them to think that you are even thinking about it. The only thing that took place between that offer and April 25 was that Chris continued to play his behind off. He won a couple of games at the buzzer. People were beginning to talk about him as the NBA's most improved player, and you know my thoughts about that. This shouldn't have been very hard for him to win, considering how horribly he had played the year before.

On April 25, Bernie called again to offer us $10.8 million for five years. I guess we were right to wait. It's a risk, but we both believed in Chris's ability once he got himself right. Bernie was still going with the $100,000 per year weight clause. It was at this point that I introduced the charity clause, whereby the player will donate a figure such as $10 or $15 per rebound, assist, three pointer, and so on, and the team will match it dollar for dollar. Most teams go along with this, but you might be surprised that some don't. We had already done this with Scott Skiles, and it had led to the forming of the Skiles Assist Fund, which did a lot of good for inner city teens in Orlando.

I countered this time at $14 million (and people think I'm tough to deal with). On April 30, I found out that Chris Dudley, of the three-point-per-game average, had been offered $16.5 million for six years. How Dudley got by me, I still don't know. Interestingly, centers are usually more valuable than guards, even backup centers.

In the meantime, Chris Jackson had become extremely serious over the past couple of years about converting to Islam. In accordance with this, he was planning a pilgrimage to Mecca between May 22 and June 7. We agreed that I would not conduct any further negotiations while he was away out of respect to him and his trip. Chris also explained to me that he was, on his return, going to legally change his name to Mahmoud Abdul-

Rauf. The only problem I had with this was in the pronunciation. Once I learned that, we were fine.

Bernie called again on May 12 and upped the offer to $2.3 million a year and eliminated the weight clause. (I was starting to look forward to his calls). The offer was for $12 million over five years. We were getting there. If you notice, we actually were where Chris wanted to end up. The rest, as they say, was gravy. Later that day I called to reject their offer. I was still having too much fun.

Chris left the country for the Middle East, and on his return on June 8, Bernie called. It is relevant to understand that Chris was to become a free agent on July 1. This explains the timing on the Nuggets part. I always have a number in my head that I want to get to ultimately, which naturally changes up or down due to circumstances. In Chris's case, that number was $13 million. Bernie offered $13 million on June 8, and I knew then and there that we would in some form have a deal with the Nuggets in the foreseeable future. My charity clause was in there, too, and now I just needed to hear from Chris. He called on June 14 and was naturally thrilled at where we were. He accepted the offer at $13 million.

I was proud of the job that I had done for him, and he was almost overwhelmed with how things had gone. A slight glitch arose when we had to redo the contract several times because of Chris's name change. There was some concern in the league office about which name he had to actually sign with. For the record, I recall negotiating a contract for Chris Jackson and having it signed by Mahmoud Abdul-Rauf.

All right, enough with the business side. I promise. I've probably told you more than I should have anyway. I want to try and give some insight into Mahmoud as a person, as a human being. No matter what we believe in, no matter what we call ourselves, that essence of who we are should grow, but at the same time, should basically remain true. I will let you be the judge in this case.

As I indicated earlier in this chapter, I really did start to like Mahmoud the second time we met in Denver. He seemed very sincere, but at the same time, extremely naive about certain things that were happening around him. The paternal instinct to protect or shield him from some of the negative comments and criticisms of his play was almost automatic. This is not unusual for me, but in Mahmoud's case, it was stronger than normal.

I have described the Follow Thru Fund earlier in this book. The first year that I held it was the year that the little girl had passed. After the funeral, I decided that rather than wait to act on the idea, I would call my players so that they could feel my anguish and emotion. That year I had nineteen players in the NBA. I called them all that afternoon, and in the end, eighteen of my players showed up at the Jersey Shore, to help people that they had never met. Only Olden Polynice had failed to come. A remarkable turnout to say the least.

What I specifically remember about those nineteen phone calls was one in particular. Mahmoud listened quietly to the story and then, almost puzzled, said, "Keith, I don't understand, what is it that you want me to do?" I told him that I needed him to come to New Jersey and play in a golf tournament in July. Again he sounded almost confused and answered, "I'll be there, and you know you really don't sound good. I can come now if you need me." I needed that then, and I remember it now, even though so many things have happened since.

My guys came for the event that by this time turned into a happening. There was a basketball game scheduled for the night before the golf tournament featuring believe it or not, the Keith Glass All-Stars vs. the Jersey Shore All-Stars. The game was held at St. Rose High School in a little gym and an hour and a half before tip-off, the place was packed. Mahmoud and Scott Skiles shot foul shots against people paying for the privilege. Good luck against those two. Mahmoud even tried his hand at golf the next day. He had never played before, but he trooped through eighteen holes, and the people that he injured that day with some of his drives have all fully recovered.

The final event of the weekend was the dinner and auction. The entire event was truly unbelievable. We set out to raise about $27,000 to pay one family's medical bills and ended up, through everybody's efforts, with about $47,000. This left us with an unexpected surplus of cash and prompted us to continue to raise money for other families in similar situations for the next six years. We ultimately gave grants worth over $400,000 to families in New Jersey who had suffered similar unfortunate circumstances and needed a hand.

I was the auctioneer, and the final item to be auctioned off was a pair of plane tickets that United Airlines had donated. From the back of the room, I saw Mahmoud bidding them up. I was more than a little curious since we had just recently signed a contract for $13 million and everybody flies professional athletes free and in first class. I just didn't understand what he needed with two coach tickets on United. As I was a little busy running the auction, I really couldn't deal with it at the moment. The goal was to raise money, and we were.

Mahmoud simply would not lose those tickets. He kept on bidding no matter what someone else bid. He ended up buying them for $1,250. He walked up with his checkbook, and after asking him for two forms of ID, I gave him the tickets. I asked him if he knew what he was doing, and he just shot me a look that told me he certainly did.

The evening was at an end, and there was obviously a lot of emotion as the parents of the little girl who had passed embraced me after I got off the podium. From the back of the room, however, I was being summoned. It was Mahmoud. He had something to say to me. He said almost sheepishly that he really enjoyed the weekend and that he thought it was a great event. Then he said, "You know, I really came here to show you what I thought of you, but after seeing what happened this weekend, I want to help more." I started to say that he'd already done plenty just by being there, but he continued. He said, "These tickets here; I didn't buy them for me." I knew that there was a mistake, and I was just about to run back to the stage to resell the tickets when he finished by saying, "I bought them for them. I think they should get away, don't you, Keith?" He motioned toward the parents who had so recently lost their little girl. He asked me to give the tickets to the parents, but I insisted that he do it himself. They couldn't believe his kindness. After resisting at first, and being completely overwhelmed by Mahmoud's generosity, they accepted.

Sometimes I feel that your life is condensed into little moments like these, and I couldn't help but think of that moment in our lives together when I saw all the hate and venom that would come to be directed at Mahmoud some years later. I loved him for that then, and even though so much has transpired since then, I still love him for that now.

In spite of these emotions I felt toward him, it was becoming increasingly difficult to communicate with Mahmoud. There was no question that forces were at work to come between Mahmoud and myself. There were increasing numbers of people around him. In fact, there were many people, apparently of the Muslim faith, actually living in his house. The religious aspect to this I don't believe bears any great significance. To me, it was just something they had in common with Mahmoud, which they could use to get something that they really wanted. It was the hook.

Every time I called the house, I got a different person on the phone. I would leave message after message that would never be returned. To this day, I am certain that Mahmoud never received these messages. For the last two years of our business relationship, I resorted to only calling him when he was on the road and therefore at a hotel, since there was no interference and Mahmoud was fine and happy to hear from me.

I have since found out that certain individuals were hard at work trying to get Mahmoud away from me. I am clearly not an expert in the Koran, but I am certain that somewhere in there it says that you can't have a Jewish agent.

I have always contrasted my experience in dealing with Mahmoud and his lifestyle with that of Hakeem Olajuwon, who up till the 1995–1996 season, was the only other Muslim in the NBA. I was particularly aware of Hakeem since I represented Robert Horry, who was his teammate on their two world championship teams. I would pay close attention when Robert talked of Hakeem and when I would actually be around him after a Rockets game or in the hotel. Whereas Hakeem seemed to be a solitary and peaceful person who was very comfortable with his religious beliefs and lifestyle, Mahmoud seemed to be harried and pressured. Hakeem lived alone and seemingly without the pressure of others, while Mahmoud was living in a house with so many people he eventually gave up one of his homes to house the overflow.

It also became increasingly more difficult for the Nuggets to contact Mahmoud. There were incidents that were always relayed to me whereby Mahmoud changed his phone number without notifying the club. This is a blatant violation of league rules and is usually met with some type of fine. The Nuggets tried to help him through this period. They were concerned, but Bernie had a job to do, and although I truly believe that he cared a great deal during those years about Mahmoud the person, a line eventually needed to be drawn. After missing a mandatory team function because they couldn't reach him, the Nuggets had no choice but to fine him.

Mahmoud also started to become more difficult as far as showing up where he was supposed to, with his entourage intimately involved in his affairs—all signs of a situation going to hell.

A gentleman named Sharif Nassir, who to this day I have never spoken with though I made several attempts, was beginning to emerge as a major player in Mahmoud's life. On August 29, 1995, I received a letter from Mahmoud telling me that Sharif would be handling his endorsements. To receive the letter at all was completely unnecessary since Mahmoud had called me weeks before to see if it was all right. I said fine.

I did not view the letter as an imminent threat. I wasn't really concerned about losing income from endorsements because there really weren't any besides shoe contracts, which I had been negotiating all along. America can be a very strange place when it comes to anybody different. There was a definite palpable fear on the part of endorsers of Mahmoud in my opinion, due to his name change and conversion to a religion that many Americans were blindly fearful of. Again, I am no expert on the Muslim religion, but its tenets seemed to me to be founded in good common sense, and like most religions, if followed, they can only be a constructive force in our society. I never had any problem accepting Mahmoud or his religion. I did have a hard time digesting what I thought were people abusing the religious link with Mahmoud for their own purposes.

The single most interesting part of the letter from Mahmoud regarding his endorsement situation was the return address. Although the letter was signed by Mahmoud, it was sent from his old house where coincidentally Sharif Nassir was now residing. (Anybody out there have Sam Spade's number?) I discussed this with Mahmoud, who insisted that I shouldn't be concerned about our relationship at all or about his relationship with Sharif.

It was in this environment that Mahmoud started to begin a practice that, incredibly, would make him the most infamous citizen in the country. At the end of the 1994–1995 season, with virtually no fanfare at all, he began not to stand for the National Anthem. We didn't even discuss this. Personally, I didn't care all that much. I knew it would be unpopular, but with Sharif handling his marketing and public image, how could they go wrong? I was also aware that Mahmoud was continuing this practice throughout the next season as well. Again, there was no mention of this between Mahmoud and myself, or for that matter, with the league or even with the Nuggets.

My thoughts on the issue were very simple and one that most reasonable people would concur with. I didn't agree with it. Not so much from the view of popularity but basically as a citizen of this country. It didn't bother me, however, as long as it remained private on Mahmoud's part. The arrangement for most of the season had been that Mahmoud would go either back in the tunnel or to the locker room until the anthem was finished and then return to the floor for pre-game introductions. This seemed reasonable to me.

Mahmoud's reasoning for doing this was supposedly religious in nature, but again, we never got into it as it seemed to me to be irrelevant. I didn't even feel that it was necessary for Mahmoud to have to explain his own reasons for doing anything that wasn't infringing on somebody else's rights. The method that had apparently been worked out by the Nuggets and either Mahmoud or Sharif had worked just fine.

On March 12, 1996, I was minding my own business. I was still in my office at 9:30 p.m. or so, which was late for me. I had just wrapped up a

Leaving the back door open. Guarding Dave Stallworth of the Knicks in an exhibition at Camp Keeyumah in 1966.

Me and my dad. In 1963 we had no thoughts of some day representing NBA players or anyone else.

Bright futures. Hall of Fame coach Larry Brown *(left)*, Director of the National Museum of American History at the Smithsonian Brent Glass *(right)*, and me after a workout in my parent's backyard in 1972.

Fill in your own caption. P. T. Barnum and Commodore Nutt, 1862, left; Tim Duncan and Commissioner Stern, 1997, right.

A hands-on coach. John Wooden at his camp, 1975, where I had the privilege of his company during our daily drives.

Coach Glass. Coaching the UCLA junior varsity team at Pauley Pavilion, 1979–80.

UCLA Basketball Team, 1979–1980. Front *(left to right):* Michael Holton, Randy Arriaga, Rod Foster, Tyren Naulls; middle *(left to right):* Vic Sisson (manager), me, Larry Brown (head coach), Elvin "Ducky" Drake (trainer), Kevin O'Connor

(assistant coach), Larry Farmer (assistant coach), Skip Bennett (volunteer assistant); back *(left to right):* Chris Lippert, Darren Daye, Cliff Pruitt, James Wilkes, Gig Sims, Darrell Allums, Kiki Vandeweghe, Mike Sanders, Tony Anderson

Good Times. Richie Adams rising above the crowd at UNLV in the early 1980s.
Bad Times *(inset)*. Richie Adams as a suspect in the 1996 death of a fourteen-year-old Bronx girl.

Big man off campus. Tommy Hamilton, the 406-pound center, was the Will Rogers of eating—he never met a meal he didn't like.

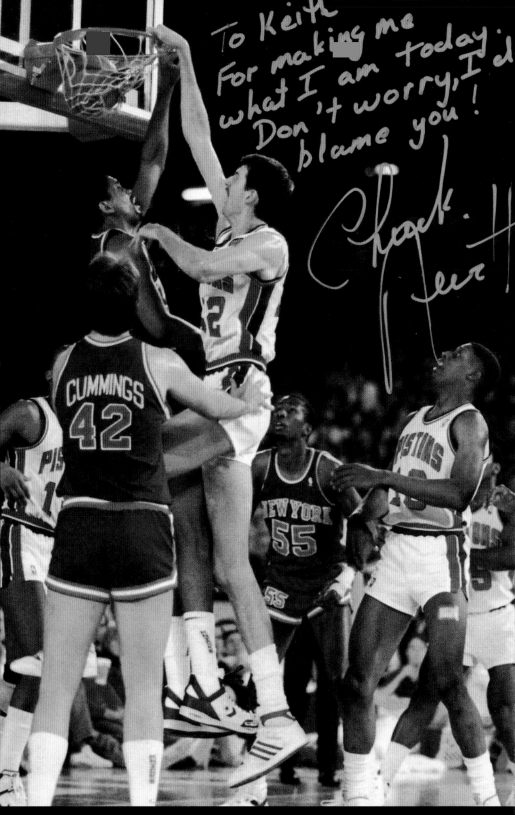

To Keith
For making me
what I am today.
Don't worry, I'd
blame you!

Chuck
Nee...

Another ringing endorsement. Chuck Nevitt, then a Detroit Piston, dunking against the Knicks. I made him what he is today. A stunned Dennis Rodman can only watch.

EARNINGS	HRS./UNITS	CURRENT. AMOUNT	YEAR TO DATE	DEDUCTIONS		CURRENT AMOUNT
REGULAR:	.000	350000.00	350000.00	Federal Wh	108090.75	108090.75
				FICA	4245.75	4245.75

1991-1992
Season

ROCKETS

HOUSTON

national basketball association

PAY RATE	CURRENT EARNINGS	CURRENT DEDUCTIONS	NET PAY	Y T D EARNINGS	Y T D DEDUCTIONS	Y T D NET PAY
	350000.00	112336.50	237663.50	350000.00	112336.5	237663.50

HOUSTON ROCKETS PROFESSIONAL
BASKETBALL CLUB, LTD.
PAYROLL ACCOUNT
P. O. BOX 272349
HOUSTON, TEXAS 77277

FIRST CITY, TEXAS
HOUSTON, TX 77252-2557
35-1-1130

3454

DATE 09/15/92   AMOUNT ***237,663.50

PAY
TWO HUNDRED THIRTY-SEVEN THOUSAND SIX HUNDRED SIXTY-THREE AND 50/100 DOLLARS

TO THE
ORDER
OF

Chuck   Nevitt
6236 Fountainhead Dr
Raleigh, NC 27609

Checkmate. The end result of Chuck's arbitration hearing versus the Houston Rockets.

Defending Hakeem. Utah Jazz center Mark Eaton was the
charter member of my Fighty-one Feet of White Centers Club

Low roof, or big guy? Mark with two of my
sons, Tyler and Alex, 1990

To the rack. Orlando Magic MVP Scott Skiles in action in 1993.

Relax while you can. Pat Williams, obviously before our negotiation for Scott Skiles's contract.

Religion and the NBA collide. Mahmoud Abdul-Rauf prays silently during the playing of the national anthem, surrounded by his Denver Nuggets teammates.

It's not Greek to me. Me and Efthimios Rentzias after his retirement in 2006. It was a wild ride from Thessaloniki through Denver, Barcelona, Philadelphia, and Italy.

Following Thru. The Michigan State contingent *(left to right):* Mike Peplowski, Jamie Feick, Scott Skiles, and Matt Steigenga help me out during my charity tournament.

Following Thru too. At the Fifth Annual Follow Thru Fund dinner, my guys *(left to right)* Chuck Nevitt, Marcus Liberty, and Bob McCann help out my daughter Sami at the auction.

Go for the Bronze! The NBA's poster children, LeBron James and Carmelo Anthony, accept their Bronze Medals in Athens 2004.

The moment of truth. Quincy Douby gets the call he's been waiting for all his life—he's been drafted as the nineteenth pick in the first round of the 2006 NBA draft. That's my son Tyler, the third generation of agents in the Glass family, left, and Jack Ringel, Quincy's high school coach, right.

Happy Days Are Here Again! New York Knicks president and general manager Isiah Thomas with Larry Brown. I'm pretty sure this picture was taken in November 2005, not April 2006.

Lucky at cards . . . Larry, my father, Joe Brunini of Caesar's Atlantic City, me, and my mom, after my dad and I took two out of the top three spots in a baccarat tournament in Atlantic City, 2000.

Turkish Delight. Me and my wife, Aylin.

The World According to Glass. While everyone else is sightseeing and shopping in Venice's Piazza San Marco. I'm working the phones and earning back Aylin's €17 café latte.

Still got it. Dunking at fifty-five, which is strange, because I couldn't dunk at seventeen . . .

Spinning my own yarns

board of directors meeting for the Follow Thru Fund, and we were going out to dinner in Red Bank. When I got in my car, I turned on WFAN, which in the New York area was the king of sports information, to hear Mahmoud mentioned during the sports news update given every twenty minutes. As a commercial played, I thought, *Great, he hurt himself.* I was driving down the road when the announcer returned to say that Mahmoud had been suspended indefinitely from the NBA for refusing to stand for the National Anthem.

I guess dinner and the Board could wait. I just whipped the car around and went back to the office. I sat down and dialed Mahmoud's home phone number realizing full well that I was about to get the runaround from whoever it would be that answered the phone. For the first time in probably two years, when I asked for Mahmoud and told them who I was, he immediately got on the phone.

As an aside, it was always my belief that even though Mahmoud was under tremendous pressure to dump me, he resisted for three years. The reasons for this were twofold. First, deep down, he knew what I could do for him in this league and that we had signed a very good deal and had together rectified a failed situation. Second, and at the risk of being totally wrong and thereby looking like a fool, I thought Mahmoud liked me.

Whenever there was something really wrong, it would be me on the other end of the phone. A month or so earlier, it was rumored that he was about to be traded. That's when Mahmoud called. I didn't know who or how exactly he had gotten into this mess, but I did know that he wanted me to help him get out of it.

With some of my players, I can always draw an analogy to something my youngest son, Lucas, said when he was nine. Clearly disgusted with the tactics of his older siblings, Alex and Maggie, in dealing with any situation involving trouble, Luke informed them to contact their Mom when they get into trouble, but Dad to get them out.

The conversation I had with Mahmoud that night regarding his suspension for not standing for the National Anthem was easily the most in-depth talk we'd had on a matter not directly relating to business. I merely

NATIONAL BASKETBALL PLAYERS ASSOCIATION

March 13, 1996

BY FAX AND BY UPS

Mr. Mahmoud Abdul-Rauf
c/o Denver Nuggets
McNichols Arena
1635 Clay Street
Denver, CO 80204

Dear Mr. Abdul-Rauf:

This letter is to confirm that you have informed us that you refuse to comply with the NBA rule requiring that all "[p]layers, coaches and trainers are to stand and line up in a dignified posture along the sidelines or on the foul lines during the playing of the American and/or Canadian national anthems." (NBA Operations Manual, paragraph I.E.2.)

Your refusal to comply with this rule constitutes conduct detrimental to the best interests of the NBA in violation of paragraph 35(d) of the NBA Constitution and paragraph 15 of your player contract. For violating these provisions, you are hereby suspended without pay, effectively immediately, until such time as you inform us that you are willing to comply with the rule.

Sincerely,

Joel M. Litvin
General Counsel

/rf

cc: National Basketball Players Association
     Keith Glass
     Bernie Bickerstaff

asked him what was going on. He did most of the talking. His response was a sort of unloading of his emotions. We talked for some forty-five minutes. In the conversation, he said specifically that according to his beliefs, standing for the anthem was impossible, that it was clearly against his religion. His rationale didn't add up to me, but again, I wrote my confusion off to an apparent lack of knowledge of the Koran and the Muslim religion.

I did wonder why this issue had never come up before in the sporting world, with Muhammad Ali, Kareem Abdul-Jabbar, Hakeem, and many college athletes never having much of a problem with this issue. Ali, to my way of thinking, is obviously a man of tremendous conviction and obviously has no fear at all of any consequences. I immediately thought of him while I was listening to Mahmoud. Even though I couldn't totally understand the reasons, I found myself admiring Mahmoud for taking the stand and for his courage in doing so.

I started to become concerned when he sort of rambled on about the political posture of the United States around the world. He complained to me about actions that our government had taken over the years. The implication clearly was that he could not stand and honor the flag of a nation that had done such terrible things to other nations. My concern stemmed not only from the rhetoric, but also from the fact that I didn't grasp the connection between his political differences with America and the statement that he was making this stand based on his religious convictions. Which was it—religion or politics?

We ended the conversation with me letting him know that I would support him and that I felt he had the right to stand or not to stand as an American citizen. The final statement he made to me was, "Keith, I will not stand!" I sincerely believed at that moment that he would not play again that season and possibly wouldn't ever play in the NBA again.

It wasn't really until I arrived home that I realized what was going on and why. I saw the CNN interview with Mahmoud. The interview filmed earlier that day, or even the day before, was about one minute long and Mahmoud, still dressed in his practice gear, said the reason he wouldn't stand was that when he saw the American flag, he thought that "it represented tyranny and oppression." Granted, he said more than that, but as usual, it was edited and that statement was all anybody heard, or at least remembered hearing.

It was obvious now why this was going down on this day rather than three months earlier, or, for that matter, last year. The NBA may be the most public relations–oriented organization in the world. This is a tremendous strength, but it can, at times, be the league's biggest weakness. Under Commissioner David Stern, the NBA has done a remarkable job of marketing this league and its players. They have made millions and millions of dollars for everybody. However, this same marketing-driven force could not in a million years allow this to go on, at least not out in the open, not on CNN. The tunnel was one thing, but not this.

In defense of the league and to be fair, there was another factor that forced the situation, which Mahmoud didn't inform me of in our forty-five minute phone call. It appears that now instead of remaining out of sight in the background during the anthem, Mahmoud had recently taken to coming out before the anthem and stretching or looking aimlessly around while the anthem was playing. This was incurring the wrath of people in Denver, and it was beginning to get some play on the local sports radio talk shows. The public nature of the situation made the league's position intractable. The NBA would not back down; it really couldn't.

The stretching angered me the most. To me, this was inexcusable. This wasn't religious or even political in nature. This was just plain rude and disrespectful. I was trying to be sensitive to and respectful of his religion, but I was offended by this conduct. While I'm no flag-waver, I do stand for every anthem and I'm proud of it. I've probably coached, played, or attended over a thousand sporting events in my life, and I stand for every one. I think one of the reasons I do stand is in part because Mahmoud doesn't have to.

I actually found myself thinking of my father, who fought for this country in World War II. I was upset for him, even though my father told me later that night that he supported Mahmoud's right not to stand.

As I wrestled with these issues all night and while the phone kept ringing, I kept thinking about two people, Ali and Hakeem. I wondered what Hakeem thought of all this. I would soon find out. I also thought of Ali because I have always considered him a great American. I was in college when he refused to take the step into the Armed Forces. I remember the vilification of Muhammad Ali. I remember the vast majority of people questioning his sincerity at the time. There are very few doubters today.

The next two days were easily the most tumultuous ones I have spent in this business. I was first and foremost trying to get a handle on the issues here, so I could counsel Mahmoud in the best way possible. But I was being inundated with interview requests the entire time. It was a very uncomfortable position to be in. I do not mind the media at all. There are times I actually enjoy it. I know that they have a job to do, and I respect that. It was, however, strange in that they would usually interview me about how I felt about something, and in this case, they wanted to know how Mahmoud felt. Since the truth was that I couldn't understand or was unclear about why and what he was doing, I certainly couldn't see myself going on the *Today Show* to expose the religious beliefs of a person that I didn't truly comprehend. That would have been just a bit presumptuous, even for me.

I spent much of that first day turning down interview requests other than some print media and radio stations. They were all things that I could do from my office in Red Bank. I said no to *Good Morning America*, *Nightline*, *20/20*, *Dateline NBC*, and *48 Hours*. These people were well meaning, but I also realized that they were really after me and Mahmoud, and there was a very slim chance of his appearing any time soon. In fact, after what I considered to be the ill-advised CNN debacle, it was my suggestion to Mahmoud that he not do any media at all unless it was a situation where we could select the show and Mahmoud would at least have an opportunity to express himself fully, without being edited to death. I did feel that to a degree that was the case the night before with the CNN interview.

Later that afternoon, the interview that I'd been hoping to see was aired for the first time. It was Hakeem Olajuwon, the only other Muslim in the NBA. Unlike my talks with Mahmoud, Hakeem spoke very calmly, very confidently, and very logically. He basically said that he didn't quite understand the issue, and whoever was teaching or advising Mahmoud had been wrong. He said that to be a good Muslim was to be a good citizen of the country you are living in, end of story, end of religious argument. Fifteen minutes after Hakeem's interview aired, I got a phone call from Mahmoud.

Apparently, he had seen the interview, too, though he never mentioned it. The league had fined him one game's pay already for the suspension, about $32,500. Mahmoud wanted to know if I thought he could get his fine back. It is hard to explain how I felt at that moment. Here was a client who some eighteen hours before was taking the stand of his life, and he was now reduced to a guy hoping to get back his $32,500. All I could muster was that I would try. Nobody ever said this job would be easy!

At this point, there were several different factions or groups involved in trying to bring about a solution to this very public problem. On one side of the fence was the league. On the opposite side was Mahmoud and whoever had advised him of the religious significance of the National Anthem.

The other two entities were the NBA Players Association and of course me. The role of the Players Association was an interesting one. During the summer before this incident, the Players Association and the league found themselves on opposite sides of another national issue, the lockout of NBA players for the first time by the league.

This time around, the association was headed by Alex English, who was the acting executive director. Coincidentally, my father and I had represented Alex in the last year of his career when he played in Italy. We were both very fond of him, and I knew him to be an extremely intelligent and sensitive man. I was fairly confident about on which side of this issue he would land. I wasn't disappointed.

Alex, along with Ron Klempner, legal counsel for the Players Association, called me several times the day after the story broke out. I discussed the situation in as much detail as I could. I always felt that even though Mahmoud was calling me three or four times a day that there was another force at work here. After Hakeem's interview, things started to spin. Other Muslim leaders throughout the nation, but specifically in the Colorado area, really came down on Mahmoud. They basically corroborated what Olajuwon had said. They didn't, in essence, see the connection to the teachings of the Koran. It seemed that the only ones who did were Mahmoud and whoever was advising him.

Let's stop tip-toeing around the issue—I'm starting to get on my own nerves! It appeared to me that Sharif was orchestrating this affair. As if that wasn't bad enough, Sharif really seemed to be enjoying it. I sure wasn't, and neither was Mahmoud. I truly believe that Mahmoud was overwhelmed by the commotion this thing had caused. He was upset that he had offended millions of people. He did not intend it to be taken in this way. But Sharif was enjoying the attention.

I tried three times at Mahmoud's request to contact Sharif during the critical two- or three-day period after the story broke. I never heard back. He didn't want to relinquish any control of this one—as if I wanted any. This first became blatantly obvious when a statement was read on behalf of Mahmoud the day after the story broke. I was horrified and at the same time amused after seeing Sharif organize a press conference and then himself read a statement for Mahmoud. Get this. The graphic under Sharif's likeness said "Sharif Nassir—Abdul-Rauf's agent." I thought to myself, *Not yet, but soon.* It got a little tedious explaining to family and friends that 1) I had not become a Muslim, and 2) I had not changed my name to Sharif.

I proceeded to call Mahmoud to discuss what I had just witnessed. My concern, I told him, was not with the graphic. This certainly was not the time to worry about my future as his representative. However, his reaction was one of annoyance with Sharif. He said they must have made a mistake at the studio and that everybody in his camp knew that he was with me. I told him that at that moment I really didn't care about that and that my advice would be to make any future statements himself. I thought that most people were turned off by Sharif and would be by anyone speaking on Mahmoud's behalf. The country really wanted to hear from *him*. This also was the reason why I didn't want to do any media on this story. The sports fans of America didn't want me; they wanted Mahmoud. If they didn't want me, then they sure as hell didn't want Sharif!

As far as Alex English's and the Players Association's involvement, they were exceedingly helpful to me and Mahmoud whether Mahmoud knows it or not. They orchestrated the arrangement with the league whereby Mahmoud would stand for the Anthem, but he would be allowed to say a silent prayer during it. And Mahmoud would get his $32,500 back. The March 13, 1996 press release issued by Alex said it all. It represented the most eloquent and accurate statement of these events that were issued in the matter.

I had implied and so did the Union and others in the legal community that Mahmoud had a right to sue for religious discrimination. The more the event took shape that appeared at least to me to be a long shot. Nevertheless, I was hearing quite often from attorneys, mostly from New York City, concerning their willingness to sue the league on Mahmoud's behalf. Obviously, this never got any further than the talking stage.

The fourth faction in this was me. My agenda was clear. If Mahmoud didn't make money, then neither did I! We are all paid on a percentage basis, so obviously, I had a vested interest in his continuing to play. This never came up in our discussions and believe it or not, I wasn't really concerned because I always thought, except for that first night, that he would play. Mahmoud, as I have said before, is a sincere person, but he also likes the financial rewards that playing in the NBA affords. I'm sure some of those around him liked those rewards as well.

As all of this was coming to a conclusion, I did some isolated interviews with the media. I remember some vividly, and others blur together. It wasn't easy to defend someone who was being vilified across the country. But I honestly felt that Mahmoud had the right as an American citizen to do what he did even if he was wrong. It is not a requirement to me that I agree with a person to defend him, and I didn't even have to go to law school to learn that. It's should be common sense, something that you pick up just by being raised in this country.

NATIONAL BASKETBALL PLAYERS ASSOCIATION

FOR IMMEDIATE RELEASE

**NBA PLAYERS ASSOCIATION STATEMENT
ON MAHMOUD ABDUL-RAUF**

New York, March 13, 1996—Alex English, acting director of the NBA Players Association, issued the following statement regarding the NBA's suspension of Mahmoud Abdul-Rauf yesterday:

"Our union respects the free expression rights of any individual, and NBA players are no different. We support Mahmoud Abdul-Rauf, and we support the American flag, which symbolizes Mahmoud's right to take precisely the action he is taking.

"Legally, the union does not believe that the NBA has the right to impose this discipline, and we intend to support a challenge by Mahmoud to the league's actions. The rule that the league relies on was not one agreed to in collective bargaining, but was imposed by the league unilaterally in an operations manual, without any input from the players.

"We also are disappointed that the league took this action without trying to resolve its concerns in a less confrontational manner. There are many ways to deal with this situation, and had the league made a good faith effort to approach the player and the union, this entire dispute could have been avoided."

The interviews and interviewers were varied, and their responses were as well. One local sports reporter who had interviewed me during the day called me from his home that night to congratulate me on how I handled a tough situation. That was a classy thing to do. On the opposite end of the spectrum was my experience on the CNN show *Burden of Proof.* Of all the requests I had done during that week, this was the only TV show I accepted to go on. I did this one because, believe it or not, since I really am a lawyer and I thought this would be a forum for me to discuss the actual constitutional issues involved here in some detail.

Not a good decision. What I discovered was that Greta Van Sustern and Roger Kosack, the hosts, had invited in about six other lawyers to talk over me. I was on a monitor, and the only word I can conjure to sum up the way I felt is *rude*. Issues? We don't need no stinkin' issues. The show seemed geared toward giving the hosts and panel a chance to demonstrate how clever and impolite they can be, not to air the issues. My mother called after the show was broadcast on CNN. She was so mad after watching the show that she said *she* was not going to stand for the Nation Anthem anymore. Mom is nothing if not loyal. But maybe there is a better way.

The only time I almost lost it was listening to the *Bob Grant Show* on the radio in New York City. For those of you who've never had the pleasure, Bob is just to the right of Archie Bunker. What specifically annoyed and worried me was that Grant was spewing forth sentence after sentence of misinformation. He and his callers did this all with tremendous emotion to go with their lack of knowledge on the subject. What worried me about Grant and the others of his ilk on both sides of the issues was that I wondered if this was the way they went about all of their discussions on the other topics of the day.

To my surprise, I called in from the car. This was the only time I reached out. Grant's people put me right through. I must admit he was more gracious than I had anticipated, especially since I was disagreeing with his position. One of his views that were widely held was that Mahmoud was breaching his contract. The theory was that here was this overpaid selfish brat making $3 million a year, and he couldn't even follow the clauses in his contract.

I pointed out that even though it made for an effective argument, it wasn't factual, and for the record, there is no clause in Mahmoud's or any other player's contract in the NBA that says it is mandatory that they stand for the National Anthem. In fact, what the league hung its hat on in this case was an NBA operations manual. As the press release of the Players Association correctly pointed out, this is a unilateral document that the league officials drafted themselves with no agreement from the association. This is hardly a breach of contract. I don't believe Mahmoud's infraction carried any hard time.

Late in the afternoon of March 13, 1996, Mahmoud or someone on his behalf issued a hand-written statement. I found the statement curious to say the least. Besides being drafted in an amateurish style, the statement did not in any way explain how this was a religious issue in the first place. It instead talks about his view, that he meant no disrespect or harm to anyone. But the main thrust seemed to be his description of his attempt to lead a more perfect life on and off the court. I was looking forward to getting some insight, some reasoned explanation of why this entire matter had even taken place. I heard very little from the press questioning this statement. It doesn't surprise me. If you are an athlete in this country, they will let you get away with saying almost anything, as long as you say it to them.

We allow explanations and clichés to come from the mouths of both college and professional athletes that would be laughed at in any other setting. Take it from me—I've heard them all. When you challenge these flights of triteness, you only get silence. Look, I make my living from these guys and I love them, but I rarely get my philosophy, sociology, or religious training from a basketball player. Why would anyone? Think about it. I know, football star Reggie White was a preacher, and I could see people listening to what he has to say, but overall, I'd rather listen to others on these matters. If you don't agree, come by later. I'm a lawyer, but I'll be happy to drill your teeth!

One of the more unusual happenings during this uproar occurred the afternoon following my interview on WFAN. I received two phone calls. One was from a person who just hated Mahmoud and now was basically threatening to come over and get *me*. The other was from another guy who was pissed with me because I wasn't defending Mahmoud enough. They both obviously didn't care for me and I realized that no matter what I did in this situation, somebody was going to be angry. I just found it interesting that off the same interview, two opposite poles of thought found something to be angry about. My only hope was that they would run into each other on their way to my office.

While the actual incident and the controversy that followed were interesting, educational, exciting, and frustrating, the return of Mahmoud to playing was painful for me, despite everything that happened. We discussed everything, and it was arranged that he would return on Friday night in Chicago against the Bulls. I immediately began to feel what he must be thinking. The pressure on him at this point was enormous. Now he was going to return under the glare of the entire nation. For the first time in years in Chicago, the fans were saying, "Michael, who?" that particular night.

My own personal emotion while watching that bizarre National Anthem was sadness. It was clear to me that this was the lowest point to which we could have stooped. What the league and the citizens of this country gained out of making a young person stand for our national song when he clearly did not want to was not a sign of respect, but a twisted display of power and the impact of money in our society. I include Mahmoud and myself in that last sentence.

Mahmoud stood surrounded by his teammates during the playing of the anthem. He held both hands slightly in front of his face in the traditional Muslim position of prayer. He prayed, with many Americans in attendance that night in the United Center booing and jeering during the playing of the National Anthem.

I don't think anyone out there who hasn't been through something like this can understand what it must be like for a young man, in that setting, to be forced to symbolically do something he doesn't want to do and then perform at the professional level. The fact that Mahmoud hit his first two shots was remarkable. It showed not only his amazing ability but also his focus and determination at the beginning of that game. Unfortunately, in hindsight, that was going to be it for him for awhile.

In retrospect, it is interesting to note that this incident occurred some five years prior to September 11, 2001. The atmosphere even then was a charged one. Our reactions in a general sense to different viewpoints or religions was and is not exactly one of universal acceptance and understanding. Muhammad Ali was stripped of his title and prevented from earning a living in his chosen field because he didn't want to kill his fellow man. This was decades before men claiming to be from his religious persuasion flew planes into the Twin Towers, the Pentagon, and crashed one in a Pennsylvania field.

Of course, the reality is that these nineteen men were not from the same religion as Ali or any other true Muslim. Unfortunately, most religions have their fanatics, and Islam is not exempt from this curse. I was no longer representing Mahmoud on that tragic morning, but suffice it to say that it would have been easier to represent him on September 10, 2001, than September 12.

Mahmoud and the Nuggets proceeded on to Toronto, which at least I felt better about. Being out of the country and specifically going to a city with a large Muslim population could only be positive. Mahmoud enjoyed that trip, and it was widely reported that he had made statements that he would love to play in Toronto. This was true, but it was also obvious that he was flailing around and really was looking for a soft place to land.

The next stop for the Nuggets was coincidentally New Jersey. Mahmoud had registered under an assumed name (I suggested Lew Alcindor.) There was tension everywhere Mahmoud went and a certain charged atmosphere. I had a meeting with the Players Association and the Agents Advisory Council on the day of the game with Nets. I went over to the hotel to try and get together with Mahmoud. There were security people to deal with. Judging from the limited threats directed at me, I could only imagine what it was like for Mahmoud. However, the doors to the elevator opened, and Mahmoud alone strolled off into the lobby. Here was the most infamous person in the United States that week, and he just walked off the elevator. I had been told that all security had been arranged for Mahmoud both through the league and "his people." I was shocked to see him alone.

What happened when he saw me is something I will never forget. He almost ran to me and grabbed me in a bear hug that some of my dates from college would have been proud of. He hugged me for what seemed to be a very long time, and I felt for him. I felt that he didn't want to let go. He asked me incredibly what was I doing there? It was at least good to see him smile. He asked if I would go to the mall with him because he didn't have any shoes for the game that night. I found this very interesting since we had turned down an offer from Nike for about $100,000 a year for two years about six months ago. But then I remembered Sharif was doing his marketing now. I hope he wasn't planning on using that incident as a recruiting tool.

We went into the store section of the Embassy Suites Hotel in Secaucus. The walk itself was memorable for me for two reasons. First, the gawking was incredible, but Mahmoud took it all in stride. There was nothing nasty said, and I was relieved about that. The second thing was that, as it turned out, I was eleven days away from emergency back surgery, which I had fought off for seventeen years. I was hurting. I noticed that whereas Mahmoud had lost some things that week, his quickness was still there. I was struggling, but I kept up. We went in to Foot Locker, and he bought himself some sneakers that he was to wear in about three hours on national television at the Meadowlands Arena. He put down a $100 bill and got eight bucks back. In all my years of representing players, I had never seen this before. A professional athlete with a game in three hours running around a mall in search of the tools of his trade.

We went back to his room and discussed everything that had happened to us that week. In the privacy of his room, our relationship was the same as it had always been, though he was a bit more nervous. Mahmoud asked the obvious questions regarding what I felt his future in the league to be. We talked about trades. Mahmoud curiously brought up the possibility of playing in Europe. I told him I thought this was premature.

I also said some things that maybe I shouldn't have, but I was trying as always to give it to him straight. For example, I told him that I respected his religion and I respected his conversion to that religion, but I added that when you convert to anything, you are always learning, and you should be always searching. It is not the same as being brought up in any particular religion. I told him Hakeem *was* a Muslim, and that he, Mahmoud, was *trying* to become one, and that the next time he made a stand on a religious foundation, he ought to understand the religion first.

That night at the Meadowlands I watched the playing of the National Anthem more closely than usual. I was touched by the reaction of Mahmoud's teammates. They literally surrounded him as if to try to protect him from harm. The coach in me looked at that scene and thought, *Now that's what a team is for.*

Six minutes into the game, Mahmoud suffered a foot injury and never played for the Nuggets again. The team was in a fight for the playoffs, and Mahmoud was their leading scorer. There were many on that team and in the organization who felt that Mahmoud quit on them; that maybe it wasn't so much about his foot as it was about his not wanting to face what awaited him in Denver for the rest of the season. Who knows? I'm convinced that the Nuggets traded him to the Sacramento Kings more for that reason than any other. I know Bernie Bickerstaff, and he is a fighter. He wouldn't have quit on Mahmoud.

On April 27, 1996, after returning from a trip to Greece, I received the letter that deep down I knew was coming as soon as I heard Sharif's name for the first time, two years before. Mahmoud had terminated me as his agent. It wasn't a surprise, but it still hurt. As noted previously in this book, these firings are commonplace and actually enabled by the union.

Although it has worked both ways, even for me, it is still wrong to allow the players the right to terminate their agent at will. It cheapens the process from the beginning to the end. It doesn't matter who you sign with as an agent because you can change him the following day with no consequence. The signing of any contract should mean something, the first thing a player does with his agent, signing their NBPA contract, means absolutely nothing.

Mahmoud and I had had an in-depth discussion while we were to-gether in Phoenix just two weeks prior to the date of my firing. We dis-cussed trades again, and in fact, I had met with the Nuggets that same day and discussed the possibility of Mahmoud's return to Denver. Things were fine, at least with Mahmoud. When I thought about the timing, I realized Mahmoud had to have written his termination letter at virtually the same time as our discussions in Phoenix.

So Mahmoud and I were done. In these situations, an agent can be comforted by the fact that even though fired, he still receives his fee. That is, if there is a fee to be had. Since I had already done his deal and the con-tract was in effect for another two seasons, I would get paid my percentage until that contract ended. Nice consolation!

I have joked in this chapter about having a limited amount of under-standing about Muslims. It is so much easier to generalize about a race or religion than it is to learn about it. I was as guilty as anyone else. It is not until we are truly exposed to different kinds of people that we all realize that all of us are basically the same. Education is the difference, and I was about to get my master's!

IT'S A SMALL WORLD AFTER ALL

"When one writes a novel about grown people, he knows exactly where to stop—that is, with a marriage; but when he writes of juveniles, he must stop where best he can."

—MARK TWAIN

This chapter was written primarily as it happened in 1996. Time moves on, and new events constantly take place in everyone's life. At the same time that Mahmoud was going through his turmoil, so was I. I went through a fairly contentious divorce in 1996. The conflict arose from how to split up the money, just like in the NBA. This battle lasted several years—a lot longer than in the NBA. In fact, according to the family courts of the State of New Jersey, I am still going through it, in 2006. I have always struggled with the concept that says "you earn the money, and then we'll split it." I actually believe that one hundred years from now when they study our culture, future generations will have two basic questions: The first will be what did men do to the women back then that prompted the courts to force them to pay sums of money to get away from them, and second, what was up with the salary cap?

Suffice it to say that after my second divorce, I swore off getting married again for the rest of my life. More importantly, I promised my mother, weekly, never again. I remembered the expression: "First time shame on you, second time shame on me." Who would I possibly blame the third time? I require someone to blame. It would be too confusing without someone to take the fall.

So off I went, single and dating. I was having a ball, too. My daughter, Sami, wasn't. She did not approve. She thought that I was born forty-six in a pair of brown shoes. I wasn't—I was born with a clean slate and bare feet. I joke about it now, but the divorces were painful and I was just doing the best I could.

At a basketball tournament in Virginia in 2002, I ran into a business associate from Turkey. Tolga was probably Turkey's most prominent agent. He represented his countryman Hedo Turkgolu, who was playing for the Sacramento Kings at that time. I had a break in between games, and Tolga, who I was actually annoyed with, asked me to dinner. Tolga and I were friends as well but not close ones. In the middle of a conversation about business, Tolga looked at me strangely and said, "You know, Keith, I have seen you with many women, but I don't think you are happy with them."

I told Tolga that obviously if you are dating several women, then you are not in love with any one of them. What I really wanted to say was, "What the hell do you care?"

His next sentence was even more unusual. "I have the perfect woman for you!" I laughed and asked where she was from, and when he replied Istanbul, I laughed again. Istanbul was not my usual dinner spot.

Tolga, however, proceeded to describe a woman that was impossible to construct. Her name was Aylin Guney. She had been a former professional basketball player for one of the biggest teams in Turkey, Fenerbache. After she stopped playing, she became the most popular female sportscaster in the country. She covered basketball and soccer, Europe's biggest sport. Tolga went on and on. The last two things he said were, "Keith, everyone who meets her loves her because of her heart" and "Oh, and by the way, she is gorgeous!"

Obviously, I was not interested. Who would be? I thanked Tolga for thinking of me in those terms, but clearly she was geographically undesirable. I mean, even if she lived in Queens, she would be geographically undesirable. Tolga left me with one final thought. "I am going to show you that I am a better agent than you!"

Three days after the tournament, I received a call from Tolga. On the extension with him was Ms. Aylin Guney. Tolga hung up, and Ms. Guney and I talked for an hour. Thankfully this was on Tolga's dime, or whatever passed for a dime in Turkey. That would be the last financial savings I would have in this matter.

She was the most charming person I ever spoke with. We started talking every three days or so. This went on for months. I started to notice that when I would be out with a woman, I was wondering what time it was in Istanbul so I could call her. Not a good sign for the date I was with. I was out on the town, and yet I preferred being on the phone with her.

In short, we were falling for each other over the phone, six thousand miles away. Strange? This is me we're talking about! I didn't want to be a pain in the ass to her, so I consciously tried to stagger my calls, but one day, we had the following conversation:

AYLIN: Why don't you call me every day? How come every two or three days?

KG: I don't want to stalk you. What if you're out with someone? I don't know. You could be dating someone.

AYLIN: (*laughing*) Oh, don't be ridiculous. Everybody is after me, but I'm waiting for you.

Now I'm starting to think that I'm being scammed in some way. I can't figure out how, but I must admit I was remembering that if something seems too good to be true, it usually is. She just seemed too perfect to me—at least on the phone. We still had never even seen each other. This was a distinct advantage . . . for me!

After Aylin invited me for dinner in Istanbul, I remembered that I had to be in Italy for the Euroleague Final Four, the next month. I also had five players playing in Athens that I needed to check on, or so I told myself. Realizing that this phone situation was not going to last forever, I turned down the Istanbul dinner invite and asked her to meet me in Athens for dinner. My mom, upon hearing this plan, said, "You're meeting a girl from Istanbul for dinner . . . in Athens? Who do you think you are, Cary Grant?" I guess it was a little unusual.

That must have been some meal in Athens. Eleven days later, Aylin flew to New Jersey, and we had dinner in Atlantic City with my parents, Larry Brown, and his wife, Shelly. After two hours, Aylin and Shelly went to the ladies room. My mother, who for five years had made me give her those weekly promises never to marry again, said only, "Are you waiting to be struck by lightning? Grab her!" Larry put in his two cents as well. "Keith, I overachieved when I married Shelly, but this is ridiculous." My dad continued smoking his cigar calmly, another very positive sign.

Two days after that meeting we were engaged. We have been fighting for the last four years over who asked who, but this is my book, so it was definitely her. Anyone who has seen the two of us together can easily tell that she pursued me. She stalked me! My choice was to call the police or marry her. There isn't a jury in the world that would convict me!

Turkey is a secular Muslim country. Aylin is a Muslim. I was fired by Mahmoud, in part, because I am Jewish. Aylin and I never discussed that seeming difference between us. Four years later, we still haven't, except to wonder at the insane notion that one's own religious beliefs can take precedence over the rest of the worlds', that one's beliefs are superior to those of others, that instead of just trying to live a good life, which is the bedrock of all religious, there are currently thousands of misguided individuals who are plotting a way to kill in the name of their own particular religious belief system. People who have hijacked or perverted their own religion to accomplish these misguided goals are not limited to Muslim extremists, though they are in vogue today. But this has been going on with almost all religions for thousands of years. The thought of the millions of people who have been killed in the name of religion numbs the mind. As usual, whenever I get in trouble expressing myself, I go back to Mark Twain:

> History is full of blood that was shed because of the respect and the veneration in which men held the last resting place of the meek and lowly, the mild and gentle Prince of Peace!

After Mahmoud terminated his contract with me, he never signed another NBA contract again, even with the expert guidance of Sharif. He did, however, secure himself a contract with one of the biggest professional teams in Istanbul, Turkey. The team was Fenerbache—the men's version of Aylin's old team. Mahmoud was having a difficult time in Istanbul. He was hard to approach and would not do any interviews with the Turkish media. The only solution was to have a former player and current top sportscaster try to break the ice.

Aylin had no trouble at all. She interviewed Mahmoud immediately, and he was gracious as he could be. She also took him to the mosques to pray. She showed him and his family the real Istanbul, which, for those who haven't been there, is a remarkable place. Six thousand miles from New Jersey, my former client and my future wife became good friends.

TEN

THE SQUEAKY WHEEL GOES TO GREECE

All right, we now know that Europe is a terrific place to find a wife. The NBA, however, discovered that there are other redeeming features there as well. When I first began traveling to Europe for basketball reasons, it was a place for me to send players who were just short of making it to the NBA. It was a good source of income for my players and for me. It was a great alternative to a job in the real world.

Today, European basketball has grown to the point where the NBA now has scores of talented and contributing players from Europe and around the world. When you think of the recent history of the NBA draft, you get a very clear message. The first pick in one draft was from China, Yao Ming. Both the 2005 and 2006 drafts saw a player from outside the United States, Andrew Bogut from Australia and Andrea Bargani from Italy, who were selected first overall. This would have seemed impossible a few years earlier.

My experience with this phenomenon didn't take the normal route. How could it? I didn't sit down with a recruiting plan and identify these top choices. That would have been too obvious, too messy, and a lot less fun.

I don't know how things happen to other people, but they do seem to happen to me in the strangest ways. In 1996, I had some health problems for the first time in my life. My back, which had been injured in that law school basketball league game, hampered me the entire winter. For seventeen years, I had been able to fight off the pain and stiffness. All the while Ducky Drake's words "you don't cut on a back" echoed in my brain. However, on Super Bowl Sunday, I was shoveling some ice after the blizzard of 1996, and that night I knew I was in trouble. For two months after that I tried to stretch it out. Nothing was working this time. I had three injections while being X-rayed trying to calm down the fourth nerve in my lower back. No luck.

The real problem, or so it seemed, was that I was in the middle of what would prove to be my last season as the head coach at Mater Dei. I was finding it increasingly more difficult to even get in and out of the car to go to practice or to work. Sometime in February, I couldn't get out of the huddles. I could get in, I just couldn't get out. My two assistants had an added responsibility—get coach up after the time-outs, one under each arm and lift.

Just when Mahmoud decided to misinterpret the Koran, I started to lose feeling in my right foot. This was the bad sign that I had always been warned about. On March 27, I finally had surgery on my lower back. I was operated on at 10:00 p.m. and was happy to leave at 1:00 p.m. the next afternoon with a very valuable assist from my mom.

A very unsympathetic nurse had come in and told me if I didn't fill up her jar with a urine specimen, then she would have to catheterize me. You know how there are things that you can see yourself doing or going through, and then there are things that you just can't? Well, catheterization definitely fell into the latter category.

My mom was in the room when the nurse gave me her ultimatum. Right away Mom told me to relax, and everything would start operating at usual. I started drinking the rest of the morning. I don't know if it was the pressure or the morphine drip, but nothing was going on down there.

Nurse Ratched had given me an hour or so to come up with the goods, or else. I didn't really notice, but my mom had vanished for a little while and returned with about fifteen minutes left on the clock. She had her big black pocketbook with her, which usually means trouble. She very calmly examined the jar, noticed it was still empty, reached into her purse, and pulled out a large plastic cup, which she had procured in the hospital cafeteria. Hot tea to go. She matter-of-factly opened the jar, poured the tea into the jar and went into the bathroom where she added water so as to get the correct color. She returned to her chair as if this is what mothers are supposed to do. The nurse picked up the sample, I mean the tea (no honey), and I was going home. As we were leaving, I did have to make a quick pit stop where I proceeded to urinate like a small horse. Nobody knows me like my mom.

I bring all this up only to relate how this affected my business in the spring of 1996. To a basketball agent, the winter is supposed to be a time for recruiting and the spring a time for finishing up your efforts by traveling to the various sites to assess and hopefully sign your recruits. I was always behind when the spring came due to coaching Mater Dei for twelve years, but I always seemed to be able to scramble in the spring and keep going. The surgery and what led up to it was going to kill my year as far as business was concerned.

On a purely personal level, it was putting my trip to the Portsmouth Invitational Tournament in Virginia in jeopardy. This was not only the first stop for prospects of the coming draft in June, but more importantly to me, it was the annual male-bonding trip for me and two of my sons. Tyler and Alex looked forward to it the whole year. After sixteen years of attending, I have never been to the Portsmouth tournament without any of my three sons. One week after the surgery, the three of us were on a flight from Newark to Portsmouth.

I had somehow managed to pick up two players who would be participating in the tournament. One of my guys, Mike Peplowski, from Michigan State, had introduced me to Jamie Feick the summer before Jamie's senior year, at which time the three of us had lunch in East Lansing. (Jamie paid for his own sandwich in case the NCAA is reading this). I was lucky to sign Jamie. The other player was Matt Maloney from the University of Pennsylvania. Matt would go undrafted, but would later sign a $17 million contract with the Houston Rockets. Is this a great country or what?

TED

Tyler, Alex, and I, complete with my walking stick, limped into the lobby of the Holiday Inn on April 4. I was in no mood to socialize. I was looking for a bed to lie down in. As I was checking in, a little fellow who I sort of recognized approached as if he had been waiting for my arrival. He was a coach from Greece who I had met some six or seven years earlier. His name is Theodoros Roudoupoulos, but I'll call him Ted. In retrospect, he has become, in my opinion, the most important of all the Greek philosophers.

I'm still not certain exactly where we had met. I think it was at a summer league in White Plains, New York. Maybe I had given him a ride back to his hotel or something like that.

He ran up to greet me, and I sort of brushed him off. I did, however, tell him to call me in a few minutes. He did. Contacts like this from overseas guys happen quite regularly to me, and I assume to other well-known agents in the United States. The point of these contacts is simple—they want *money*.

Most foreign agents are trying to get in between me and an overseas club. Since the clubs pay the agent's 10 percent fee, these guys are merely looking to be cut in. This can range from one-third to half of my fee. This totally differs from the situation in the NBA where agents are regulated as to how much of a fee we can charge (4 percent), and we receive payment directly from the player.

Ted's purpose for seeking me out was completely different from what I was expecting. He asked me directly if I had ever heard of Rentzias. He used only one name. Since I had been so out of it during the past several months, I had no clue who he was talking about. For all I knew, this could have been some Greek delicacy. But I faked it. He asked me if I would have an interest in representing him. It was then that I realized that this was not about food. (You don't have to hit me over the head with a brick, even if I am on Vicodin.) I told him that I would check it out and get back with him.

About thirty minutes later, I went down to the lobby to try and find someone from the league that I could question about this Rentzias guy. The first person I ran into was Stu Jackson, the former Knicks coach and currently the NBA official in charge of discipline for the league. I mispronounced the kid's name, but finally, Stu perked up and asked, "You mean the big kid from Greece? Oh, he's a lottery pick." Meaning he'd be one of the top thirteen draft choices in the next NBA draft. My first thought was, *Where the hell is Ted?*

The only problem with this was that as you have read, his real name was not as simple as Ted. His last name was a lot more involved, and, quite frankly, I just couldn't remember it. The name sounded to me like trying to pronounce an eye chart. I called down to the reception desk and spoke to a woman who had luckily remembered me from previous visits. She was great. In fact, she thought that she had even seen him around the lobby and said that she would look out for him and call me if she found him. You must understand that in this business, especially in a hotel with two agents per square foot, an hour alone could mean anything. Ted could be bound and gagged in the luggage room for all I knew.

Believe it or not, ten minutes later the phone rang. It was my girl from the front desk, and she had Ted. I explained to him how unbelievably interested I was in Rentzias. In fact, I amazed myself with what an expert I had become in just forty-five minutes on Rentzias's game, life, dreams, etc. It's amazing what a potential lottery pick can do for your creativity and enthusiasm, not to mention your back.

Now I had to make sure that I signed him. I didn't know how this had fallen in my lap, but I wanted to make sure it stayed there. It turned out that Ted was an advisor to the Rentzias family. They were looking for an agent, and he had come to the United States to find the right one. Ted told me that he had gone up to three GMs that he had known in his travels as a coach. He asked them all the same question, "Who are the top three agents in the NBA as far as knowledge and integrity were concerned?" He then told me that I was the only one who was on all three lists. That was it for him. I was the guy they wanted. He must have found the only three that liked me.

Ted asked if I could come to Greece to a place called Thessaloniki because the family wanted to interview me. I said, "Sure, no problem," as I reached for my back. First, I had to make a trip to Phoenix for the Desert Classic. To be honest, I really didn't think this was going to pan out anyway. I am constantly approached by well-intentioned people who sincerely believe they can deliver the first pick in a particular draft. I almost feel sorry for them, since I know how deceptive some of these players and the people around them can be. The people approaching me were just about to find out.

Anyway, for the rest of Portsmouth and the following week in Phoenix, I continued to gather as much information on Efthimios Rentzias as I could, just in case. The news was all good. Glowing in fact. He was six feet eleven inches tall with great offensive abilities. He was the best prospect in Europe. He was the best player in the junior nationals the summer before. He had kicked the ass of Samaki Walker, the University of Lousiville sophomore who had just declared for the draft and would subsequently be taken with the ninth pick overall by the Dallas Mavericks.

Holy crap, this was ridiculous! I called Ted in Thessaloniki from Phoenix. Everything was the same. He would let me know if the family wanted me to come to Greece. I was a little ambivalent about this trip. Obviously, I wanted them to want me to come, but I had serious concerns about making the trip with my back being the way it was.

I arrived home from Phoenix on Sunday night, tired. I was clearly doing too much too soon. Monday morning, back in the office, the first call I received was from Ted. He wanted to know if I could come to Thessaloniki on Wednesday. No problem. Actually, there were some problems. For example, "Where am I going?" All day Tuesday I could not get Ted on the phone. His mother, a very nice woman who couldn't speak English, had the adorable habit of hanging up on me whenever I called, and Ted wasn't there. I was getting really concerned and was just about to cancel my flight when I finally reached him. He laughed and told me that his mom simply couldn't understand me due to the language barrier and that he would pick me up at the airport. *What airport? What the hell—Newark to Frankfurt to Thessaloniki, my usual commute.*

Here's a free travel tip. If you're going to Thessaloniki after back surgery and you happen to have an extra $3,000 lying around, go business class. The trip took about nine hours just to get to Frankfurt. My connection from Frankfurt took me right into Thessaloniki. I really didn't know whether Ted would be there or not. What if he wasn't? I would be in a foreign country alone and unable to communicate with anyone. At last, my second marriage had prepared me for something.

Ted's was the first face I saw after going through customs. I have never doubted him again. We had a meeting scheduled with Rentzias and his family the following day. I was really entering uncharted waters. I was trying to get as much information as I could about Rentzias and his family. What I have always felt is that if you are going to try to sign a foreign player, you should at least attempt to understand their culture and priorities.

The reputation of the "ugly American" in many of the European countries is richly deserved. Many players and their representatives treat the coaches and general managers in foreign lands as if they know very little about the game. Whereas in many cases we as Americans have a distinct edge as far as talent and the ability to play the game is concerned, it does not automatically follow that they have nothing to add. It always struck me that this arrogance and condescending attitude would lead to our downfall basketball-wise.

I was in a foreign country to try to sign a player for the NBA draft who had never had the advantage of playing against the greatest players in the world, but had still risen to a level where the league was extremely interested. I respected that. The Greeks, Italians, and Spaniards were, at that point in time, still not as good as the Americans, but I knew if they continued on their current path and we continued on ours, then it wouldn't be long before they were equal. The American game had become a selfish one-on-one type game. In Europe, they still played as a team.

The meeting took place in the Rentzias family apartment, which was very nice. Efthimios was the only member of the family who could speak any English at all. He could speak very well but had trouble understanding when I spoke to him. Actually, so do a lot of people in New Jersey. I have since come to marvel at Efthimios's ability to master a foreign language. Today, his English is perfect. When he played in Spain, he ended up speaking fluent Spanish in three weeks.

His parents were very good, solid people whose sole concern was their son's well-being. The meeting lasted for about three hours. Ted had clearly laid some groundwork. The family trusted him completely, and he impressed me with the fact that he too was truly interested in Efthimios's welfare. Incredibly, I left that apartment with signed contracts from Efthimios Rentzias. I was thrilled and relieved that the trip had been worthwhile.

I decided that I would next travel on to Rome to visit another one of my players, Steve Henson, on the way back to the United States. Steve picked me up at the Rome airport. He had a playoff game that night against Benetton, a major team in Treviso, Italy. Steve had scored thirty-seven points in Treviso to upset Benetton in the first game, and the second game was that night in Rome in a best two-out-of-three series.

I went to the game with Steve's wife, Cindy. After all the NBA games with their interminable post-ups and one-on-one plays, I found this play-off game refreshing. The enthusiasm of the crowd was great. In Italy, as in other foreign countries, the crowd sings songs of support the entire game. Not just during time-outs, but for the entire game. The place was packed and even though Steve played valiantly and virtually alone, Benetton won to even the series.

Steve, Cindy, and I ate pasta outside, next to the Pantheon, where we actually discussed seriously what the chances were of Steve getting back to the NBA, to a city maybe as beautiful as Detroit. I looked at the Pantheon, shook my head, took another bite of my pasta, and realized that's why they make chocolate and vanilla.

PRE-DRAFT

I said *"Arrivederci, Roma,"* one of my favorite cities, and headed home to New Jersey. I had to begin to plan my strategy for Efthimios. Being twenty years old, he first would have to enter his name in the draft. This was accomplished by a letter that I wrote for him and sent to the NBA league office. The letter merely informs the league that the player wants to have his name entered in the upcoming draft.

I next turned my attention to discussing Efthimios's situation. I have found through the years that talk is cheap. Unless a club specifically guarantees that they will select your guy if he is still available, then you never really know. I had received one specific guarantee from the Knicks, and I had informed Efthimios's family of that fact. I was very comfortable with the Knicks' position since not only had their general manager Ernie Grunfeld guaranteed this himself, but they also even had the luxury of three first-round draft picks: 18, 19, and 21. I was safe in that even if something strange occurred the night of the draft at 18, they could take him at 19 or 21.

The Knicks were adamant, however, by saying, "Keith, if he's available at 18, then I guarantee we'll take him." I verified this with the general manager's assistant who had seen Rentzias play. He was even higher on the kid than his boss. His assessment was basically that Rentzias wouldn't even be available for them to pick at 18, but if he was, then he would be their selection.

Great, I thought. *I'm guaranteed at 18, so let's see if we can't get higher.* I started to notice that this draft would not be a typical situation for me for a couple of reasons, the biggest of which was the subtle fact that Rentzias was already under contract to his existing team, PAOK. He had signed, as many kids do in Europe, a five-year contract beginning when he was only sixteen years of age. The coming season was to be his last under this amateur agreement.

Efthimios was not considered a pro, but PAOK was desperate to keep him, and they made it clear that they were going to fight me. Technically, he was only under this agreement until his twenty-first birthday, which was coming on January 11. PAOK was maintaining in the Greek press that Rentzias would not be leaving. What was more threatening was that they indicated that he must sign an additional professional contract covering the next five years.

Whether this was true or not, it was having a definite chilling effect on the NBA general managers as far as their view on how high to draft Efthimios Rentzias. Why waste a first round draft pick on a player that you can't have right away? For the first two weeks of May, I constantly found myself in the position of having to explain his contractual situation, which was clear as mud. Every time I spoke to someone, I got a different interpretation. What I was becoming increasingly aware of was not so much the problem of not knowing what the rules were going to be concerning this matter, but that I was going to become involved in some sort of morality play over this. I could sense that with no real direction or definitive ruling, the teams in the NBA were going to have to rely greatly on my say-so. In other words, the general managers were going to question me on the real meaning and validity of Rentzias's agreement in Greece, and my credibility was going to be an issue. My credibility was going to get a real test.

I decided that I was just going to tell the truth as I knew it. When I didn't know the answer, I would say so. If I was asked whether Efthimios could get out of his agreement with PAOK, I would say, "Probably not." Let's get one thing straight. I am not Pollyanna. I know the overall reputation of agents is one of deceit and lies. This is richly deserved. I believe I have a reputation different than that for several reasons: 1) I always wanted to maintain relationships. I wasn't in this for a quick buck or for a temporary time period. I assumed that if you are constantly lying or misleading people, it will catch up to you; and related to the first point, 2) if you lie to make a deal for one of your players, then you are in essence screwing the rest of your clients. You are effectively eliminating not only your credibility in the process, but theirs, too. So I would tell the truth. It was a novel approach.

As if we needed a further complication to unfold, Rentzias's teammate from PAOK Predrag Stojakovic also decided to make himself available for the NBA draft. He was a six-nine small forward who had great potential, but at that point, was considered to be a second-round draft choice, clearly behind Rentzias. It was also apparent to me that this was an important situation for Rentzias and his father. The competition between the two players was clear, and it was important to the family that Efthimios be drafted ahead of Stojakovic.

Stojakovic had come from the former Yugoslavia, which had become a real hotbed for basketball before the war tore that country apart. The Croatians and Serbs had produced some of the finest players outside of the United States. Players like Drazen Petrovic, Vlade Divac, Toni Kukoc, and many more thrived not only in Europe but also in the NBA. Petrovic, in fact, was named third team All-NBA two months before dying in a tragic car accident on the Autobahn. Today, his jersey hangs in the Meadowlands, the home of the Nets. Stojakovic was only nineteen years old and was said to possess a great jump shot with tremendous range. He actually was more equipped to come over and play in the league than Rentzias. The balance shifted to Rentzias in that centers or big forwards were harder to find.

As the early days of May rolled by, other factors started to complicate the draft status of Efthimios Rentzias. As in any draft year, underclassmen can declare for "early entry." In 2006, we are accustomed to fifty to eighty players submitting their names for early entry into the NBA draft. Back in the early 1990s, most years saw five to eight underclassmen apply. By May 15, 1996, there were twenty-six.

Compounding this was the fact that two quite highly regarded high school seniors, Kobe Bryant and Jermaine O'Neal, had also announced that they would enter the draft. The position of Rentzias, which just three weeks earlier looked like a sure top ten, was being severely challenged.

I kept in touch with Ted and the family almost every day. I would explain who was entering the draft and who was considering doing so. For example, Lorenzen Wright of Memphis State would later declare. Being a seven-footer, he would have a direct impact on Efthimios, especially since teams in the league didn't have to deal with a contractual obligation from across the ocean. The problem wasn't a reflection of his abilities, but more out of the league's concern about his contract. I started to sense that we were dropping.

I called the Knicks again. "Keith, stop worrying about it. I guarantee we'll take him if he's available." Well 18 is not so bad. Ernie went so far as to suggest that I stop pushing Efthimios in front of other clubs. He was in essence selling me on the positives of having Efthimios in New York. He not only spoke of the quality of the Knicks themselves and the first class way they ran their organization, but also of the fact that there was such a large Greek population in New York. He knew that this had to be appealing to Efthimios and his family. It was. Souvlaki, anyone?

Maybe some information on what my options were in this situation would illuminate the position I was in. The rules stated that I could withdraw Rentzias's name from the draft. In 1996, if I did so, it would have to be within forty-eight hours of draft day. All of these calls and discussions with clubs were designed for the specific purpose of trying to ascertain, as best I could, where Rentzias stood so that we could make an informed decision about remaining in or withdrawing.

My decision to keep Rentzias in the draft or withdraw was a critical one. I knew that he would probably go higher in the following draft since so many underclassmen had already declared, thereby, weakening the next draft. The guarantee from the Knicks was the pivotal reason for staying in. We discussed it in detail and determined the money we would receive at 18 would be fine. Factoring in the thought that 18 was the lowest we would go clinched the deal. I will admit that it placed a lot of faith in the Knicks and Ernie, but I had always considered him a friend and I couldn't see any reason or what he would have to gain by misleading me.

Looming in the distance, only days away, was the last leg of the showcases designed to determine the order of the draft. The NBA pre-draft camp is really the only one totally run by the league. They invite some sixty players, underclassmen included. As a general rule, if an agent or player feels that he is a top twenty pick, or at least in that vicinity, he doesn't play in Chicago. He will attend, but only to take the physical administered by the league. This saves the player the time and aggravation of having to possibly take five, six, or more physicals on possible individual team visits right before draft day. In 1997, the league switched this process by having the players play first and then take the physicals. The hope was that more guys would play instead of just showing up for the physicals. I personally don't think it matters that much.

The league and the public sometimes question and criticize agents and their prospective clients for not having the courage to play one more time in front of the critical eye of the league and its coaches, general managers, and scouts. This is the most absurd thing I have ever heard. For the most part, these kids have played three or four years with more than ample opportunity for teams to scout them. The NBA is a critical group. They're looking for flaws. That is the nature of things. A player who has waited his whole career to be drafted and finds himself as a possible twentieth pick has a lot more to lose than to gain. The twentieth pick in a draft these days is looking at approximately $4 million over a three-year period. This money is guaranteed to the player regardless. If he should fall, let's say to number thirty-one, he is guaranteed zero. For the nonmath majors in the audience, that is $4 million down the toilet. At this point in a player's career, this is business. There are countless examples of players who made the wrong decision about attending one of these camps and either fell in ranking or dropped out of sight completely, resurfacing in Japan. Please, if your son told you, "I have $4 million guaranteed already, but I just want to play one more tournament to show that I'm not afraid to put it on the line," you would probably either tie them to the bed until the tournament was over or hire a cult to deal with him for a week. Me personally? I'm putting him in a large mayonnaise jar, and hoping he doesn't spoil.

Both Rentzias and Stojakovic were invited to Chicago. The problem with Rentzias was that he was on the Greek national team. This was a tremendous honor for him, but it was also a tremendous pain in the ass for me. I never knew where he was going to be. The Greek national team were all over the place. What's more they had qualified for the Olympics in Atlanta, for the first time in history of Greek basketball. Efthimios was a national figure in Greece, but it was clearly getting in the way of the draft. Stojakovic had no such problem. He was not on any national team. He was not Greek. He had been signed under some strange circumstances by PAOK out of Croatia and had in some way become a Greek. He was not, however, eligible for the Greek national team.

Back in Red Bank, I was still leveling with everyone. Efthimios was not free. I told the truth. I must have been out of my mind!

I was now getting the distinct feeling that we were down to two possibilities. The first was the Golden State Warriors at number eleven. Dave Twardzik, one of my friends on the other side of the table, had just gotten the job as the GM of the Warriors. They were interested in Rentzias. In fact, Dave and Rick Adelman, their head coach, took the long trip to Athens to watch Efthimios play with the national team. They spent three days over there and called me every day. They liked what they saw and were especially excited about his offensive skills. There was an excellent chance that they would select them at number 11.

Two other teams had made plans to go over to Greece. The Pacers decided at the last minute that they would decline the trip. Ernie Grunfeld and Ed Tapscott from the Knicks also considered making the trip. Ernie called, however, and said that it would be better if they didn't go so as to not tip off the other NBA teams as to the Knicks' interest. This is not at all unusual around draft time.

I was continuously informing Rentzias and his family through Ted. I informed them that I would make one last call to the Knicks to lock up number eighteen. I spoke with New York exactly two days before the draft. For approximately the twenty-sixth time, they assured me that Rentzias would be picked by the Knicks if he was still available at number eighteen. I remember pressing them on that occasion. I explained that this was not a college senior who had to take his chances in the draft. I told him we could and actually were considering withdrawing his name and entering again the following year. I said to the Knicks that the only reason we would remain in the draft was based on their word that the Knicks would select him. Once again, I was informed that they would select him.

Things got very interesting the day of the draft. All day long, there were calls regarding Efthimios and another one of my clients, Jamie Feick from Michigan State. Jamie had visited Milwaukee, who was looking at him with the thirty-third pick. And I started to fudge a little about Rentzias's availability, but it never honestly crossed my mind to mislead anyone. I just couldn't imagine lying about Efthimios's lack of availability, having a club draft him high and then saying later, "Sorry about that."

I had been on the phone periodically the day of the draft with Dave Twardzick of the Warriors. All talk centered on when they could actually have Rentzias in a Golden State uniform. Earlier in the day, I had organized a conference call between Rentzias, Twardzick, Rick Adelman, and myself with Ted acting as interpreter. One other member of that call was George Irvine, assistant coach with the Warriors and my best friend for some twenty-five years. The conference was mainly a discussion with Rentzias about his desire to play in the NBA. The Warriors were very concerned (and rightly so) about his burn to be the best. They felt that if a guy didn't want to come over, then they didn't want to select him at such a high level. The call went well, and I felt pretty good about our chances.

My moment of truth actually came at about 5:30 p.m. when I had a call between Dave, Adelman, and me. They basically were telling me that they were going to select either Efthimios or Todd Fuller, a center out of North Carolina State. At the end of the call, Dave asked me point blank: "Keith can you guarantee us that when we open up training camp in October, Rentzias will be there?" They were in essence begging me to lie. It was not tough to answer. "No, I can't promise that," I said.

There was no doubt in my mind that if I had just led them on a little more, the Golden State Warriors would have selected Efthimios with the eleventh pick. Instead, they went with Fuller. It was the safe thing to do. It hurt at the time, but I understood the move. The Warriors were not a very good team. As it turned out, they also would have been building a team for someone else. Rick Adelman was fired at the end of the season. To illustrate the cyclical nature of the NBA, in 2006, Rick Adelman was fired by another team, the Sacramento Kings, after a very successful stint there. Dave Twardzick is currently the player personnel director for the Orlando Magic.

IT'S A LITTLE DRAFTY IN HERE!

I had always watched the draft on television, but I had never gone. Usually, it's an awful night for me for some reason. With the exception of 1992, in which I represented three of the first twenty-eight picks, it invariably turns into a disaster of varying proportions. I have usually signed a particular type of player. They are usually fundamentally sound guys, but they lack the flair that the league seems to be attracted to. On most draft nights, this has led to my clients dropping further down the draft list. In the 1986 draft, Scott Skiles, for example, went twenty-second, while the more flashy and promoted "Pearl" Washington was drafted at number thirteen. In that same draft, Johnny Dawkins of Duke went eleventh. Scott's career dwarfed the other two, but you get the idea. Multiply that by twenty drafts or so, and you get the total picture.

The 1996 draft, however, was in New Jersey at the Meadowlands. After my call with the Warriors ended, I headed up the Garden State Parkway to the draft. The league had made arrangements for me to sit in the Green Room, which is where all the agents with the top players gather with their hopefully soon-to-be-millionaires in freshly bought suits. I ended up sitting in the arena with the fans. My client was sleeping in Athens, and besides, I had no clue about the proper protocol regarding hugging and handshakes. Thus began the worst night of my career.

There were key spots for Rentzias in the first round. The first seven or eight picks didn't really matter. All I was concerned about was that there were no major surprises. What happens when you get a surprise is that a team may be all set to take your guy, then all of a sudden somebody gets left on the table that they honestly never thought would be there. The best example of this would be the 1985 draft. I'm sure that the Utah Jazz had scouted and prepared diligently for the draft that year—they had the thirteenth pick. When Karl Malone from Louisiana Tech was still available at number thirteen, whoever they had been planning on taking was out.

I was looking at the tenth pick, which belonged to the Indiana Pacers, who had periodically expressed interest in Rentzias. They were really interested in getting Kerry Kittles, Lorenzen Wright, or Eric Dampier—whichever one was still in play. My concern was that if they were all gone, the Pacers might take Stojakovic, leaving me with some serious explaining to do. The Pacer's GM passed a folded piece of paper to David Stern, who announced, "With the tenth pick in the NBA draft, the Indiana Pacers select . . . Eric Dampier from Mississippi State." One hurdle crossed.

The eleventh pick was also critical. It was our chance to really come out on top. Twardzick had told me that he honestly didn't know if it would be Efthimios or Fuller. "With the eleventh pick in the NBA draft, the Golden State Warriors select . . . Todd Fuller from North Carolina State." That hurt, but we were still okay. Only seven more picks to number eighteen, and this part will be over.

In the meantime, John Wallace, who had led Syracuse to the national championship title game against Kentucky, began doing a very good Karl Malone draft day impersonation. He was too talented to stay available much longer. I wanted him out of the way. With each pick, the crowd at the Meadowlands got more and more excited. Holy crap, I realized, John Wallace was heading toward the Knicks, and the savvy crowd sensed it. "With the thirteenth pick in the NBA draft, the Charlotte Hornets select . . . Kobe Bryant." This was rumored earlier and was actually part of a trade that sent Vlade Divac from the Lakers to the Hornets and made Kobe Bryant a Laker.

Next up Sacramento. "With the fourteenth pick in the NBA draft, the Sacramento Kings select . . . Predrag Stojakovic from PAOK of Greece." Ouch!

We got to number seventeen. The end of the line for John Wallace certainly. "With the seventeenth pick in the NBA draft, the Portland Trailblazers select . . . Jermaine O'Neal." Another high school kid. David Stern was starting to get on my nerves!

Now the entire arena was exploding. They were chanting Wallace's name. Here we were at my lovely number eighteen, and the entire world, it seemed, was in some kind of conspiracy to screw it up. But I understood that despite their promises, the Knicks would have to take Wallace or be killed in the papers the next morning. They also held numbers nineteen and twenty-one, so we were fine. "With the eighteenth pick in the NBA draft, the New York Knicks select . . . John Wallace of Syracuse University." Bedlam in the arena. It's okay; we were next.

"With the nineteenth pick in the NBA draft, the New York Knicks select . . . Walter McCarty of the University of Kentucky!" *What? Did he just say Walter McCarty?* Amid more cheers and happiness around me, I don't recall ever feeling that down and betrayed in this business.

"With the twentieth pick in the NBA draft, the Cleveland Cavaliers select . . . Zydrunas Illgauskas from Lithuania."

We were now up to the third and last of the Knicks' picks. I figured, "Alright, they took a gamble that we would still be available, and they won." It cost us a little money, but what the hell." "With the twenty-first pick in the NBA draft, the New York Knicks select . . . Donta Jones of Mississippi State."

The thought crossed through my mind in my state of panic that we now had a chance to actually fall right out of the first round. To understand the difference between going thirtieth, which was the last pick in the first round, in 1996, and thirty-first, which is the first pick in the second round, get into your car and drive off a cliff. The part that comes after your wheels become airborne and gravity takes over—that's the second round.

"With the twenty-third pick in the NBA draft, the Denver Nuggets select . . . Efthimios Rentzias from PAOK of Greece." I never had the urge to kiss Bernie Bickerstaff before, but I was tempted. Well, not really.

I can never hope to explain my feelings at this moment. It wasn't so much the business aspect of it. I knew deep down I would survive this. I did think that there was a chance that Efthimios would terminate our contract, but more than that, the sense of betrayal I felt from Ernie Grunfeld would be the lasting effect. I just couldn't understand why. Why would the Knicks do this? I guess, it is a question for them to answer.

I called Efthimios when I got home that night to tell him the unfortunate news. I also called Ted, and he was devastated. I understood. Rentzias was upset, but I will not forget his attitude. He said, "Keith, everything is okay. You tried very hard, and you did your best." I appreciated that more than I could explain, and still do.

I left the Meadowlands in a very foul mood after Rentzias was selected. I had waited for about ten more picks to see if Jamie would go at number thirty-three. "No way, not tonight." I must have left around the forty-sixth pick in the second round. No Jamie Feick yet. That was all I could stand. When I finally got to my car, I put on the radio to catch the rest of the draft. They were up to number fifty, and I listened in horror as Jamie's name was never called. I called up Mike Peplowski just to vent a little bit. It was Pep who had helped me sign Jamie. As I launched into my diatribe on my evening and the fact that Jamie had been passed over, Mike informed me that Jamie had been picked by the Philadelphia 76ers at number forty-eight. They must have watched me leave the building and, to finish off my perfect evening, picked him. Jamie was selected by Philadelphia where he had the distinct pleasure of joining the number one overall pick, Allen Iverson. Jamie would spend parts of four months playing with him while trying to earn a spot on the roster. Within that time, Iverson would pass Jamie the ball three times.

Two weeks after the draft, the Knicks called trying to get me to give them Lloyd Daniels, another client—about whom I could write an entire book—for their summer league. I told them off. But nothing could change what happened, not to me and not to Rentzias and his family. This was his one chance at the draft, and he was badly deceived. "I'm sorry" didn't quite cover it!

ELEVEN

PUTTING THE ODD IN ODYSSEY

As in any field of endeavor, when you take a hit, you either lay there and feel sorry for yourself or you get up. The real interesting part of all this is that having a player drafted is not even what we are hired to do in the first place. If you read the contract signed between players and their agents, we are supposed to "conduct individual compensation negotiations." In other words, the Players Association, which drafts this agreement, is holding to the popular belief that the public shares, that an agent sits behind his desk with a big cigar fielding offers for his clients. There are many times during the day that I wish that was the case. In my case, however, I clearly felt responsible for the Rentzias draft day disaster. His attitude of loyalty and understanding toward me was duly noted, and I was determined to make his and Ted's faith in me as his representative pay off for them.

The summer is when most of the contracts actually come for a basketball agent's players. By September or October, most of your guys should be signed either in the NBA or overseas. The situation regarding Rentzias would complicate my summer drastically. Every agent who ran into Rentzias would undoubtedly take his shot at me and suggest that if Rentzias had signed with him, he would have gone fourth. There was really nothing I could do about this, so I didn't worry about it.

The position of PAOK was this: Since they had signed Rentzias to an amateur agreement, they took the old Greek position that he had to sign a professional contract with them for at least the next five years. My position would be that on January 11, his twenty-first birthday, Efthimios would be free to sign with other teams, including the Nuggets. Nobody but me wanted this to happen. First of all, the club didn't want to lose Efthimios in the middle of their season. Secondly, due to his popularity and the fact that his family lived in Thessaloniki, Efthimios didn't want to leave in the middle in the season. Lastly, the Nuggets didn't want to have him for only half a year because under the new collective bargaining agreement, all teams had to sign first rounders to three-year contracts. And, FIBA, the international governing body for sports, had already indicated to me that they would not support this. It didn't stop me from using the suggestion as a threat, but it really wasn't going to be an option.

THESSALONIKI

A few months later, the Atlanta Olympics went poorly for Rentzias, but not too badly for the team as a whole—they finished fifth. It still seemed as if the Greek powers-that-be were limiting his exposure and, thereby, limiting his minutes on the floor. Efthimios went home to Thessaloniki. PAOK wasn't discussing anything specific, continuing to believe that they owned him anyway, so why bother with some guy in New Jersey.

About a week after the Olympics, that attitude would change 360 degrees. Almost out of nowhere, I got wind that a certain team in Thessaloniki, Greece, wanted very badly to sign a specific American point guard named Scott Skiles.

Scott had retired from basketball after playing with the Philadelphia 76ers the season before. Playing for that version of the 76ers could do that to you. The Greek team was talking about a lot of money, and when I realized that the team that was making the offer was PAOK, I couldn't believe it. *How convenient*, at least for me and Rentzias. This was the crowbar that would now open things up for us. The only problem was that Scott didn't want to live the next nine months of his life in Thessaloniki, Greece. The thought of leaving his two sons in Indiana didn't thrill him. He really agonized over this one before deciding to take it. But the money was over a million dollars, and he ended up becoming the highest paid player in the history of PAOK.

It wasn't going to hurt Efthimios or PAOK to have Scott running the point. I figured this was a win-win situation if I ever saw one. Scott would not only make great money and have a fantastic experience, but also Efthimios would benefit from playing with and learning from Scott. I also realized that the stronger and more successful the team was, the better off Rentzias would be at the end of the year when his contract was up.

The next move was just as big. I had another one of my clients, Anthony Bonner, with a major team in Italy, Kinder Bologna. Anthony had taken the place of the injured Orlando Woolridge the season before as a temporary replacement and had played extremely well. In fact, after he returned from Italy, I was able to get him hooked up with the Orlando Magic for the playoffs. His reputation was growing overseas. We had received several offers from leading clubs, including Maccabee Tel Aviv of Israel. They had made an attractive offer and were, in fact, meeting with me on Long Island, which was the site of that year's NBA summer league at the Nassau Coliseum, to discuss a contract. Anthony and I met on Long Island as well to discuss this, along with the two other offers that I had just received that day. One was for over a million dollars from Efes Pilsen, the top team in Turkey, and the other one was for just under a million from guess who—PAOK.

After much discussion, Anthony took the deal with PAOK. Whereas I was happy to be straightening out PAOK as a team, part of me was concerned. Was I putting too many eggs in the same basket? What if things didn't go well? What if the chemistry between my three guys wasn't good? This is why I always have my clients make the final decision. It is true that I will strongly voice my opinion and sometimes even exert a lot of influence on the final choice, but they have to call the shots.

So two of my better players, and favorite guys, were off to Thessaloniki to join my latest. This changed everything. Firstly, I started to understand a little bit of what Rentzias was going through with the media. I began to face intense scrutiny as well, even though I was back in my office in Red Bank. Ted would call every other day to ask me if what was in the Greek paper was true. "Glass is coming next week to talk face-to-face with PAOK" was their favorite headline. None of this was accurate until September when Mr. Economides, who was the general manager, invited me to come to Thessaloniki to talk about a contract for Rentzias. The nicest thing about the invitation was that they were paying for the trip. Business class, here I come!

My second day in Thessaloniki, I met with Mr. Economides and Mr. Alexopoulos, the president of the team, at PAOK's offices. The meeting did not go well. It became apparent that they were going on the assumption that Efthimios and I owed them five years of service after January 11. I tried to take the high road by suggesting that we all cooperate and try to make a deal where everyone could benefit.

My plan was to sign an extension for maybe two years with PAOK. After that time we would be free. During these two years, Efthimios would be allowed to go with the Nuggets during the summers. I figured that this would help with his development and that would benefit PAOK, Efthimios, *and* the Nuggets.

PAOK would have none of it. They felt that they owned Efthimios and were adamant about it. They also made it clear to me that they felt that Efthimios was a mere child. That he had not accomplished anything yet, and that they were entitled to reap some benefits since he had contributed nothing to them during his first years.

The unfortunate thing for PAOK about this situation was that I, with the help of the Nuggets, had already received a preliminary finding by FIBA, the international governing body, that Rentzias would indeed be free after this coming season. I tried to convey this to Mr. Economides and Mr. Alexopoulos without directly alluding to FIBA, but they were stubborn. The meeting ended with me getting pretty pissed off and leaving. I returned to the Rentzias apartment to relay PAOK's offer to them of $1.6

million over four years and to also explain my disappointment with the results of the meeting. PAOK was basically saying, "Take it or leave it." We were going to leave it.

Efthimios was going to get anywhere between $1.6 million and $2.4 million over three years from the Nuggets depending on how the negotiations went, and I already had an understanding with Denver that it would have to be the $2.4 million figure or they wouldn't get him.

Efthimios's family was annoyed with the president of PAOK. Turns out he had been trying to go behind my back during the summer with Vasillas Rentzias, Efthemios's father. The key thing for me to accomplish on my trip was to make certain that Vasillas realized that if he discussed contacts directly with the PAOK president, then he was going to cost us all money. This is an old trick that teams use. It is obviously a lot easier to negotiate with a guy who doesn't do this for a living. I had to rely on Vasillas's integrity and the efforts of Ted after I left. All of us agreed that I would not contact PAOK again; instead Rentzias would play out the contract and proceed after the season.

When I returned to my hotel, there was a message from Mr. Economides. He was coming by to meet with me. Mr. Economides was a very savvy and direct guy to negotiate with. He came by the hotel, and we met outside on the patio with the sea behind us. It was romantic, but Mr. Economides was not my type.

He and Mr. Alexopoulos must have realized that my position might be the correct one and that I was also genuinely angry. Mr. Economides suggested that I come up with a proposal when I returned to the United States. He was making it seem like he was the good guy trying to do what he could with Mr. Alexopoulos—that old "good cop, bad cop" thing. My problem was that I never could figure out who had the real power and, therefore, who I should be talking to.

After my return, I worked on the proposal that Mr. Economides had suggested. I also focused on the play of Rentzias specifically and PAOK in general. The team was really struggling. Scott hated it and was driving me crazy. He hated his car, his apartment, his shower, the team, the coach, etc. When Anthony joined the chorus with the same complaints, I knew this was going to end badly.

The coach was the real problem. I had learned a long time ago that with Scott, everything boiled down to basketball. Simply put, if his team was winning and he was playing well, then life was great. The coach, a guy named Gomez (not the guy from the Addams family), was absurd. He had been a successful coach in France for several years. He had a real hard-on for Scott. His attitude was that he wasn't going to be impressed with this NBA stuff. He was putting both Scott and Anthony through things that were just ridiculous, such as running them up mountains. It was all non-sense, and it was driving both of them nuts.

There are many aspects of overseas basketball that I find fascinating, but in some instances, you get people over there who have a built-in bias against American players. They feel a certain resentment before they even meet the guys—a defensiveness that is not only unnecessary, but also clearly counterproductive. Gomez definitely felt that he was going to es-tablish that he was the man, not Scott or Anthony.

Gomez's solution to Scott's unhappiness was brilliant. He decided not to start him. Great move—that's the way to win! In his place, he put a Greek point guard who would have had trouble starting at Disco Tech. This went over very big. Scott continued to play his game. He scored twenty-three points in nineteen minutes one game. But he just couldn't crack the starting lineup. Thessaloniki is a tough town.

Eventually, through the direct intervention of management, the situa-tion was corrected. The short of that conversation was probably along the lines of " Hey Gomez, do you think we brought this guy over here for $1.1 million to sit on his ass and watch?" Scott was back in the lineup. But it was one thing after another.

It was obviously bad enough that $2 million worth of my players were basically being driven out of their respective minds, but remember that I also had my prized Greek hero in the mix as well. At least, I figured, he would escape the foreigner resentment. But he was also struggling. He couldn't stand Gomez either. What I came to reluctantly realize was the simple fact that Coach Gomez was a nut. I don't care how many championships he won in France; he was awful in Greece. He wouldn't have played too well in Peoria, either.

I then started to wonder if maybe it was me. To have all three of my guys tormented and unhappy in this way was almost too coincidental. I felt ridiculous even thinking that way until I casually mentioned it to my Greek agent at the time, Gus, an American from Chicago who had been living in Athens for the past eight years. There are times when an American agent is contacted first by a European agent. The European agent figures if he can get to me before the team does, he can get a piece of my commission. In the case of Scott, Gus was successful. Gus informed me that my concerns were possibly due to the fact that Gomez was one of the first coaches in Greece to have an agent. That agent just so happened to be Luciano "Lucky" Capicchioni, who just so happened to represent Predrag Stojakovic. The world was shrinking up on me.

Gus insinuated that Gomez and Capicchioni were busting my chops and anyone that I represented. He then casually mentioned that Gomez didn't want Scott in the first place and that Scott was the decision of the owner Mr. Alexopoulos. Lovely! Well, if anyone could fight through this, I knew it was Scott.

When PAOK made their offer directly to Vasillis Rentzias, they didn't bank on the loyalty of the Rentzias family. I had fortunately predicted this move on the day I left Thessaloniki. At breakfast in the Macedonia Palace, I told Vasillis, Efthimios, and Ted that this was exactly what PAOK would do. Think about it. I'd be 6,000 miles away; what kind of control could I possibly have? I guess I had a little more than they thought. In any case, PAOK offered the same basic deal they had done with me in their PAOK offices, the equivalent of $1.6 million over a four-year period. Vasillis told them what I had told him to say: "Talk to Keith." He would continue this refrain for the next eight months.

We turned down the offer and said that now that the preseason schedule was over, we wanted to concentrate on the season at hand. No more negotiating. We wanted everyone in Thessaloniki to realize that Efthimios was a good guy, which he is. I was trying to paint him as the anti-Stojakovic, who had to stay with PAOK rather than join the Kings. This idea came to me after my visit in September. During my three days there, Stojakovic and his agent "Lucky" Capicchioni staged a walkout on PAOK. They backed PAOK up against the wall, and Stojakovic actually left the team. He missed several games and the reaction to him and Capicchioni was not very positive.

The Rentzias family and I quickly decided that his was not the way we wanted to go. There was a fundamental difference between the two young stars from PAOK. Efthimios was a true Greek, born and bred. He felt an affinity to his country and was very concerned with how people perceived him. Stojakovic, however, was basically a hired gun transported from the war-ravaged former Yugoslavia. He was a Greek in documentation only. There are several disparate stories on how he became Greek, but few know the truth and I am not one of them. However this Greek transformation evolved, it obviously has been a sincere one. With all the stops Stojakovic has made since, Thessaloniki remains home.

The Stojakovic holdout actually helped me in another way. There was so much attention focused on him that the Greek press really didn't follow me around Thessaloniki, after that first press conference. PAOK would, however, report every detail of our discussions to the media. It was putting undue pressure on the Rentzias family, and I just didn't need it. It was also more than a little unnerving to do an interview and not be able to see or understand how it was being interrupted. It did start to cross my mind how dangerous it could be to be completely misunderstood, either by mistake or intentionally.

I left Thessaloniki with no semblance of a deal for Rentzias, but seemingly with an even closer relationship with Efthimios and his family. I did, however, meet Natalie Cole in the lobby of the Macedonia Palace and got tickets to her concert that night as well as her autograph: "To Keith, with love." I'm currently working on some sort of elaborate untrue story to go with that. I'll let you know when I'm done.

On my return to the States, I realized that I now needed to more actively involve the Nuggets. The Nuggets' position was clear but limited, due to the new collective bargaining agreement. They could pay a maximum of $2.4 million over a three-year period. They hadn't formally agreed to that number yet, but they would if pushed.

In Greece, some more events were taking place, which would further serve to complicate matters. Scott was still struggling with everything about the place, but now he developed a physical problem. During the end of one of the games, he severely injured his shoulder. Those who have followed Scott during his career know that he is not the type who gives in to anything, including injury. But sometimes an athlete has no choice. Although Scott continued to play, the shoulder was getting worse with every outing. We finally decided that it was enough. To be honest with you, I was strangely relieved that this part of the saga would be over. I could get Scott home and relax.

I called the people at PAOK to inform them of the problem. They had initially reacted to the injury with the attitude that basically it was nothing and that they could treat it themselves. I firmly let them know that this was not the case and that we should begin to try and make a settlement so that Scott could return home. We had a totally guaranteed contract, but many times overseas, they want to make some kind of a deal to save some money. They have no legal right to do this, but they always try. Scott, no surprise to me, didn't mind making a deal. Scott is a throwback. He is old-fashioned in many ways. He felt badly that he was hurt and that they were paying him so much. He authorized me to make a reasonable settlement.

After several discussions, we were able to do just that. PAOK, however, never really believed the entire story. They felt that we were maneuvering in some way. They never thought that Scott was leaving. The boxes and suitcases in his house told them otherwise. Scott was scheduled to leave on a Friday. He was packed and ready. On Thursday, I received a frantic call from PAOK offering the following mind-boggling proposal—they would fire Coach Gomez and hire Scott as their head coach.

Historically, nobody offers a thirty-three-year-old American with no coaching experience of any kind the head coach's job with one of the top teams in all of Europe. It obviously was a reflection and tribute to what they thought of Scott.

Scott was thrilled, but packed—he really wanted to come home. It was now February. It had been six months or so, and he missed his kids. We had often talked about Scott's career after playing. Coaching was as far as we ever got. I saw this as a fantastic opportunity for him to get experience and a reputation as well. I always believed that someday he would become an excellent NBA or college coach. I wasn't going to let him make the mistake of passing this by.

After much discussion, he accepted, causing startled reactions both in Greece and the U.S. But it made a lot of sense. Even though the team was not playing well, they were in almost every game. No one was playing well for Gomez. From the outside, it appeared to me that Gomez was the wrong guy for the job. I knew Scott could improve things. I knew that Anthony would do better, that Efthimios would do better, and so on. I also knew that Scott was in a no-lose situation. If he could turn them around, he would be a savior, and if not, then the situation was too screwed up for anyone to salvage.

In typical Skiles tradition, PAOK won their first game under their new coach. They beat a team on the road in Athens that they hadn't beaten in years. Even better news for me was what I learned from Anthony after that game. He called to tell me that in the tunnel during post game interviews, Scott had asked several members of the media who had been previously trashing the team to simply step outside, so they could get some things straight. Anthony and I laughed, but Scott was apparently beginning to feel very much at home.

WELCOME TO CLEVELAND?

The Denver Nuggets, while watching the activities in Greece from afar, were trying to devise a way to make the Rentzias family feel wanted in the

United States. To that end, they arranged for myself, Vasillis Rentzias, and Ted to meet them at the NBA All-Star game in Cleveland.

The Nuggets sent their assistant general manager, Todd Eley, to meet and discuss the future of Efthimios with their team. Vasillis and Ted were clearly excited to be at an NBA All-Star game. I was excited because Matt Maloney, another one of my clients, had made the Rookie All-Star game. He had been starting for the Houston Rockets the entire first half of the season and had really distinguished himself as their starting point guard. You think things were a little wacky in Greece? Welcome to Cleveland.

Things went along fine the first day. Todd, however, seemed a bit distracted. At the rookie game, I began to understand why. Carroll Dawson, who had taken over as the general manager of the Rockets, grabbed me out in the lobby of Gund Arena and asked if I had heard about the Denver situation. He informed me that Bernie Bickerstaff had left and was going to be named as the head coach of the Washington Bullets, who had just fired a friend of mine, Jimmy Lynam. My initial reaction was why would Carroll Dawson, who I really hardly knew, at that time, be part of a massive conspiracy to bust my balls.

Thankfully, I quickly came to my senses. But what did this all mean? Is Todd Eley still employed by Denver, since he is basically Bernie's right-hand man? If so, great! If not, why are there two gentlemen from Thessaloniki staying with him on the outskirts of Cleveland?

This situation was beyond awkward. Here Todd was in Cleveland trying his best to get the Nuggets draft pick comfortable enough to leave his homeland and sign with Denver, and yet, it was obvious that he didn't really know whether *he* would be in Denver. Under the circumstances, he did a remarkable job. If you didn't know, you would never suspect that he was a man facing the loss of his job.

That night at dinner one of the owners of the Nuggets joined us for dessert. When Vasillas heard about the shake-up in Denver, he was concerned. I was surprised at how much of his concern centered on the Nuggets' representative and his status. I made it my business to get the owner alone to discuss it. I informed him that the family was very concerned. He looked me right in the face and promised me that Todd was going nowhere. In fact, he informed me that they knew how valuable an employee Todd was and they weren't going to let him get away. This was reassuring, and I informed everybody.

The following day was the annual NBA All-Star game. I will admit that I was not looking forward to it. I see so many games that the purist in me likes to see somebody guard someone every quarter or so. Couple that with the ultra-hyped All-Star Saturday, and I'd had it.

What I didn't bank on was that this was the fiftieth anniversary all-star game. To commemorate the anniversary, the league had been conducting a year-long extravaganza. They left nothing out. There were books, videos, commercials, new logos for the uniforms, and throwback uniforms. The marketing was brilliant. This is what the league does best, and they had, in my opinion, outdone themselves.

Into this setting came the jaded version of Keith Glass. They proceeded to knock me on my cynical ass. They invited the fifty greatest players of all time to the game. Forty-eight showed. The sight of these gentlemen in the same building, on the same floor, is something I will not soon forget. This was reliving my childhood. I couldn't help being thrilled. They were all individually introduced. One great immortal after another: Wilt, Russell, Elgin, Oscar, Magic, Bird, Michael. It was incredible! Mikan, Julius, Rick Barry. The crowd was electric, and the feeling was just indescribable. Actually, sitting there with these men from Greece made me feel so proud. It was as if I was saying, "Yeah, these are our guys! You wanna play?"

I really don't remember who won the game, but the half-time show was spectacular—all they did was call out forty-eight names. No fireworks display, no music, no dancing girls; they didn't need it.

I returned home to New Jersey and let Ted and Vasillas go on to Denver. They stayed for three days. The Nuggets had something planned almost every minute. Vasillas was sold. He returned home and was going to inform Efthimios that he thought this would be a great place to live and that he had his blessing to sign with the Denver Nuggets. A job well done.

As soon as the plane to Greece left the runway at Stapleton Airport in Denver, the Nuggets fired Todd Eley, the guy who had done all of the work and had done such a great job of making it happen. I'm not sure if the landing gear had even retracted yet. Ironically, Todd learned that dirty deals were not made only on my side of the table. Today, Todd is an agent, competing with me instead of cooperating. I informed the Greeks on their arrival back to Thessaloniki. Their reaction was this—if they would do this to Todd, then they will do it to Efthimios. It's hard to argue with people when you agree.

Into the middle of this fiasco, which clearly seemed incapable of getting any worse, stepped Allan Bristow, who immediately proceeded to make things worse. Allan had been picked to replace Bernie Bickerstaff. Allan and I had known each other for some years and had done various little deals. In fact, after he had been fired as the coach of the Charlotte Hornets, he had contacted me to represent him but I declined. Now he was being named as the new general manager of the Nuggets, and I was going to have to deal with him on the Rentzias matter. I tried to bring him up to snuff about where we were with the Rentzias situation. Allan made it plain to me in that first conversation that he didn't want to discuss the old regime again. So much for tact.

Allan indicated that he was going to have to go and check out Efthimios. He plainly was dreading the trip. He did not understand what the fuss was all about. His attitude was, "Damn it, Keith, we drafted this kid in the first round; either he wants to play for us or he doesn't." It was obvious that Allan was not going to deal with the Greek culture or have the sensitivity necessary to make the family feel comfortable.

Reluctantly, off to Thessaloniki he went. Later that week, Scott Skiles told me that the game Allan saw was one in which Efthimios played really well. He had twenty-two points and twelve rebounds. Allan called me from a stopover in Athens and said that he was really impressed . . . with Scott! "What?"

According to Allan, Efthimios wasn't ready, but he wanted to know if I could arrange for Scott to interview for the head coaching job at Denver after Allan fired Coach Dick Motta. Although dazed a bit, I said I would. However, I, along with everyone else in basketball, knew that Allan was going to hire his long-time assistant Bill Hanzlick. But what the hell, just the mere mention of Scott's name in conjunction with an NBA head coaching position would be very beneficial.

Of course, I was extremely disappointed for Efthimios, but I learned a long time ago that NBA opinions, even based on limited information, are very difficult to change. The most important thing was to keep these opinions confidential, so that Efthimios's value would remain high in the league.

As soon as Allan returned, he immediately told the press that Efthimios was not ready for the league. This basically destroyed any chance the Nuggets had of successfully trading Efthimios.

Whereas Allan clearly had the right to his opinion, the decision to tell the media was something that Allan immediately regretted. It was not only reported nationally here, but also it was the subject of great documentation in Greece, as you can imagine. This had a ripple effect of undermining our bargaining position with PAOK. Overall, in a few short weeks, the Nuggets in general, and Allan specifically, had turned my prize recruit of 1996 into a pile of manure.

RISING FROM THE GREEK RUINS

My approach from this point on was twofold. I needed to try to get Efthimios traded to a team in the NBA that actually wanted him. And I needed to try and negotiate the best possible deal with PAOK. This was going to be difficult with the lack of leverage that I had. Another problem with the second strategy was that PAOK had not called me since September. This was March. The only positive thing was that the team was starting to gel, and Scott was actually becoming extremely popular. Incredibly, they were about to add the title of general manager to Scott's name. This meant that I would basically be negotiating Efthimios's contract with my "little brother."

I couldn't decide which scenario was worse, the night of the draft or this latest disaster in the bizarre case of Efthimios Rentzias. One thing that I have always understood, however, is the fact that the best way for a player to get out of a negative situation is to play his way out. I must admit that I was beginning to wonder if Efthimios could do that. He was still struggling, big time. Scott was down on Efthimios as well. This concerned me greatly because the entire family viewed everything that Scott did as tantamount to me doing it or saying it myself. My efforts would now be centered solely on making sure Scott didn't quit on Efthimios, or worse, that Efthimios didn't quit on himself.

In Greek basketball, as in the other European countries, the regular season is fun, but the single most important measure of the success of a team is whether or not they qualify for the European Cup. If they do, they get to play in the cup tournament the following season. Sponsorship money flows in much greater amounts, and the fans of that particular team have the entire off-season to gloat that their team is in. In Greece, the top three teams qualify. PAOK continued to languish and finished sixth overall in the Greek league. They were, however, getting better every time out. They were playing much better defensively. When I spoke to Coach Skiles, all he would do was go on and on with great pride about how well they were defending. Scott was officially now a basketball coach!

Another by-product of PAOK's improvement was that Scott kept indicating how Efthimios was getting better and better. Additionally, Anthony Bonner was starting to justify his salary and reputation. PAOK entered the Greek league playoffs as a long shot, but they were favored to win the opening round. They did.

When the team won the second round in an upset, people started talking. The fans of PAOK were becoming a little crazy, and the object of their fascination was Scott. By the time they made it to the league's final four, Scott, Anthony, and Efthimios were finding it difficult to go out in public. If people saw Scott in his car, they would surround it and start chanting "The bald one is crazy!" In Greece, apparently that was quite the compliment.

PAOK lost in the Final Four to the second place team in Greece, AEK. But since the top three teams qualify for the playoffs, the winner of the third and fourth place series qualifies for the cup the following year. Therefore, the series, which would be played against Peristeri, would be the most important series of the year. Peristeri had finished third in the league and was the favorite. I actually had another player—Marlon Maxey—on Peristeri, but my rooting interest was clearly with PAOK. Marlon knew it, and we actually joked about it.

The series was a best three out of five. After losing the first game badly on the road in Athens, PAOK won the next two. Game 4 was at home in Thessaloniki. If they lost, it was back to Athens where they knew they would be in trouble. PAOK won game 4 by twenty-seven points. It was a professional ass-kicking. Efthimios played great ball and was a key element in the playoffs. Anthony had become the best overall player in Greece. Scott passed into legend. I think he was made an honorary Greek god, somewhere to the left of Zeus.

Scott was paraded around the streets of Thessaloniki on the shoulders of the fans. The media was in a frenzy, but all Scott really wanted was to go home. PAOK won the series on a Friday night, and Scott, Anthony, and the entire team partied the night away.

On Saturday afternoon, I got a call from Scott. He was in Orlando, Florida, in the house he had bought when he was with the Magic. I guess he wasn't kidding all those months when he said he wanted to be home. During the phone conversation, he tried to warn me about the pressure I was going to get about re-signing Scott as the coach from the president of PAOK. I was more concerned about Efthimios and finding some form of alternative career route for him.

Sometime in May I got the call I needed. It actually was a call from my father. He called to say that an agent in Spain said that Barcelona was interested in talking about Efthimios. Barcelona is one of the top teams in the world, and since the Bristow barrage had sunk our NBA plans for the moment, both Efthimios and I were very interested in speaking with them.

As usual, news of the interest in Efthimios by Barcelona seemed to be in the Greek media almost as soon as I received the call. This was becoming almost comical. Was there a Greek basketball FBI that had tapped my phones? Whereas the Greek hoops fans had become resigned to the possibility that they might lose Rentzias to the NBA, they never contemplated having their guy go to another team in Europe. All season long, Greek sports page readers were being told that "this Glass character was wrong." The fans felt that they owned Efthimios and his rights and that this would be proven in the end.

In early June, it all came down. While Scott was deciding his future with PAOK, Efthimios and I were simultaneously trying to get out of playing for them. The Rentzias family felt betrayed and belittled by the owners, and they viewed PAOK's refusal to negotiate properly with me and going behind my back as an insult to them.

I was in a precarious position—forced to walk the line between Scott and Efthimios. In all my years, I had never been in such a strange spot. And you know from reading this far just how strange some of my previous spots had been. Scott understood completely that Efthimios had to do what was best for him. At the same time, it was a factor for Scott whether or not he would have a center to coach the following season if he returned to PAOK.

From a purely business point of view, the Rentzias predicament was ridiculous. Here was the best Greek prospect in many years (if not ever), a member of the Greek National Team, and a first-round NBA draft choice, and he was making a grand total of $65,000. PAOK's refusal to negotiate would now prove to be their undoing. Rentzias felt trapped by PAOK, not only financially but also as a player. He was not developing properly. It was as if they were consciously trying to keep him under wraps, under control, under them. It wasn't going to work this time, but it didn't mean that PAOK wasn't going to try.

I did feel some pangs of sorrow for PAOK, so I decided to at least give the team an opportunity to get back into the negotiating picture. I did this by leaking the story to the press that Barcelona was interested in

Efthimios. PAOK's response was twofold. First, they said I was lying, and second, they clung to the premise that Efthimios couldn't leave.

In June, Efthimios Rentzias signed a professional basketball contract with Barcelona. It was a three-year contract that gave us an "NBA out" after two years. Barcelona would pay for Efthimios's house, car, and so on. The total package was worth the equivalent of $1.1 million per year.

Two weeks later, PAOK sued Efthimios in Athens, essentially saying that they held his rights because of the contract he signed when he was sixteen years old. Three weeks after that, the courts disagreed.

The reaction in Greece was mixed. Naturally, PAOK put out some scathing stuff about Efthimios and me, but many fans in Thessaloniki plainly blamed the club's owner and general manager. However, the more critical and public decision regarding Scott was now an issue. He clearly wanted to get started on his coaching career either at the NBA or college levels but nothing was happening on those fronts. The pressure from across the water from PAOK and the media was relentless. The final offer for Scott's services climbed to $3.6 over a three-year period. This was a staggering offer! Even more maddening was the simple fact that Scott didn't want to go.

Scott is nothing if not intelligent. It was now the middle of June, and he realized that he had nothing else going, even though I was trying every day to rustle up some interest in the NBA for him. He reluctantly decided to return to PAOK. I just needed to dot some *i*'s and cross some *t*'s. I was upset for him, but hey, the 10 percent I would receive as well as the salary Scott was about to earn would probably ease our dejectedness.

I faxed PAOK and asked for some final clarifications to close the deal. They did not immediately respond. Later that same afternoon, out of the blue, I received a phone call from Danny Ainge, who was the head coach of the Phoenix Suns at the time. Danny was finishing his rookie season as the head coach and had done a wonderful job of turning around the club. He and Scott had actually been fairly hostile competitors during their careers. I was more than a little surprised when Danny asked me what Scott's plans were for the coming season.

I explained that we were on the verge of signing a lucrative contract for $3.6 million. Danny said he would love to have Scott join his staff in Phoenix. That Friday, we signed a three-year contract with the Suns for a total of $900,000. I know what you're thinking: *Isn't $3.6 million more than $900,000?* Correct! But this was the absolute right move for Scott. He began his career in a great place with a great organization.

It had been a little more than a year since I had flown into Greece, unknown and on Vicodin. During that time I had signed their national hero and sent him to Spain. I had brought them Scott Skiles and Anthony Bonner, who led them to the European Cup. Scott and I had subsequently opted to stay in the States for a quarter of the money offered by PAOK, breaking many hearts in the process. The fact that Efthimios and Scott had left seriously decreased interest in the team, and therefore, financial support from sponsors who bankroll the season. This precluded them from having enough money to sign Anthony.

My plans for running for public office in Thessaloniki are on hold.

TWELVE

THE $706 MILLION BRONZE MEDAL

Eight years after my own invasion of Greece, Larry Brown led the United States' men's Olympic basketball team into that same European country. To view the results of the 2004 Olympics and realize that something was drastically wrong doesn't exactly take a genius. To look underneath and try to identify some of the root causes of such an embarrassment is another matter.

The breakdown in coaching and teaching and the attendant lack of respect shown for those professions has been going on for so long that I don't even think people notice anymore. The burdens that are placed on coaches and teachers increase yearly. These burdens have subtly forced many good coaches and teachers to the sidelines.

The notion that lack of control or discipline is okay as long as a kid can play is obviously unacceptable. The notion that in America we do not have to teach because we are simply better than the rest of the world is nonsense. All of the years that the basketball community moved away from truly teaching and setting examples finally caught up with us.

When you get older, the tendency is always to blame the younger generation. They don't work as hard as we did. They don't have any discipline. They don't care as much! These are common themes. In basketball, and sports in general, that is not true.

Having been around these players all this time, I can tell you, without question, that NBA players work themselves like most of you reading this would not believe. The physical work ethic of 99 percent of these players is incredible. It is also not like the past when players would have a true off-season. They work on their games all year long.

The players are in better condition than their predecessors, and their individual skill levels are far more advanced than what we have witnessed in years past. Whenever I look at a player now, I instinctively realize just how much time and effort he has spent on becoming as good as he is. While I am often critical of the player's attitudes and conduct, their work ethic on their own games is incredible. When fans call professional athletes bums and worse, it strikes me as humorous. They have no idea what has gone into the making of that player, at least in a physical sense. They also have no idea as to just how good the guy they are yelling at really is.

Almost all players are taught the game at the beginning of their careers. Young people are going to do what is *demanded* of them. Yet, it is practically in their job description to try to get away with whatever they can. I have never coached a player who wanted to run sprints or suicides after practice. I *made* them do that.

This country is currently full of enablers—guys who are around kids telling them as early as the fifth grade how *great* they are. Players are not taught about the beauty of being a member of a team, but rather how great *they* can be in the future. To totally blame that early identified eleven-year-old as the source of the problem is ridiculous. He becomes the problem later. Through the further encouragement of adults, he becomes the selfish twenty-five-year-old that we see on TV.

DOES NCAA STAND FOR NO COMMON SENSE AT ALL?

In Europe and in other parts of the world, teaching and discipline remain in fashion. Working together, like a team, is paramount. Meanwhile, there are regulatory bodies in these country, but there is nothing like our NCAA. Whatever their intentions, the National Collegiate Athletic Association has legislated their members' institutions and athletes into an almost comatose state. If you were to really examine the NCAA rule book, you would not believe it. There are restrictions on everything a coach or a player can do—when a coach can even teach his own players, how many days he can coach, how many days a player can be in a gym working out.

The rules go on and on. I am aware of the supposed reason for all of this legislation, but at some point, a dose of common sense can be very useful. As I wrote this, I was "advising" Quincy Douby of Rutgers University on whether or not to remain in the 2006 NBA draft. I say "advising" because that is the required word that the NCAA uses for any underclassman to maintain his collegiate status.

To "advise" him, I have to run everything through his college coach—any contacts with NBA teams, any workouts, etc. If I set up a workout, the kid is ineligible. The fact that this particular coach is already on record as telling the kid that he needs to stay in school doesn't matter. The fact that this coach's livelihood is, to a great degree, linked with this player remaining at the university doesn't seem to be a conflict of interest to the NCAA.

To expect college coaches to orchestrate the departure of their best players is unrealistic and unfair to both parties. April 29, 2006 was the date set by the NBA for any underclassmen to submit a letter declaring for the draft, thereby renouncing his remaining collegiate eligibility. The draft itself was not until June 28, 2006.

To understand fully what a player faces here, it goes like this: The NCAA has the player's college coach direct him before April 29 on whether to enter the draft. He issues this advice in part by getting the opinion of an NBA committee that tells the prospective player approximately where he will go in the draft on June 28. Therefore, all of this is done without either of these entities actually knowing who is in the draft to begin with. How can anyone predict in good faith where a player will go in a draft when they don't know who is in the draft?

But wait, there's more. There is another date: June 18, 2006. This is the day when the player can now withdraw his name from the draft or choose to remain in it. He does this by finding out where he stands. He now knows who's in, but he doesn't know where he stands specifically. All players find this information out in part by attending workouts given by all NBA teams prior to the draft.

Sounds reasonable, but that's too easy. Here comes the NCAA again. We need more rules. How about this one? An underclassman has to pay for his trips to these workouts! Yeah, that'll do it. His family can pay! No one else, not the university, not a friend, not his high school coach, and certainly, not an agent. If a kid's family cannot afford, say, the $15,000 to $20,000 expense, which is necessary for their child to pursue his dream, well, that's too bad. Keep in mind that the NBA teams are anxiously waiting to pay the kid's expenses—and in a first-class manner. This edict against NBA teams paying for expenses extends to airlines tickets, hotel accommodations, and even transportation to and from airports and to their workouts. If a player lands, for example, in Los Angeles from New Jersey, he cannot be picked up at the airport.

This last rule prompted me to call the NCAA agent enforcement division for the eleventh time in a month. Like a fool, I had been doing this to try and comply with their rules. Since the player I was "advising" had been invited to work out for the New York Knicks, I called to find out how to physically get him there. For example, can I drive him? No! What about his coach? No! What about my son, Tyler, who works for me and was the player's teammate at Rutgers? No! Miles Brand is the director of the NCAA. I asked if he could drive him! No response. No sense of humor either.

They didn't have an answer for me, so they told me they would e-mail answers to all of my questions that day. It's thirteen days later. I still haven't received an e-mail or any further clarification. I had warned the NCAA that what they were really going to accomplish was to frustrate these kids so much that they would be forced to sign with an agent to get away from all of the regulations and nonsense.

In this case, that is exactly what happened. Tired and frustrated, Quincy decided that I am no longer his advisor, I am his "agent." Quincy signed earlier than he, I, or anybody else associated with him wanted. He felt he had to in order to pursue fully something for his and his family's future. He cannot return to college. Another job well done by the powers that be.

Joe Lapchick, the late, great coach of St. Johns University years ago, advised us that we should be careful about having too many rules because it's always your best players who get caught. I would pay big money to watch him read the NCAA rule book today.

THE PARENT TRAP

While we are at it, I can't possibly leave the subject of enabling without devoting a little time to parents. I am the father of five. I am divorced twice. I have made many mistakes, too many. All of us have. After all, we don't have a rule book to guide us.

But not to understand the damage that today's parents are responsible for is simply to ignore the obvious. The role that parents have had in turning athletics into a selfish exercise is obvious. At least now there is some recognition of this conduct. Parents today in the field of athletics are interested in only one thing—how their kid is doing. The team is merely a convenient vehicle so their child can shine and some of that light will reflect onto themselves. The team is just a prop.

Because of this attitude, the fundamental lessons of sports are lost. If you keep in mind that every sport was not developed for the glory of one of its players, but as a way to teach youngsters, then you can see the problem. If teamwork and the lessons learned from getting along with your teammates is not the focus, then we have lost the battle before we even "lace up."

Why parents take this approach is the most puzzling notion of all. I coached high school basketball for twelve years as the head coach at Mater Dei High School in Middletown, New Jersey. My cumulative record was 206 wins and 63 losses. In other words, the teams were fairly successful over the years. Over the course of twelve years there, three players of mine went on to play some form of college basketball. One player went on to Princeton to play for a great coach, Pete Carrill. Another ended up as a walk-on at

Rutgers University and later became a scholarship player. And the third player received a scholarship to a Division II school in Connecticut.

I point out the preceding to illustrate the question further: What do these parents want? I speak of the meddling and overbearing parents who every high school coach in this country is currently, if quietly, screaming about. It clearly can't be about the money. Even from successful programs, there is a lack of scholarship opportunities. Any thinking parent would see that there is a much better chance of their child receiving financial benefits if they applied themselves with the same effort in the classroom. In my own family, my son Tyler worked all of the time on basketball and ended up as a walk-on at Rutgers University. He loved it, and it was a life-enriching experience, but there was no financial benefit to him at all. My daughter Sami, in contrast, stopped playing basketball in high school and received $20,000 worth of academic scholarships to college.

You may think I'm exaggerating this problem of parental interference, but I'm not. On one of my very good Mater Dei teams, which had won its first twenty-four games, I remember one player refusing to pass to another in the state tournament. I sat him down and found out that his father had told him specifically to exclude the other kid. After twenty-four wins in a row, this guy now felt the need to take over! This crossing-over-the-line interference can rise to a level that is more than just intrusive and destructive. Sometimes it is downright dangerous.

THE GRAND JURY AND ME

Even with the sometimes odd occurrences that I have been involved with in my life, I had never been close to being in trouble with the law. Naturally for me, that all changed during a basketball game.

While coaching at Rumson-Fair Haven High School in 2003, I had a run-in with one of my players. He was what I would call a punk. He was nothing but trouble for me, my assistants, and his teammates the entire year. I felt that we could help him. He became proof-positive that you can't help them all. This is true, especially when there is an overbearing parent in the mix.

In this case, his mother was a beauty. To call her an enabler would be an insult to enablers. Naturally, her child was an angel who never did anything wrong. I later learned that before I ever met him, he had changed schools several times and had been disciplined by several different teams. For example, he had been disciplined right before our basketball season by the New Jersey State Athletic Association (NJSAA) for allegedly telling an African-American official to "go back where he came from" during a soccer game

He had transferred from a parochial school nearby for reasons that I'm still not totally clear on. During his two months or so with me, he had received several technical fouls and had several fights with other teams as well as his own teammates. To be brief, I had just about had it with him after he threw a ball at a teammate in early February.

The day after he threw the ball, we were in Freehold, New Jersey for a game. We had just qualified for the state tournament two days before. After acting up for the forty-third time, I took him out of the game. I pointed to a chair and told him to get a good one, a comfortable one, because he was going to be there for a long time.

As I turned to walk away, he "chirped" something else at me. I went back to him and said "If you ever speak to me like that again, I'm going to take my foot and shove it up your ass!"

Now, I understand that hearing that sentence out of context, it sounds crass and inappropriate. During a basketball game and within the context it was said, I considered it a cordial warning. That exact phrase has been said to me during my playing days, and I admit to saying it a thousand times during my coaching career. Any coach who says he hasn't uttered those or similar words is lying.

I never put him back in the game. In the locker room afterward he kept going. Instead of sitting and listening to our post-game meeting, he started undressing. I asked him to stop—three times. He just wouldn't listen. I had my two assistants remove him from the room. These things happen on teams all the time. I thought it was finished. But not with this kid and mommy dearest.

Realizing that their time was now up with me, they had to devise a plan to get rid of me. It started immediately. The kid did not return with the team on the bus. I didn't know this because I always drove my car to the games. My assistants handled the bus. This gave me more time at my office. I returned home with my son Alex, since Alex was a member of our freshman team and was at the game.

When we were almost home, I received a call from mommy dearest. She was crazed. She started screaming immediately that her baby was lost. He was not on the bus. He could not be found. Did I have any idea where he was? "Call the police!" she screamed. I said I didn't know, but I started calling my assistants who were on the bus. Neither of them answered.

I decided to return to Freehold to try and locate the kid. After I got there, the gym was empty. I remembered that the gym was empty when I originally left, as it was always my habit to check and make sure everyone was gone. After all, I had been coaching for sixteen years and never lost one of my players before.

That's when it hit me. *How did she know he wasn't on the bus? She wasn't on it either.* I called her back to ask that specific question. I'll never forget her answer or her frightening tone: "Cause he's sittin' next to me!"

Okay, at least now I knew who I was dealing with. When you are confronted with a liar anything is possible. When you are dealing with a liar, all bets and sanity are off. I knew that she was not going to stop there. Her plan evolved into trying to get me fired, but that didn't work.

When she failed at that, she took the unusual step of going to the Freehold police to start an investigation into criminal charges against me for assault and abandonment. She did this even though she laughingly admitted lying about the bus situation to school and public administrators. The police did an investigation and found what you might expect. This woman was a nut job, and they refused to file charges against me.

That should have been it, it wasn't. She was just revving up. She apparently had an acquaintance high up in the county prosecutor's office. A month after being told that no charges would be filed, I was informed by my attorney, Fred Klatsky, that she had personally signed a criminal complaint, and the case was to be submitted to the grand jury.

These types of antics continued for a year and a half. Understand that as ludicrous as it sounds, I could have actually been indicted for coaching. You never know what a jury or grand jury would do. What if there were twelve of *her* on that grand jury? Actually, now that I think about it if there are twelve of her in the whole country, then I'm emigrating. As dramatic as this sounds, my liberty was at stake. To compound my concern, I was dealing with people who lie without any conscience getting in their way. A grand jury and liars equals a dangerous combination.

The school district had also been sued in civil court. They, therefore, had to defend themselves against this nonsense as well. They actually not only had to pay for their defense, but also issued a check for $9,000 to pay for my attorney.

Once the grand jury actually heard the facts of the case, they threw them out on their ear. The kid perjured himself several times under oath. I read the transcript. If that was not the case, then I suggest they try me again!

Once the grand jury indicated that they wanted no part of this twosome, the case was automatically returned to municipal court. In municipal court, my exposure if found guilty of disorderly conduct would be a $100 fine. The mother showed up at municipal court and offered to dismiss the charges with no hearing. There was one catch. I had to admit that there was probable cause to bring the matter in the first place. Why? She had heard that I was merely waiting for this crap to be dismissed to prepare a counter-suit against her and her little devil for slander and malicious prosecution.

This was not true. I was not preparing anything. It was already in Fred's briefcase, ready to be filed. In other words, no deal! As I thought, she dismissed the case anyway. I think she was having trouble now finding a lawyer even to show up on her behalf. We filed the same day, and that lawsuit is still being litigated. By the time you read this, I will probably have already been paid damages for her and her sons' behavior. My goal is to take some of that money and open the gyms here in New Jersey, so something good can ultimately flow from this nonsense. In my travels, I have noticed something troubling about our country, not only New Jersey. Everybody just wants to go home. Being involved with young people as a coach and being a father for so long, it is obvious that rather than keeping gyms and ballfields open as much as we can, we devise and accept any excuse to keep our own kids out. Some of my favorites are "They need adult supervision," or, the best one, "We don't have insurance!"

These excuses are camouflage. They hide the real goal, which is merely to have janitors, teachers, and administrators . . . go home. Dedicated coaches who want to do their job or kids who just want to play or work on their sport are fought at every turn. I've been there. There are people at all of my coaching stops who didn't care for me because I wanted to do a good job. There are kids all over this country right now who would be in gyms if the authorities in their towns would just open the doors. I guess we want these kids some place else.

The "adult supervision" argument is even sillier. Excess adult supervision is ruining our kids. Open the gym, and let the kids play. Let them sort it out. Let them settle their own disputes, call their own fouls, and so on.

I bring this up here for several reasons. The misguided parent does not usually go this far, but this incident taught me some other valuable lessons—lessons that I should have learned earlier. I have already discussed my surprise when the coaching community did not, in my opinion, have P. J. Carlesimo's back after the choking by Latrell Sprewell incident. I felt I was in a very similar position.

Privately, every coach and administrator was shocked and offered their sympathy. Publicly, they ran for cover. As a member of different coaches' associations, I believed that this was a great opportunity for coaches to say enough is enough. They have bitched about these issues with parents for years, but they let the opportunity go.

Coaching is not a way to teach anymore. To many coaches, it is merely another source of income. When coaches, officials, teachers, and administrators view their jobs as purely their way to make a living, then we are indeed in trouble. The sadder part is that because the way things are set up today, I don't blame them, but this fear of rocking the boat is a huge negative in our society.

The most illuminating point of all was the reaction of the other parents in the program at the time. Whereas I did receive great and emphatic support from most of my players and their parents, an interesting development occurred. As on any team, only a certain number of players start—five. In general, though it varies, you can comfortably play about eight or nine kids. Since you carry around twelve players, there are going to be some unhappy players, and in today's world, very unhappy parents. Coach Al McGuire, who won a national championship at Marquette in 1977, quoted Casey Stengel when he said: "The key to being successful in coaching is to keep the five guys that hate you away from the five that are undecided!"

On that Rumson team, I had one player and two fathers who clearly felt that I had some mysterious vendetta against them. The fact that they weren't making a contribution to the team was irrelevant. Coincidentally, it was these two fathers who agreed that my conduct was wholly unacceptable. Anything to get their boys a bit more playing time. I can only cringe at the thought of the other lessons these kids are getting as they continue on in their development. When I was an assistant at UCLA, we had a theory that went as follows: A prospective player should play one level below where he thinks he should play and two levels below where his father thinks he should play. I used to think that was a funny thought. Not anymore.

Even though I would like nothing more than to somehow blame a mother and two fathers from Rumson, New Jersey for our Olympic failure in 2004, I realize that can't be the case. There were many factors involved in that debacle. We had and continue to do so much enabling and legislating that we have enabled other countries to steal our game.

THE BRONZING OF AMERICA 1964–2004

The Olympics were always special to me. Not only did I enjoy the basketball competition, but also almost every event I watched. I felt a great deal of national pride in all of our teams. The Olympics were special before marketers and agents got their grubby little hands on the NBA, the NFL, and Major League Baseball. The days before we were instructed on what and how to watch. Before we were told who was great before a particular event even occurred. Does Bode Miller come to mind?

As with many watershed events in my and my family's lives, my initial interest in the Olympic games began in earnest through Larry Brown. It was 1964, and Larry had received an invitation to the U.S. basketball Olympic trials. Even better for my family was the fact that the trials would be held at St. John's Alumni Hall, which was twenty minutes away from our house. Larry had already graduated from the University of North Carolina and was playing for the Goodyear Wingfoots, a company team, in the old AAU league. They had won the league championship, garnering invitations for about half the guys on the team to the trials.

Along with Larry and his Goodyear teammates, there were some sixty other players from across the country—the best college players in the land. Cazzie Russell was there. So was Willis Reed. Walt Hazzard, who had just lead Coach Wooden to his first of ten national championships at UCLA, was there as well. Bill Bradley, who would later play for the New York Knicks and did some other less important things with his life, was also trying out.

The whole family was excited with Larry's invitation. There were to be twelve games over a three-day period at St. Johns. Four games a day. I went to every game. I was thirteen years old. My father, being the most singularly efficient human being ever to live, had purchased tickets so early and often that we had quite a surplus. In what may have been my first entrée into becoming an agent, I was sent outside in Queens with the only instructions being to dispose of the extra tickets as best I could. Suffice it to say that we as a family, forty-two years later, have some of that money left. We use it for emergencies.

Larry played extremely well during the trials and amazingly made the team. Four or five of his Goodyear teammates also made that squad. They were not the best players that we had in the country, but they had earned their spots on that team through their overall play. Better players were cut. This would happen again throughout the years. In 1984, Charles Barkley was released from the Olympic trials by Coach Bobby Knight for similar reasons. This was, however, 1964, and we were more concerned about putting together a team than what we would subsequently become obsessed with: putting on a show.

The 1964 U.S. Olympic basketball team won the gold medal. They beat the Soviet Union 73–59. In the final game of the qualifying round, the United States was led by a five-nine point guard from Long Island named Larry Brown, who scored sixteen points. After the gold medal victory, Larry (very uncharacteristically) had a couple of drinks. He climbed up a flag pole and took down an Olympic flag for me. I was as thrilled with the flag as I was that he made it back down.

Forty years later, Larry was named the head coach of an updated version of that same team, our 2004 U.S. Olympic team. There had been many stops for him along the way which have been well documented. He had changed along the way as had the entire process of competing in these games. After the United States lost in 1988 with our college players, the Olympic committee (along with the NBA) decided that this would never happen again. We decided to send our professional players into the Olympics.

We brought together the greatest single collection of players that have ever been assembled in any sport. You want to argue that statement, save your breath. To Barcelona, we sent Michael Jordan, Larry Bird, Magic Johnson, Patrick Ewing, David Robinson, Karl Malone, John Stockton, Scottie Pippen, and even Charles Barkley made it this time. What a mismatch! In 1983, Ronald Reagan sent the U.S. military to invade Grenada. In 1992, David Stern sent the "Dream Team" to Spain. The results were similar.

In the next three Olympiads, the United States' teams went twenty-four and zero and obviously won three gold medals. The original Dream

Team scored an average of 117 points per game. They beat some teams by fifty and sixty points. At the Atlanta games in 1996, the team (led by David Robinson, Penny Hardaway, Scottie Pippen and Charles Barkley) won the final against Yugoslavia by the lopsided score of 95–69. The average score of the games in 1996 was 102–69.

In Sydney in 2000, it was more of the same for the rest of the world. There, Kevin Garnett, Jason Kidd, and Vince Carter led us to another eight and zero record. Things did, however, start to tighten up some, and the U.S. squad got a major scare from Lithuania. Actually, they survived a last second three-point shot by a point guard named Sarunas Jasikevicius to hold on to an 85–83 escape. Jasikevicius actually played his college basketball at the University of Maryland, but he went undrafted by the NBA and was deemed not good enough. We would hear from him again.

Even though it was not an Olympics, American basketball people should have received a wake-up in 2002 at the World Championships. These games were held in Indianapolis, with Aylin and me in attendance. She was excited because the Turkish national team, with several of her friends on it, was playing. I was settling in for a good four days of gloating as my U.S. team would obviously manhandle the competition. We came in sixth.

It wasn't just the fact that we lost. It was the way we lost. No passion, no fire, no passing, no defense. It was, to say the least, an embarrassment. During our last day in Indianapolis, we went to watch the U.S. team play against Spain. I left during the first half of that loss. It was that upsetting.

In many instances, basketball mirrors our society. In the year 2006, we have more than any other country. We spend more. We have acquired more and more things. We don't always get our money's worth, but we continue to spend. We think this spending guarantees us success. But many times the opposite is true.

Ask George Steinbrenner. The New York Yankees' recent past from 2000 to the present, I believed, would be the lesson that would finally teach us that money cannot buy everything. Certainly it cannot buy championships in sports. The fact that the Yankees have spent incredible amounts of cash and have not won a title in six years should have been the signal for all sports to realize that there is more to constructing winning teams than money.

The NBA and the USA basketball committee needed season tickets at Yankee Stadium. Our Olympic basketball team that was assembled in 2004 by the above-mentioned entities will go down as the biggest embarrassment and debacle in the history of sports in this country. With committed salaries of $706.5 million to the players alone, we took on countries that, only a few years before, looked on us as role models and heroes. At the Barcelona Olympics in 1992, players from opposing teams were known to ask our players for autographs before we crushed them. In 2004, they decided to skip the autograph session and merely kick our asses.

Forgive me for not buying into any of the excuses made for our showing in Athens. I've heard them all: The world is catching up. The play around the world is getting better. Our dream team of 1992 inspired the world, etc.

Let's set the record straight. We stank. We didn't play together. We were outhustled. We were outsmarted. We were outeverythinged.

Larry Brown is part of my family, and he doesn't need me to defend him. He is a tremendous basketball coach. In the interest of family unity, suffice it to say that the 2004 Olympics were not Larry's finest hour. The problem, as I saw it develop, was that one of Larry's great strengths, specifically his ability to teach the game, turned into his biggest weakness. In the Olympics, where you have a very limited amount of time together, teaching needs to take a distant back seat. The object is merely to win in the Olympics. Larry saw young players who had been selected by the organizing committee, and he saw great players who could get better instead of talented guys selected to simply win today!

Try and get your head around the following: The *bench* on that 2004 Olympic team consisted of Lebron James, Carmelo Anthony, Dwayne Wade, Carlos Boozer, and Amare Stoudamire, who couldn't get six minutes of playing time a game. This was who was on the bench! This team lost to the likes of Puerto Rico, Argentina, and Italy in exhibition. This team finished third behind Argentina and Italy. The Italian team finished second, yet not one player on that team was deemed worthy of a contract to play in the NBA. I was actually asked to represent one of the players on that silver medal–winning Italian team. His name was Giacomo Galanda. He is a six-ten forward who has an uncanny ability to shoot threes. I couldn't get one NBA team to pay for his flight over here to play in an NBA summer league. Earlier in this book, I used the word *arrogant* in certain sections. You can put it in this chapter as well.

How can a team that, according to the experts and sages in the NBA, does not have a player worthy of inclusion to the NBA finish ahead of a team that those same experts have deemed worthy of $706.5 million worth of contracts? Either the decisions on awarding contracts are seriously flawed or the way we play the game is.

To blame Larry for this failure is understandable. It is also unfair and simplistic. He made mistakes, but he also unknowingly found himself in the middle of the perfect basketball storm—the recipient of years of enabling and selfishness. Our style of play was and still is so selfish and uninspiring that prior to the games, at least half of our own country was pulling against our own team.

From my own vantage point, it was particularly disturbing. The man who I had assisted many years before and who had prided himself on playing the game "the right way" was now lording over a collection of stars who would forever be remembered for their failure to play together or even stay together. The 2004 men's Olympic basketball team lived on the Queen Mary 2 with family members and entourages. They couldn't stay in the Olympic village with the other athletes of the world. They are, after all, multimillionaires. They are entitled.

They stayed first class . . . and they finished third.

THIRTEEN

THE MALICE AT THE PALACE

As if the Olympics weren't bad enough, Larry's year would get worse before it got better. It was almost as if the basketball gods were was trying to level him off. So many accolades and so much success had come his way, so maybe this was some form of reverse compensation.

In 2001, Larry had been named the NBA coach of the year for leading the Philadelphia 76ers into the NBA finals, where they lost four games to one to the Shaq/Kobe Lakers. In 2002, the entire Glass family was present as Larry was inducted into the Basketball Hall of Fame in Springfield, Massachusetts. That same year he was named as the head coach of the U.S. Olympic men's basketball team. Karma? He became the coach of the Detroit Pistons in 2003. He would proceed to lead that very talented group to the NBA championship, where they spanked the favored Shaq/Kobe Lakers. In other words, Larry was on a major roll right up until Athens in 2004.

I watched the brawl at the Palace in Detroit on TV. Larry was coaching the Pistons, who had won the NBA title some six months earlier. The Pistons, playing at home, were being thoroughly whipped by the Indiana Pacers. The Pacers had to feel pretty good about themselves, having beaten the defending champs so soundly on their home floor. Little did they know that with under a minute to play, they would be playing with their full lineup for the last time that season.

Ben Wallace of Detroit committed a hard foul on Ron Artest of the

Pacers. After being fouled and having a towel thrown at him by Wallace, for some reason, Artest chose to lie down on the scorers' table. He was then hit with some kind of liquid that had been perfectly thrown from the stands. Without seeing who threw it, Artest and Stephen Jackson of the Pacers proceeded into the stands in the general direction of the cup thrower and began to beat anyone they could. They weren't really successful in this effort, but it was the whole shocking scene that was remarkable. At the same time, Jermaine O'Neal of the Pacers, though still on the court, had more physical success, cold-cocking another fan who inexplicably ran onto the court. O'Neal actually landed the best punch of the whole sordid affair.

All of us have seen the pictures a hundred times. They are burned into our memory. The picture that I came immediately away with, however, was the one of O'Neal leaving the court and entering the tunnel to return to the locker room. He was pelted with drinks, popcorn, and anything else that the fans could get their hands on. To me, it was the most disturbing image of the night. There was hatred in those stands. Jermaine O'Neal was taking the brunt of it. I also couldn't help but think that not one of these fans would have had the audacity to do anything with Jermaine O'Neal except ask for his autograph if they met thirty minutes later in the parking lot. However, protected by railings and as anonymous parts of a mob, they felt safe to hurl verbal invective as well as physical objects.

Since many of those people brought their children to the game, what did they say to their kids about why they threw soft drinks on another person's head below them? After they finished that noble act, did they take down the posters of Jermaine O'Neal from their kids' walls?

Where does that kind of anger come from? It doesn't come from being a Pistons fan. It doesn't come from your team getting beaten by the other team. Some have said it is racial: Jermaine O'Neal being black and the fans being primarily white. Is there anything in today's society that isn't racial? I can't think of a serious issue today in which one group or another isn't claiming racism. Nine out of ten times I actually have trouble trying to think about a particular issue in terms of color. I guess I have to start.

Wait a second, let me think about this. Can a person simply be rude, unprofessional, disrespectful, disgraceful, or classless? Or is every form of previously unacceptable conduct now explainable through some form of subliminal racism? For example, can a black person like thousands of whites and other races, be a hypocrite? Can a black person, like thousands of whites and other races, be a phony? Can he be cheap? Can he be dishonest? If a black man can become a head coach or general manager in the NBA, can't he also have the distinction of being a bad one? Not today, apparently. We are living in a time of such political correctness that we have become paralyzed to even suggest such things. It is as if the pendulum has swung so far that now we apparently have a race in our midst that has no flaws at all. I know I'm being ridiculous, but no matter which direction prejudice flows, it is still prejudice.

Americans used to able to discuss these issues more openly. As a college student in the late 1960s and early 1970s, I naturally thought I had all the answers. I didn't, but I tried. My generation could actually have meaningful discussions on race without worrying constantly about being labeled a racist. We could even joke about it, which was always my way. The joking can make a certain irrational belief system look like a joke.

Whenever I see or hear the racism explanation applied to any and all issues, I think of the great Bill Russell. Eventually, everything always gets back to basketball. Bill Russell was the greatest winner in the history of the NBA. He was known in his playing days as a fierce competitor. But the way he was depicted through the media to kids like me was as a nasty, arrogant, and militant type of black man—someone actually to be afraid of. The truth of the matter was that he was, in reality, a highly intelligent and proud man who happened to win eleven NBA championships in thirteen years. This will not be done again. He also spoke his mind and didn't take any crap from anybody.

Russell was an extremely complicated person. It is only after many years that the public has come to understand him. As a player in the 1950s and 1960s in America, he was actually discriminated against. This was not subtle discrimination. This was not perceived slights. You don't have to create a racist argument when your neighbors defecate in your bedroom to show their excitement about your moving into the neighborhood.

Beyond all this winning and excellence, I also remember Bill Russell for an extraordinary appearance on *Saturday Night Live*. In his sketch, Russell plays himself. Everywhere he goes he sees racism. No matter what happens to him, he declares, "It's because I'm black, isn't it?!" The kicker comes at the end of the sketch when his mother disciplines him as mothers do. He utters the same tired refrain to his mother, "It's because I'm black, isn't it?"

The only problem here is that the sketch was aired in 1979. They were poking fun at this cop-out excuse thirty years ago. In 2006, this way of thinking has increased to such a proportion that we literally cannot have an opinion on anything or anybody without being labeled a racist by someone. Am I really a racist because I think that Barry Bonds and all the other steroid users of that era should be thrown to the curb? Does it really take a genius to understand, even while it was happening, that Mark McGuire and Sammy Sosa were not legit? Let's see. Roger Maris in 1961 sets a record that stands for over thirty years and then *two* guys obliterate it in the same season. Bonds then breaks that new record shortly thereafter. *Please.* Do you mean to tell me that if I found out that during his career Michael Jordan was having shock absorbers surgically implanted into his feet before games, it would be racist of me to think differently about what his accomplishments really were? What the hell, I'll take the risk. Barry Bonds was not as good as Willie Mays or Hank Aaron. I'm sure that somehow makes me a racist in some quarters, and I'm looking forward to hearing the rationale.

I rather think that most of the animosity of that evening in Detroit comes from a disconnect. And guess what? Yup. It all comes down to money. There is a lot of frustration about Jermaine O'Neal's $110 million contract and what the fans have to pay to watch a product that is not worth the admission price. I know that it's all out of whack. I know that the numbers are crazy. The fans' frustration may well be real, but their actions were a disgrace. Does it mean that Jermaine O'Neal has stopped being a person because he makes that much money? Jermaine O'Neal and all of the others merely said "yes" when the money was offered. What I saw directed at O'Neal that night scared me. What I saw directed at the fans by the players scared me. The Buffalo Springfield line, "Nobody's right if everybody's wrong," rang in my head.

This is occurring not just in the NBA. How else can you explain the reaction of the fans of the New York Yankees to Alex Rodriguez? Months after being named the American League's most valuable player, Rodriguez was being booed every time he did anything. This is not a good player. This is a great one! I don't think he is being booed; I think his contract is. Making $25 million per year is great when you and your wife go the bank, but it obviously fosters quite a bit of resentment when you don't perform in the clutch.

Commissioner Davis Stern said as much, in reacting to Latrell Sprewell's comment about "feeding his family" on only $14 million a year. He admitted to a "widening gulf between professional athletes and the fans."

No matter what spin the league chooses to put on the 2004–2005 season, the year will be most remembered for the night that the players and fans came face to face and both lost. "Spinning" is unfortunately exactly what the NBA has been doing in varying forms for some twenty-five years at least. Spinning, promoting, and selling seems to have been the strategy.

So maybe the issue is why that money is being offered. Where did it come from? In Boston in 1964, at the first televised NBA All-Star game, Elgin Baylor, Oscar Robertson, Jerry West, Bill Russell, Wilt Chamberlain, and others refused to go out for the second half until their owners relented and provided them with some form of health insurance benefits. When Jack Kent Cooke, the owner of the Los Angeles Lakers, sent an aide down to the locker room to inform West and Baylor to return to the court or suffer the consequences, Baylor and West informed the aide to instruct Mr. Cooke what he could do with his ultimatum. They and the other players prevailed and thus began the infant steps of their union.

Some forty years later, that same union took up the cause of defending the players who entered the stands and pummeled whoever was in reach. Believe me when I tell you, those Pacers players had health insurance, as well as pension benefits per diem, travel rights, and numerous other benefits that most people can only imagine. The winding road from that Boston locker room to Detroit sheds a lot of light on how this entire distortion of reality has come about. This sense of entitlement obviously didn't simply appear one day out of the blue. It was nurtured and, in most cases, acquired through the efforts of agents, the NBPA, the fans, and, ultimately, the league itself.

I don't believe for one second that any of this was caused by evil people. On the contrary, I happen to be fond of everyone at the NBPA. I particularly respect the executive director, Billy Hunter. I think he has done a very good job in very difficult circumstances. He and everyone else at the union have to represent about 425 players. These players have different needs and different agendas. Most confounding of all, they have different agents. And the agents all have their own agendas, too.

Nothing I have said in these pages has not been said directly to the faces of the staff at the players association. Whereas they have tolerated me and been amused by me over the years, they have, for the most part, treated my suggestions with a nod but without any reform. This is my turn, and I'm taking my cuts.

Interestingly, I believe David Stern is starting to get it. Recently, statements he has been making regarding his disappointment with the subculture of basketball in the United States had me thinking that he could have coauthored parts of this book. Sorry Dave, I'm not sharing my royalties. But he seems to understand what he has helped to create. But can he truly implement the changes necessary to reclaim the game?

The NBA is run by incredibly competent people. But the league has grown and changed so much that we've gotten away from Dr. Naismith's game. Although basketball was originally invented to give the kids at the YMCA in Springfield, Massachusetts a game they could play indoors during the cold weather, Dr. Naismith turned it into a vehicle to teach kids how to play together. And to play together, they needed to listen to their teammates.

When people, corporations, leagues, or countries get too big and too successful, their downfall usually occurs when they stop listening. When I look at the NBA, I think about that lack of listening. I remember the picture on Ducky Drake's wall of the Olympic broad jumper with his head in his hands after faulting on his last jump because he didn't listen to his coach.

My other thought is much more ominous. George Armstrong Custer was an American hero to me and thousands of other kids who read, watched, and therefore, bought into the stories we were told. The fact that a closer examination of Custer reduces his valor to a series of broken treaties and promises is besides the point. The relevance here is that Custer was outmaneuvered and killed by the Sioux at the Little Big Horn.

Custer had been warned by the Sioux many times. After his death, he was found with blood coming out of each ear. It was clarified later that the Indians punctured both eardrums so that he would be able to listen better in the next life.

FOURTEEN

AND HERE COME THE ELEPHANTS!

Since the theme for this book was inspired by the great P. T. Barnum, who furthered the popularity of the circus, it is fitting to begin to wrap it up with a discussion of the 2005–2006 New York Knicks. If comedy was the goal, there would have been no complaints coming. The problem was they weren't really going for laughs; they were actually trying to compete in the NBA.

The whole thing started with the old sports cliché: "You can't rebuild in New York!"

That has passed for the gospel for a long time. It's not an actual written rule, and it also is not true. If a New Yorker actually thought about it for a few seconds, he would be insulted more than anything else. A short explanation why that is the common belief is that in New York, the fans are so spoiled and superficial that they cannot and will not tolerate any failure or losing. This approach has, however, created a drought of thirty-three years (and counting) between NBA championships. At what point exactly will the powers-that-be realize that the quick fix is not working? Or that it's not so quick?

If anybody in the Knicks front office remotely understood New York, they would have long ago realized that the exact opposite is true of New Yorkers, especially when it comes to their basketball. The other old sports cliché is that the New York fan is the most sophisticated in the nation. Aha! Sophistication is not always synonymous with winning. With sophistication comes an understanding of the game itself. In other words, it involves understanding effort and distinguishing real effort from the flim-flam that has been pushed at them for years.

The Knicks have been selling the following saviors to the public: Stephon Marbury, Jerome James, Eddy Curry, Steve Francis, Jalen Rose, Nate Robinson, and Quentin Richardson. The New York fans have been so desperate, they have accepted all of these saviors until they were actually called on to play together.

Naturally, the latest savior came from my own extended family. In the summer of 2005, the Knicks brain trust decided that they had to have Larry Brown as their coach. He was the answer du jour just as Stephon Marbury had been a year and a half earlier. Larry and my father had just terminated their relationship with the Detroit Pistons, and it didn't end warmly. This acrimony developed after Larry had coached Detroit in two consecutive NBA finals, winning one of them. Pistons owner Bill Davidson had some unkind things to say about Larry, which obviously did not sit too well with my family. The one thing you learn very quickly with the Glasses is that no matter what we do, our back is covered. It's actually a pretty good feeling.

Isiah Thomas, the president of the Knicks, who had his own issues leaving Detroit, had in fact reached out to me during that period of turmoil with Detroit for some advice on dealing with my father and Larry, just in case Larry suddenly became available. The New York media was already speculating about Larry coming to the Knicks. When he did become free, the media circus was ridiculous. Reporters constantly trailed after Larry and his family. You couldn't pick up any paper without reading and seeing Larry and his wife, Shelly engaged, in such news-making activities as walking the dogs, shopping, or eating in a restaurant.

My father negotiated the richest contract for a coach in any sport in all of two days. The total was in excess of $50 million for five years. This sum was completely guaranteed. I purposely never discussed any of these negotiations with my father, but I have a feeling that he said a lot of *okays* and *yeses* during the proceedings.

Larry's hiring brought waves of excitement and borderline hysteria to New York, or so it appeared. To me, most of that excitement seemed to be generated by the Knicks and their public relations people. There was an incredible press conference complete with a video tribute to Larry. My parents attended, and it was thrilling for them and for Larry. It was all perfect, and it would have remained so if they didn't have that damn basketball season to play.

The Knicks won only twenty-three games in 2005–2006. The only trouble was they had won thirty-three the year before. Understand that Larry was not the only addition they made during that summer. They added Jerome James and his $30 million contract. They traded for Eddy Curry from the Chicago Bulls and paid him $55 million. It could have been more, but Eddy had this heart problem. The Bulls, coached by some guy named Scott Skiles, were so concerned about Eddy and his condition that they would not sign him without further DNA testing. The Knicks did not share this concern. The trade not only cost them money, but also to get the right to overpay Eddy, the Knicks forfeited their first-round draft choice from this month. Due to the disaster of a season that they had, this turned into the second pick in the entire 2006 draft, which the Bulls used to draft Tyus Thomas from LSU. There were more additions. The Knicks added three first rounders—Channing Frye, Nate Robinson, and David Lee. All of these guys can actually play and can have a bright future for New York if they remain there.

When Isiah Thomas was hired as the general manager of the New York Knicks, I was surprised. Not from the point of view of his competence, but rather I didn't know how they got to him. Isiah is nothing if not bright. I have detailed to some degree my interactions with Isiah previously. But his forays into the management side of basketball before he was hired as the man in New York had been as negative as his playing days were positive.

Isiah was initially supposed to be "a Detroit Piston for life." These were his own words, spoken after his retirement as one of if not *the* greatest players in Piston history. Months later, he left Detroit after a falling out with owner Bill Davidson. He became the first president of the then expansion Toronto Raptors. That experience and the results sound eerily familiar today. The report card read shaky with the business decisions, but a real good judge of talent. In other words, he drafted well. It was Isiah who drafted Tracey McGrady out of high school when eight other clubs passed on the all-star.

It was in Toronto where Isiah and I first collaborated in the Thomas Hamilton Affair. I had signed another player with Toronto, Lloyd Daniels, during Isiah's stay there. In fact, the only reason Lloyd is not a chapter herein is because he requires an entire book.

Lloyd was toiling in the Continental Basketball Association (CBA), which is the minor leagues. I got him signed to a ten-day contract. In his first game up, he scored twenty-three points against Cleveland. The coaches were excited and kept giving Lloyd minutes. Isiah and the Raptors signed Lloyd for another ten-day period, and then they released him. When I called Isiah to find out why, it was just another example to me on how sharp he truly can be. He told me that Lloyd was better than McGrady at that point, but that McGrady was going to be great. As long as Lloyd was on the roster, the coaches weren't going to play McGrady. Lloyd was too good—obviously had to go.

The Toronto experience did not end drastically for Isiah, but it did not end the way everybody wanted it to. It was Isiah's next stop that raised eyebrows across the basketball landscape. The NBA was about to institute its own developmental minor league called, appropriately, the NBDL, or National Basketball Developmental League. The only competition for the coming NBDL was the CBA. The CBA had been around for a long time before Isiah decided to purchase the entire league. He figured that the NBA would try to buy the CBA from him to eliminate the competition. That was not how things unfolded. Isiah left the CBA in the middle of the season and left embittered team owners in his wake. Many of us in the business figured that this bit of mismanagement would haunt Isiah, at least in the short term. For the Knicks, it was apparently treated as a recommendation.

To be kind, the 2005–2006 Knicks season did not get off to a rousing start. Larry quickly became disenchanted with the roster. But this is his way, always has been. He searches and tries to figure out how to win. Way back at UCLA during our time together, he changed 80 percent of the starting lineup. That tinkering project landed us in the national championship game in 1980, which shocked the college basketball world. With the Knicks, he began to criticize the players and the makeup of the team on an early trip to the West Coast. Since Isiah was the one who was totally responsible for constructing that roster and had brought Larry in to save the day, he got a bit agitated. As he later told me to my face, he felt that Larry had tried to "throw me under the bus."

Things got progressively worse from there. Eddy Curry showed mere flashes of ability. It seemed that no one in the Knick organization had bothered to find out that Eddy, while a very nice person, doesn't actually like to play basketball. To me, that's important. To the Knicks, their attitude was "what's $55 million between friends?" Jerome James decided that whereas he enjoyed being paid twice a month on his $30 million contract, he felt that the part about his responsibility of actually playing was a mere suggestion, not a true obligation.

Into the middle of this mess comes myself with a player on the Knicks who I represent—Jackie Butler. Jackie was only twenty years old and in his first full season with the Knicks. Isiah had discovered him in the CBA where he was leading that league in rebounding at the age of nineteen. Jackie had been advised by an agent that if he would enter the draft right out of high school and forego the University of Tennessee, he would be a guaranteed first-round draft choice. He wasn't drafted at all, never mind the first round. Whereas the Knicks had committed salaries of $85 million to their other two centers, Curry and James, Jackie was making the second-year NBA minimum of $641,000, and he was in the final year of his contract. He would become a restricted free agent that summer.

To further complicate matters, Larry really liked Jackie. Jackie did what players were supposed to do—listen and try. On this Knicks team, those were rare qualities. While Jackie sat on the bench and sometimes didn't even dress for games at the beginning of the year, he slowly started to get minutes. Whenever he did get an opportunity to play, he usually responded. This caused further friction between Larry and Isiah. Larry publicly declared that in spite of the huge contracts to Curry and James, Jackie was "our best center." This didn't go over too well either.

In my opinion, the key to finding the true culprits in this mess of a year is to analyze two specific moves that were made even after all that previously transpired. In spite of the overwhelming expenditures that I have discussed, the Knicks had two assets that they had touted for some time. Specifically, they had the expiring contracts of Penny Hardaway and Antonio Davis. An expiring contract is an asset only in the sense that the team acquiring the player with this expiring contract can simply let it fall off the cap the following season.

In the NBA, a team acquiring a player is not really trading for the player in most cases; they are trading for his expiring contract. They only have to keep him until the end of that season, and then they can let him go. The team then gets the benefit of the reduction of their cap. It's pretty insulting to the player if you think about it, but nobody does.

When a team allows an expiring contract actually to expire instead of acquiring a player with an equally inflated salary under a longer contract, this is referred to as allowing the contract to "fall off the cap." Each team in the NBA has a different cap number due to their own contracts they have signed with their players. Since the Knicks have always taken the approach that "you can't rebuild in New York," they have never had contracts "fall off the cap." They go out and try for the quick fix time after time.

Instead of allowing Patrick Ewing's $20 million salary to "fall off" and then use that money to acquire free agents, they traded him to Seattle and that led to the burdening of the franchise with Glen Rice, Shandon Andersen, and Howard Eisley. At least this has always been the philosophy under James Dolan. The Ewing deal was done by a friend of mine, Scott Layden, who was the Knicks' general manager at that time. This practice has been continued by the current general manager, Isiah Thomas. The common denominator here is James Dolan. I would love to learn whose philosophy this truly is. To rebuild takes patience and a plan. You have to be willing to suck it up for a year or so and get under the cap to acquire the right free agents. If you are always over the cap, you are never a "player" when free agency begins on July 1 of every summer.

As a way of illustration, one of Isiah Thomas's first acts as the Knicks' general manager was to make a little deal with the Phoenix Suns. The Suns smartly used the concept of expiring contracts in this instance. They traded Stephon Marbury—who was making huge money—along with the same Penny Hardaway and his bloated contract to the Knicks for Antonio McDyess. The advantage to this deal for Phoenix was all about getting rid of mistakes, not about acquiring McDyess. The Suns allowed McDyess to "fall off their cap," and with the money they had by getting under the cap, they signed Steve Nash. Nash has been the most valuable player in the NBA for the two years that Marbury has been in New York.

Now, it was finally the Knicks' turn to either let Hardaway's $17 million contract fall off their cap or turn it into a huge asset for the club. The Knicks ended up trading Penny's contract to the Orlando Magic for Steve Francis. Francis was actually more overpaid than Penny, so the Knicks also had to give Orlando a promising young small forward, Trevor Ariza, to have the salaries match up. Players being traded must add up to a total within 15 percent of one anothers' salaries. Not only was Francis making slightly more than Penny, but also he came with the additional "benefit" of having three more years on his contract. The total owed to Francis as of this writing is still $48 million.

But we still have to deal with the other expiring contract of Antonio Davis. That one was also worth $17 million or so. The Knicks turned that one into Jalen Rose, whose salary matched Davis's, but included an extra year at approximately the same $17 million. Since the Knicks are capped and are therefore subject to the "luxury tax," the total expenditure going forward is double the total of these two deals, or $130 million.

Whoever was truly responsible for these two acquisitions is the problem. I understand that we will probably never know the complete answer to that question, but that is what is called in courts "the ultimate question." James Dolan and Isiah claim that it was Larry who had to have these guys and then quickly refused to play them. Larry denies this. I wasn't there, and neither were any of you.

The season mercifully came to end. Larry, Isiah, and even Stephon Marbury put on what appeared to be a united and conciliatory front for the media. I assumed that they would lick their wounds of the season from hell, dust themselves off, and get on to the next one.

On Mother's Day, Aylin and I traveled to Atlantic City to spend the weekend with my parents. I got up early at the hotel and decided to get some breakfast. I picked up the papers before going in. The front page of the *New York Post* blared COACH ISIAH! Peter Vescey, who had become relentless in his negativity toward Larry, had gotten the scoop that James Dolan, the president and CEO of the Knicks, was about to fire Larry. They went on to say that Dolan would be seeking to negotiate a buyout of Larry's contract with my father. My first thought was *good luck*! Between Brent, Jodi and myself, I was the only one able to negotiate lunch money from our father when we were kids.

The Knicks never confirmed or denied Vescey's bombshell. All this did was fuel the story. The team then went silent on this nonstory for forty-one days. The newspapers and television media had a field day speculating. Actually, it was a field month. The Knicks management were made to look even more dysfunctional than the team did during the season. In the middle of the very entertaining NBA playoffs, the Knicks had the back page of the New York tabloid papers nearly every day. It was simply embarrassing. The Knicks let Larry dangle out there for forty-one days.

I got caught up in this latest fiasco as well, but thankfully only for a few days. I had just signed Quincy Douby out of Rutgers University about two weeks before all this broke. The Knicks had interest in Quincy and wanted to work him out at their practice facility. I agreed and was invited to watch the workout.

Isiah and Larry had not spoken to each other for over a month when I arrived for the workout. After it was over, Larry called me down to the court to talk. After a few minutes, out of the corner of my eye, I saw Isiah coming over to talk to us. To say the least, it was a bizarre conference. They clearly were both using me to talk to each other. There was just some chit-chat about the workout they had just watched . . . separately. They discussed in very generic terms different players coming up for the draft the next month. It was strained and forced with very little substance. After ten fairly uncomfortable minutes, I eased away.

At the end of the forty-one day period, Larry was called into the Knicks offices for a meeting at 8:00 a.m. one morning. He was specifically told not to call Joe Glass. They talked about what Larry had to do differently to remain as the coach of the New York Knicks. Apparently Larry wanted no part of what they were selling. So, Dolan fired him for what he claimed was "just cause" and said that he would not be paying him either. Being that he owed him $40 million over the next four years, I think he realized that the meeting with Joe Glass would probably be taking place after all.

The Knicks officially stopped paying Larry on June 30, 2006, which was his next payday. My father and his lawyers filed a grievance with the commissioner's office. David Stern had been specifically named as the arbitrator in case of any dispute between Larry and the Knicks. He accepted to hear the case. If my dad and Larry had won this one, Larry would've in essence been paid over $50 million for ten months of work. Larry got $18 million.

"AND THE MAN IN THE MIDDLE . . ."

As bizarre as all of this activity obviously was, it had one final irony, and I was directly in the middle of it, of course. The day after the Knicks stopped paying Larry, I received a phone call from Isiah regarding Jackie Butler. According to leagues rules, July 1 was the first day that agents and management could discuss free agents. Jackie was a restricted free agent. As you remember from class, that meant the Knicks could match any offer I got from any other team. This is called the right of first refusal. To retain those rights, the Knicks had sent me "a qualifying offer" for Jackie three days before. The offer was for $919,320, which was the minimum they had to offer.

The fact that Isiah and the Knicks had already committed to paying $85 million for Eddy Curry and Jerome James certainly was going to make this a very interesting free agent saga. Couple that with the current animosity between the Knicks and members of my family, and you get an almost Shakespearean drama. I'm not sure which side were the Montagues and which were the Capulets.

Isiah put it on me. He told me that the Knicks liked Jackie very much. They wanted him on their team next year. There was no animosity toward me or Jackie. He was assuring me that one thing had nothing to do with the other. I already knew this since I had nothing to do with Larry's contract, and I had a long relationship with Isiah.

Isiah challenged me to go out and get an offer sheet, and then the Knicks would have a tough decision to make.

Translation: There is no way you're going to get an offer for more than the $919,320 because everyone will assume that the Knicks will automatically match.

It was actually the correct assumption to make. The hardest part for me was not going to be finding teams that liked Jackie; I already knew they were out there. The tough sell would be in making a believable case that the Knicks wouldn't match. The Knicks always match. Money seemed to be irrelevant to the Knicks. Were they printing the stuff in the basement of the Garden?

So I went out, and the Knicks figured I'd be back in October with my tail between my legs, happy to sign the qualifier for $919,320. The New York papers were full of speculation about what would happen with this situation. The most amusement I had was while at the Las Vegas summer league. I picked up a New York paper on July 11 and read a comment from Isiah that basically said that it was "going to be a long summer for Keith!"

I smiled to myself since as I was reading that statement, Jackie was physically sitting in the San Antonio Spurs' offices waiting for 12:01 a.m., so he could legally sign his offer sheet. The first day that an NBA free agent was allowed to sign an offer sheet was July 12. At 12:01 a.m. on July 12, he signed an offer sheet for approximately $7 million. At 6:00 a.m. the same day, the Spurs dispatched a member of the front office to board a plane bound for New York. He delivered the offer sheet personally to the Knicks' offices.

Under league rules, New York now had seven days in which to match San Antonio's offer sheet. Isiah was stunned at the numbers. Due to their previous mismanagement of the salary cap, the Knicks had an additional problem, which the Spurs and I had calculated. Whereas it would cost the Spurs $7 million to sign Jackie, it would cost the Knicks $14 million due to the luxury tax. The Knicks were way past the tax threshold while the Spurs, who had won three championships in the previous six years, were not.

The day before they had to make their decision, I received a call from Isiah. He told me that the Knicks would not match the offer. He congratulated me and Jackie on our accomplishment. He wished us both success and told me how happy he was for both of us. He could not have been more classy or professional, or in my opinion, more sincere. I truly believed him, and it meant a lot to me.

In spite of everything that went on between the Knicks and my family, I have never personally had a problem with Isiah Thomas. I wished him the same good fortune. I also believe that he will have his success to a degree with the Knicks. James Dolan put him on a one-year lease this year. In yet another bizarre turn, James Dolan announced at the press conference where Isiah was named head coach that if there was no improvement in 2006–2007, Isiah would be gone as well. He said this with Isiah sitting right next to him. It really did look like this edict caught Isiah by surprise. But I know they will have more success than last year if only because the bar has been lowered so dramatically. Since the 2005–2006 team had underachieved so drastically and won only twenty-three games, an improvement is automatic. A thirty-three- to thirty-eight-win season should be easily obtained.

I have observed and joked in these pages about the hypocrisy involved with all forms of attempted legislation aimed at agents and players. This overemphasis on unnecessary rules has become an almost comical attempt to control our influence and subsequent impact on the NBA. The only common denominator in these attempts is that they usually miss their target.

But changes are on the way! The union, which I have been slightly critical of, has finally moved to begin to clean up this agent-driven corruption. It doesn't involve the stealing of clients. It doesn't address the paying off of players, street agents, runners, AAU coaches, parents, etc. No, nothing as trivial as that.

Instead, the NBPA suspended an eighty-one-year-old man named Joe Glass for representing Larry Brown, basically a member of his family for a half a century. They claimed my father had a conflict of interest, since agents cannot represent players and coaches at the same time. The fact that my father hadn't represented an NBA player in six years apparently was not deemed to be relevant.

Now we're getting somewhere!

FIFTEEN

THROUGH THE LOOKING *GLASS*

When friends of mine found out about this book, I was repeatedly asked the same question: "Why do you want to write this thing?" I've been asked this so much that I figured I ought to answer it. No, I don't have a professional death wish. For many years, however, I've been troubled and conflicted by the messages we in professional basketball have been sending. I have always viewed basketball, and other sports, as an opportunity to set an example. The goal, of course, is to have an example be a positive force, but examples can also work the opposite way as well. The NBA has been setting negative examples for too long, and it's time to change some things.

I've had my fun. I have pointed out some of the problems inherent in the league from which I earn a living. I have told stories, I have poked my finger in the eye of the system, and I've thrown figurative cream pies in the faces of the people who allow these elements to fester and flourish.

I also know that it's always easier to tear something down, be it a person, a group, a system, or a league, than to build it up. It took a lot of creativity, sacrifice, and effort to create the NBA; it is now time to offer some ways to help the league get to where it should be. Professional basketball has, as an entity and a sport, lost its way.

I'm not the only one who thinks this either. Referring to the world of runners, street agents, AAU teams, and sneakers companies, which I have touched on in the book, the following quote caught my eye in July 2006: "Something is totally wrong with the development of young basketball players." This may not seem so significant by itself until you consider the source of the quote. It was spoken by the commissioner of the NBA, David Stern.

As in most things good that have gone wrong—the Chevy Impala, Sudafed, and the NBA Official Game Ball—there is not one root cause. There are several facets that have conspired to hurt the game.

RULES

Like having guns laws where only law-abiding citizens register their weapons, the NCAA, the NBA, the NBPA, high school federations, and others operate with similar results. By restricting the high school coach from even being in the gym for most of a calendar year, you give a license to the local AAU coach or sneaker representative to exert more influence. By restricting the access of college coaches to their players, you give opportunities to street agents. By legislating certified agents, the union has left itself no control over noncertified individuals. The certified ones are bad enough; the others are an out-of-control mob.

My advice on this one is real simple. Get rid of all the rules. They may be well intentioned, but all they do is create a system based on deceit. The effort has shifted from teaching or coaching kids to getting around these rules. The message to the players is clear—the rules are merely an annoyance, something to be gotten around. The people who aid in this flaunting of the rules are the guys that you least want these young and impressionable players involved with. These kids are not learning to respect these rules; they are instead learning that it's okay to break them. The concept of a respectful attitude toward any sort of authority is ridiculed.

High School Coaches

There is no denying that because of the restrictions placed on all high school coaches, we have empowered the AAU coaches. I would start to reverse this trend with one common sense rule. *Open the gyms.* I don't want to hear the excuse about insurance coverage, which is the most popular one invoked. Why anyone would argue about opening a gym for kids to play is mind-boggling. We built them, so open them. They should be opened seven out of every eight days. The eighth day they would be closed for cleaning. Also, rotate the closed day, so there is always one open in every neighborhood.

If a coach wants to be in a gym with his players, let him. Another rule: Anytime someone wants to try and get better or just play and enjoy him or herself, there should be no impediment. If coaches and their players want to work hard and live in the gym or on a field, let them. Where do we want them to go? Any kid with an interest or a passion for anything should be encouraged, not legislated.

The NCAA

This institution needs a complete overhaul. The NCAA administrators are bright people who apparently have trouble relating their legislation to the practical application of those rules. It seems to me that they have developed an obsession when it comes to any collegiate prospect getting an "extra benefit." This misguided attempt to eliminate any such "extra benefit" is really at the root of the problem. It is also why all NCAA rules, however sound, are currently held up to such skepticism and ridicule.

The reality doesn't exist on the same planet as the rule. In college athletics, there are two money-producing sports, football and basketball. Therefore, the NCAA has deemed it its mission not to allow any football or basketball players to get any extra reward besides their scholarships. Why not? Do you mean to tell me that if a member of the university marching band was offered an all-expenses-paid trip to Lincoln Center to audition for the New York Philharmonic, he or she would not be allowed in the marching band the following year? Are you now going to use the excuse that the person in the marching band is not on scholarship? Then take a case of a student of mathematics on academic scholarship. If he is offered a job interview in Chicago, would he have to pay for his own plane ticket and hotel or be barred from attending math classes the following year? Don't be silly. In what other field of endeavor is a potential employee not allowed to interview at the employer's expense?

Why the difference with an athlete? It's probably because of the high-profile nature of a college basketball or football player. It's also rooted in some form of resentment from the rest of the university community who don't feel they receive their fair share of credit, notoriety, or *money*. It probably didn't help things too much when Bear Bryant, the legendary University of Alabama football coach, replied to a math professor who complained about Bryant's salary and demanding ways: "How many people go to see you give your final exams, because 50,000 come to see me give mine . . . every Saturday."

THE NATIONAL BASKETBALL PLAYERS ASSOCIATION

My criticisms of the NBPA are centered on the word *enabling*. The structuring of a relationship between players and their agents that is so slanted toward the player enables players basically to do anything they want without any consequences. A contract that the player can sign one day and terminate the next with no ramifications isn't just unfair, but it also fosters a lack of responsibility that permeates other areas of the player's life.

I have a very close friend who works as a manager in the music industry. I recently explained to him how my contract works with all my clients in the NBA. When he realized that the clients were under no obligation to remain with me from one day to the next, he couldn't believe it. His concern was this: There are many times as an agent or advisor that you need to give tough, honest, and sometimes, unwanted advice to a client. If there is no binding duration in this agreement, how can you effectively do your job?

Clearly there is a need for a player/agent agreement to mean something. There should be at least a three-year commitment on both sides. This would give an agent who is attempting to give the right advice the footing to do so even if that advice is not what a player wants to hear at that moment. Obviously, there should always be a way to terminate this relationship "for just cause." If an agent has done something to harm the player, there needs to be a mechanism in place for terminating that agent. This can easily be done on a case-by-case basis. This, however, is not the way of things today. A player can be recruited away from the most well-intentioned and hard-working agent in the world for no reason, and there is absolutely nothing the agent can do about it. A binding commitment would at least curtail some of the overt stealing of clients that occurs every day. The message to the players would also be obvious—namely, that a contract actually stands for something. There has to be some value for signing with a particular person. A time commitment may also get the player to consider his initial decision more carefully. He may actually decide more on whom he wants representing him for the next three years rather than who is furnishing the nicest car or the hottest babes.

THE RETURN TO OLYMPIC GLORY

I devoted an entire chapter to the debacle and deterioration of our Olympic basketball efforts. What had been an interesting idea in 1992 has now become distorted into a marketing effort that has resulted in not only defeat, but also embarrassment. Like most legislation gone wrong, the problem is in the overreacting to a situation.

The Dream Team was fun, but ever since that initial foray, it has become a colossal bore. Like the NBA itself, it lacks any discernable identity or rooting interest. Who roots for the NBA as a whole? The simple truth is that the United States doesn't need to send stars to the Olympic Games to capture the gold medal. We need to assemble an actual team and not just a team of the best available NBA all-stars.

We are taking steps in the right direction. Under Jerry Colangelo's leadership, I'm sure that things will get measurably better. He is an extremely knowledgeable and successful man. Coach Mike Krzyzewski has been appointed, and he has impeccable credentials, which include three national championships and the reputation for running a clean program that graduates its players. They've assembled a team that have made a commitment to playing together for three years. The team played together in the World Championships as well in 2006. More on this later. This will no doubt help the players get ready and win gold in 2008.

The problem I have with this approach is that it does not establish American dominance of a game invented in the United States. We are merely sending the best we have to obliterate the opposition. To show real dominance, we need to show the world that we do *not* need our best to win it all.

The thrill of watching and rooting for the U.S. team in Olympiads past was that they were college kids for the most part, fighting to capture something that was special to them, and therefore to us. In addition, since the Olympic athletes were all amateurs, they were never going to have the chance to do this again. It created a feeling of excitement that has been simply lost. It is a big part of the reason why so American basketball fans rooted against the U.S. team in 2004. There was no connection to the fans. There was no sense of desperation.

To an NBA all-star making $8 million to $17 million a year, a game is just another game. There is always another game. Ask Oscar Robertson, Jerry West, and Jerry Lucas if that was the feeling in 1960 during their Olympics. Ask Bill Bradley, Luke Jackson, and yes, Larry Brown if that was the feeling in 1964. Even ask Michael Jordan if that was the sense of things in the pre–Dream Team 1984 Olympics Games.

I have a tremendous amount of respect for the international game. For the most part, its players and coaches are first-rate. That being said, there is also no way they should be able to compete with an organized group of American basketball players. Note the word *organized*. We simply have a much bigger pool of players. It is true that Germany has Dirk Nowitski and that Argentina has Manu Ginobili and Andres Nocioni. It is equally true that they should not be able to beat a team of American players.

If done correctly, the United States could form a team using two main guidelines that would help us dominate the international hoops scene. First, all players would have to be under a certain age. Let's cap the age at twenty-six at the time the team is picked. Second, every four years, we establish a completely new team. The fifteen players selected would have to make a commitment to play every summer together, and if they don't want to, then move to the next fifteen. We'd be a lock to win the gold that way. That's dominance. To say to the world we don't even need our twelve best to beat your twelve best is a statement.

Let's be specific. Using my guidelines for 2008 Olympics, you could line up the following NBA players:

POINT GUARDS:

- Chris Paul
- Deron Williams
- Kirk Heinrich
- Shawn Livingston
- Jameer Nelson

SHOOTING GUARDS:

- Martell Webster
- Ben Gordon
- Quincy Douby
- Brandon Roy
- Randy Foye

SMALL FORWARDS:

- Adam Morrison
- Ronnie Brewer
- Jared Jeffries
- Josh Howard
- Tayshaun Prince

POWER FORWARDS:

- Tyrus Thomas
- Nick Collison
- Chris Bosh
- Channing Frye
- Charlie Villanueva

CENTERS:

- Amare Stoudamire
- Jackie Butler
- Tyson Chandler
- Dwight Howard
- Joel Przybilla

That's twenty-five guys. There are another fifteen to twenty who would win it as well. That's the point. The NBA and U.S. Olympic Committee now finally understand that the rest of the world has caught up to us, but only to a degree. What foreign countries have done is teach our game better than we do. They approach the game from a team concept rather than as a collection of individuals. Most importantly, the games matter to them. The Olympics is not an NBA showcase any longer. It is a competition, and if we don't prepare for it as the other countries do, we will suffer the same fate again. And again. And again.

If a player insists on special accommodations or treatment he doesn't make the team. There are too many talented players to deal with that crap. The opportunity to represent your country in the Olympics is an honor and a privilege, not another chance for self-promotion and marketing. If his wife, girlfriend, family, or entourage have to be involved, go on to the next guy on the list. It's not a vacation. It's the Olympics.

These players, properly trained and motivated, will do just fine. Instead of continuing the glorification of Lebron, Carmelo, and Dwayne Wade, we would be generating twelve to fifteen more guys to root for. To put it in terms the league will get excited about, they get twelve to fifteen more jerseys to sell.

THE MEDIA—IMPACT AND RESPONSIBILITY

The overall impact of the media is an incredible thing. Its power is unlimited. What the public views, especially on television, has an impact that is difficult to exaggerate. When ESPN's *SportsCenter* shows all dunks all the time, it has an impact. When *Fox Sports* shows players preening and threatening, it has an impact. Why we need to see athletes trying to frighten one another with their glaring is beyond me. In the past, such behavior would be looked on as crass and silly. Today, it is encouraged.

My suggestion here is a rule limiting dunks to 50 percent of a telecast. Maybe we can set a limit of five taunts per thirty minutes of airtime. Remember while American players were dunking and being cool in Athens in 2004, they were also getting their collective asses kicked. Better yet, what if the NBA sends a directive to the directors and editors to exercise some common sense. Show us a great pass every once in awhile! Are Magic and Larry Bird really such a distant memory? I seem to recall that they saved the league from itself not so long ago.

THE SHOE WARS

The unregulated power of the sneaker companies is at the heart of many of the problems inherent in grassroots basketball in America. The growth of AAU tournaments during the summer has gone unchecked and now dwarfs the high school experience for the top players in the nation.

It is the major sneaker companies—Nike, Adidas, and Reebok—who fund these traveling teams on their journeys all over the country. Since there is no regulation of these entities, they are virtually free to do whatever they choose. In the meantime, the corresponding high school coach is sitting at home reading the rules of his particular state federation, telling him when he is allowed physically to enter the gym again with his players.

An across-the-board committee is urgently needed to try and sort through this mess. For the good of the game and for the good of the kids who play it, some semblance of sanity should be required throughout the entire process. All of us have made too much money. We, be it agents, coaches, or school administrators, owe it to the game to serve on the committee if asked.

The Keith Glass rule: If anyone asks for compensation to serve on this committee, they would be immediately arrested.

THE BIG GIVEBACK

There are many current and former basketball people who have made and continue to make significant contributions to their communities. Some of them even do it without an NBA CARES camera coincidentally nearby. However, what is necessary to eradicate some of the issues I have discussed is a policy that not only allows, but also encourages, a return to the idea of teaching the game.

There are countless coaches and former and current players who would do whatever was asked of them to right this ship. There are many qualified basketball people who could do great and constructive things with young kids today, if they weren't restricted by one NCAA rule or another. We need to get people who know the game back into the gyms at the lower levels, not to sign autographs or pose for pictures with kids, but actually to sweat with them and teach.

People did it for me. Forget all of his problems of late and think about this: In forty years, I have never seen Larry Brown turn down anyone who wanted to learn something from him. You don't have to love everything that Larry has done, but if you don't think he has a world of knowledge about the game that he is willing to share, then you are a fool.

I began this book talking about the great UCLA coach John Wooden and how I came to know him at his summer camp. Coach Wooden *worked* his camp. He didn't show up, take the money, and go home. Today, that is not always the case. One of my sons attended a camp recently at a major university. I went to the closing ceremony. The head coach of the university gave a speech at the closing of the camp. He said the right things about practicing, listening to your parents and coaches, and doing well in school. On the way home, my son told me that was the only time besides the opening ceremony that he saw the coach. I was disappointed, but not surprised.

This is where we need to begin. Coaches need to teach, not just recruit. Agents aren't the only ones recruiting full-time. At some point in time for coaches, players, and agents, it becomes payback time. That time needs to be now. Every college coach should be required to teach coaches at the lower levels. The quality of coaching in some grade schools and even high schools is appalling. This has clearly led to the usurping of power by AAU coaches in conjunction with sneaker companies and has led to a general lack of respect for high school coaches—by players, by their parents, and by everyone else up the basketball food chain.

THE NBA AND ITS GAME

I'll admit it. Watching an entire NBA game is difficult for me. I would, at times, prefer to watch a fly crawl up my drapes. The league poohbahs recognized this as well, leading them to change some rules. Much of the grabbing and holding—at least on the perimeter—has been eliminated, and this has opened up the game. This has promoted more scoring, and therefore, gives the league not only a better product, but also naturally a better opportunity to create and market new stars. After all, this is what they are all about.

Here are a few more rules of the game that need fine-tuning.

Foul Shots

Will somebody please explain to me why they do not shoot one-and-ones in the NBA anymore? All foul shots are two shots. At every other level, the pressure is put on the player to hit the first to get another shot. Fourth graders have to live with that added pressure, and they are paid much less than Ray Allen. This creates a little excitement as well. The rule is now that the first free throw in an NBA game is the time to get up and pee. Make the fans hold it in, I say!

This would also increase the need for players actually to work on their foul shooting. Giving a poor free throw shooter an extra try does not exactly pressure him to improve. Perhaps if a coach realized that by missing the front end of a one-and-one, his team was forfeiting an opportunity for two points every trip, it might shift some emphasis from posing, taunting, and dunking by the players, to actually shooting free throws.

REDUCE THE IMPACT OF REFEREES

So far, I have spared the refs. This is the official end of that nonsense. The coach part of me can no longer protect them. Let's put aside for a moment the issue of the quality of refereeing at the lower levels of basketball, which to put it mildly, needs work. The NBA refs are the cream of the crop. However, the nature of game is so fast that it makes it extremely difficult to officiate. Add in the burden of the fact that most of these officials are human beings, and you get mistakes.

All of us make mistakes. The problem with making a mistake in an NBA game is that the refs can and do completely distort the outcome of a contest. I am not only referring to winning and losing, but also to the way the entire game progresses. It is one thing to call a bogus three-second violation or miss a guy stepping out of bounds, but if an NBA ref blows his whistle twice, then he changes what everyone came to see.

I am talking specifically about fouls. When a ref misses or even correctly calls two fouls, the entire strategy and flow of the game is changed from that moment on. Kevin Garnett comes down the floor with 10:23 left in the first quarter, and a ref calls him for a legitimate personal foul. With 6:14 left, Garnett takes a position in the key outside of the circle trying to get a charge on his man. The ref blows the call. KG heads to the bench for the rest of the quarter. Beyond that is the fact that he is now saddled with those two fouls the rest of the night. In the second quarter, if he gets one more and therefore has three, he is out for the rest of the half.

Now we have the start of the third, but Garnett stills has those three personal fouls. One more in the third, and he's out for that quarter. You get the gist. Two blows of an official's whistle, and 18,435 people who have paid astronomical prices to get in to see Kevin Garnett play don't.

It is an absurd scenario when you really think about it. Nobody except maybe their mothers came to watch referees ref, and yet we have granted them extraordinary power and control of the game. Additionally, there is no other professional endeavor where a player can be forced out of the game due to official's judgments. Fouling out is unique to the NBA. Of course, in every sport an official can "run you out" for misbehavior, but the NBA officials have the added power to "foul you out" as well.

I haven't even addressed their power to call technical fouls on coaches and players. These, I can say from personal experience, usually occur right after a ref has screwed up a call, and the coach is demanding an explanation. Instead of "I missed it," they say "Technical foul!" This strategy is designed to deflect the attention to the reaction to the error instead of the error itself. Interesting.

All this being said, I understand that it is not an easy job for referees to do. Human error alone is a reason to reduce their influence, not increase it. The league understands, to a point, that the refs are fallible. Years ago, basketball leagues on every level eliminated the jump ball, except at the beginning of every game. They went to alternating possessions, which is about as exciting as a Lamaze class for men.

Do you want to really know why the jump ball was eliminated? The refs couldn't throw it up there properly! These are the same guys that the league entrusts with making the lightening quick decisions on who plays and who doesn't. So let's help them out some more.

THE NEW FOUL-OUT RULE

A player will be allowed three fouls in the first half and four in the second half. You can still foul out, but only for that particular half of play. The advantage of this is that by adding only one foul per player, you can eliminate changing the entire flow and result of the contest due to officials' calls. If a player is committing fouls, he will still be penalized in terms of minutes missed, but it gives him and the people who paid to see him play a fresh start in the second half.

Another alternative to this problem of fouling out is already in use in some summer leagues that I travel to. At the Rocky Mountain Revue, if a player gets his seventh foul or beyond, his team is assessed a technical foul. The other team gets a free throw and then shoots two more awarded from the foul itself. It is the decision of the coach whether that penalty is worth continuing to play that particular player or not. Kevin Garnett probably stays in. Jerome James, not so fast!

Another idea is to award an extra foul for each overtime period. This would enable a player who has already "fouled out" to return to the action, instead of being a well-paid spectator. It seems like common sense.

CHANGE THE RULES REGARDING TIME-OUTS

It has to be merely a matter of time until the NBA realizes how badly excessive time-outs have ruined the flow of NBA games. I have too much faith in David Stern to believe that this could be allowed to go on much longer. The first three quarters are bad enough, but at the end of the game, it borders on the unbearable.

Coaches hoard their time-outs like gold. At the end of any game, close or otherwise, there is a time-out called on every possession. In the last minute of a close NBA game, this has absolutely destroyed any possible flow of the contest.

Team 1 scores: Time-out!

Team 2 misses: Time-out.

Team 1 can't get the ball inbounds: Time-out.

Team 1 looks like they may be able to get the ball inbounds: Time-out.

The wife of a member of Team 1 can't get the proper respect from an usher: Time-out.

You get the point. It's excruciating. What in the world are they talking about in these huddles? I only ask since after 83 percent of these high-level encounters, the team that took the time-out somehow manages finally to get the ball inbounds only to clear out one side of the floor and have their best player go one on three and jack up a bad shot. Couldn't we have gotten to that twenty minutes earlier?

I am not naïve as to the reason for this. Not surprisingly, we're back to money. This is where the big advertising dollars are found. The more stoppages in play, the more commercials. The more commercials, the easier it is for the league to recoup some of the inflated money they've already spent. Especially at the end of the game, where people will stay tuned and will not head for the kitchen or bathroom because this is the exciting part!

Currently, each team is entitled to six full time-outs and two twenty-second time-outs. This amounts to sixteen stoppages of play. The only possible reduction of this number is in the event that a team does not use its twenty-second time-out in the first half; they forfeit it. They rarely forget to do so. There are mandatory time-outs for the teams as well. These mandatory ones happen if the teams do not call their own time-out within a certain period of time. Got to sell! If there is a mandatory one, at least this counts against the allotment for the teams.

Here's the Keith Glass solution to the constant interruptions of the game. Instead of allowing coaches to hoard those time-outs, and thereby use them late in the game, there should be a penalty for that practice. "Use it or lose it" should not just be a cheap slogan for Viagra! It should also apply to NBA time-outs as well. Let's say each team would be allowed two time-outs in the last two minutes of play. Period.

All these stoppages of play accomplish is exactly what the words say: They stop play! This, along with the actual level of play itself, is what makes the game unwatchable at times. All contests need a flow to them, and the end of NBA games is a trickle. Would you watch a spelling bee with time-outs? I don't think so! Even during the playoffs, when the games by their nature are a much better product, incessant time-outs kill the action.

During the 2004 playoffs, I was watching the end of a game. It stood out in my mind because it was a terrific contest. A very exciting game that held my interest all the way, and the end was the best part. It was ten minutes later that I realized that the coaches had both mistakenly run out of time-outs with about a minute left. The result was a game with action and flow, and it was thrilling.

Are the coaches really teaching during those time-outs? If the answer is yes, then I have another question. Since NBA coaches, as well as the players, make huge sums of money, why don't they teach and prepare at practice? Why do they have to do it on our time?

I wrote this chapter while traveling to different NBA summer leagues across the country. This final section on time-outs was written on a flight between Las Vegas and Salt Lake City. Three hours after landing, I was at the Rocky Mountain Revue, the NBA summer league hosted by the Utah Jazz. The most thunderous ovation of the three games played that night occurred when the public address announcer proclaimed that with 23.7 seconds left, "The San Antonio Spurs are out of time-outs." I am not making that up. There was some really good basketball played that night, too, but nothing so exhilarating as the prospect of an opportunity to watch what the people had actually had come to see.

They seem to get it out here in Utah. Hmmm . . . polygamy and fewer time-outs. . . . Can a Jew happily married to a Muslim woman possibly be a Mormon?

FROM 6' 11" TO THE 7-ELEVEN

When you represent players, you always hope that the future is kind to them. You hope they save their money. You hope they don't hurt themselves physically or personally too much. Unless they have fired you along the way, you hope they have nothing but success. Reality does not always line up with your hopes. You hope that they don't start off walking into your office measuring six foot eleven inches tall, and years later, return the favor when you walk into their office and they serve you a Big Gulp at the 7-Eleven. The following are some updates regarding some of the characters of the preceding chapters:

1. Feeding Your Family on Only $14 Million a Year

LATRELL SPREWELL, as mentioned at the beginning of this book, did indeed reject that $32 million four-year guaranteed contract from the Minnesota Timberwolves prior to the 2005–2006 season.

On March 22, 2006, ESPN reported that Jeff Van Gundy placed calls to Latrell Sprewell regarding an offer to play for the Houston Rockets. The Rockets were floundering and had very little chance of making the playoffs. Sprewell would not return Van Gundy's calls.

He never signed and hasn't played since.

2. I'm Bicoastal—Not That There's Anything Wrong with That

JOHN WOODEN is now ninety-five years old. While his health prevents him from traveling as much as he would want, he remains a constant inspiration to everyone who has had the pleasure of his company. It is particularly inspiring to see the reverence his players have for their coach no matter how many years have passed. To sum up Coach Wooden as a man in a paragraph is impossible.

ELVIN "DUCKY" DRAKE died on December 23, 1988. He was clearly my favorite person that I met during my two years at UCLA. He was my friend, and I learned so much just hanging with him. We went shopping together on every road trip. He and his wife had so many friends that I could never figure out how he kept track of them. After his wife passed, we were in Japan for two games in 1980. When I entered my room, the phone was ringing. I picked and heard a gravelly voice say "Coach, are you ready?"

The next thing I knew I was in the Tokyo subway system with Ducky. We were hunting for gifts for his wife's friends back home in Los Angeles. After getting lost in the subway, which was quite a thrill, we finally found an outdoor marketplace. Mr. Drake found some Japanese scarves to his liking. He turned to me and said, "Do the best you can." I got the lady down to about half price, and from over my shoulder I heard, "Okay, wrap up forty-seven of them!"

RICHIE ADAMS was convicted of the manslaughter death of a fourteen-year-old girl in the South Bronx in 1996. He is currently serving a twenty-five-year sentence. The last I heard, he is still housed in Attica State Prison.

4. Eighty-one Feet of White Centers

MARK EATON never left the state of Utah. He lives in Park City, just up the mountains from Salt Lake City, where his jersey really does hang in retirement. He has owned restaurants in Salt Lake City and has done well as a television color man for the Jazz and the University of Utah games.

He is also a vice president of the NBPA retired players association. Today, he, along with the other members of that association, is very active in trying to get reasonable benefits for older NBA players who did not gain the benefits that today's players take for granted. These players are referred to as the "pre-1965ers," since they retired before 1965, the year the NBA established their pension plan. Mark and this small group of other former players, with a sense of right and wrong, have been trying for years to get reasonable pension and health benefits for these older players who have struggled. You would think that with all of the money and benefits that the league and the players have acquired, it would be a relatively easy thing to accomplish. Apparently, it's not.

5. Agenting—The Truth, the Half Truth, and Nothing but Baloney

ROBERT HORRY went on to win four more NBA championships after he terminated me. Apparently, I was not as critical an element to those Houston championships as I had thought. He won three times with Shaq and Kobe Bryant as a member of the Los Angeles Lakers and one more with the San Antonio Spurs and Tim Duncan. He is currently still under contract for at least one more year with the Spurs. He will be a teammate of Jackie Butler. I hope his clubbing days are over.

6. The Scales of Justice

CHUCK NEVITT, who is to this day among my favorite people, lives in Raleigh, North Carolina with his wife, Sondra. He works for Misys Healthcare Systems, which provides software for hospital management. When I spoke to him recently about this book, his main suggestion was that we start the Follow-Thru Fund up again. I guess he's finally running out of golf shirts. If the Rockets are reading this, he weighs 258!

STEVE PATTERSON, who battled with me over Chuck Nevitt's weight, is currently the general manager of the Portland Trailblazers. Our most recent discussion occurred just last month before the 2006 NBA draft. Steve was interested in whether I thought Quincy Douby would last to where Portland was selecting at the end of the first round. I told him I didn't think he would and that I thought Quincy was too skinny anyway.

7. Leave the Napkins; Take the Cannoli

SCOTT SKILES is currently the head coach of the Chicago Bulls, in spite of having his biggest contract negotiated primarily on paper napkins. In a very objective, unbiased opinion, I believe him to be the best coach in the NBA.

I consider him my little brother. I don't know what the hell he considers me.

JUD HEATHCOTE, the man who began our relationship by basically hanging up the phone on me, retired as the coach of Michigan State University several years ago. For twenty years now, Jud and I have corresponded. He has always tried to help me, and he has succeeded many times. After my initial signing of Scott Skiles, I had the good fortune of representing Mike Peplowski, Matt Steigenga, and Jamie Feick. I know that they would never have signed with me if not for Jud. Today, I periodically receive calls from Jud. He tells me an off-color joke and hangs up. I think we're friends.

PAT WILLIAMS survived the Skiles negotiations and many more. He is still involved in a major way with the Orlando Magic. He has written several books himself, and they are very interesting.

GEORGE IRVINE is one of the best friends that I have ever had. After becoming the head coach of the Detroit Pistons and signing a new contract with them in 2000, he was terminated. There seems to be a lot of that going around.

BORIS DIAW did indeed sign an extension with the Phoenix Suns in October 2006. The numbers read $45 million guaranteed over five years, or $9 million per year. Not bad for a bust from Atlanta.

8. Running for Your Life

THOMAS HAMILTON never played in the NBA again after we parted company. It wasn't for lack of interest on the part of the league. Several teams dabbled with him, in an attempt to be the one in the room when the light went on. It unfortunately never did. Tommy lives in Chicago in the projects very near where he began.

GREG, who orchestrated the Hamilton saga and many others, kept on doing his own thing both on the periphery of the NBA and in his personal life. He never relented to do it my way. His last project with me was Jermaine Jackson. He put Jermaine and me together for the second time while Jermaine was playing in Spain. I had previously represented him and had gotten him his only guaranteed contract of his career with the Philadelphia 76ers. He fired me shortly after.

This time after reuniting, I brought him back from Spain with the goal of getting back to the league. He ended up signing with the New York Knicks for the bulk of the 2004–2005 season.

During the Eddy Curry trade, Jermaine was included as a throw-in. He pocketed $832,000 for merely being included in the deal. Chicago, I knew all along, had no interest in Jermaine. He was indeed waived by Chicago ten days later. He terminated me again, and incredibly, his new agent tried to claim credit for the deal.

Greg never made it to see any of this. He died in March 2005. He had lived a hard life, and I guess his body couldn't take it anymore. He had scammed me so many times that I ashamedly admit that when I got the call from his wife that he had passed, I initially thought it just another elaborate scheme to get some money out of me.

I wish it had been. I miss him.

9. Star-spangled Disaster

MAHMOUD ABDUL-RAUF terminated our representation agreement as per the regulations of the union in 1998. He went on to play under the terms of the contract I had negotiated for him for the Sacramento Kings and, for a short time, with the Vancouver Grizzles. The Grizzlies moved onto Memphis where they still play today. Mahmoud's trip was a little further.

He played exclusively overseas after our contract with the Nuggets was over. His initial foray into this venue took him to Istanbul where he signed to play for my wife's old team, Fenerbache. This was in 1999. Aylin and I didn't even meet until 2002.

Aylin, just in conversation, had inquired if I knew her "very good friend, Mahmoud Abdul-Rauf." I indicated that I certainly did, we noted the coincidence, and that was the end of that.

In 2003, Aylin had been "turned on" to oatmeal by my mother. That is why we found ourselves in the Red Bank Diner. My cell phone rang, and after four years of no communication, Mahmoud was calling me. He told me that he was sorry that he ever left me. He said he had made a mistake and wanted, in essence, to come "home."

I was surprised enough to hear his voice again, but looking across the table at my wife, his friend from 6,000 miles away, was even more bizarre. I told Mahmoud that before we talked business, there was someone who I think he would be interested in speaking with.

When Aylin said "Hello," I could hear Mahmoud's shock coming through the earpiece. When she told him that she had married his agent—about whom they had never even spoken—I probably could have heard him without the phone. All of us laughed at the surreal nature of this call and of the crisscrossing of our lives.

Mahmoud and I reunited, though way too late. We still are together, and while he never can pick up where we left off, he is still in demand as a player in places far away. I placed him in Italy the first year we were back together. Last year, he was injured and couldn't play. In addition, his wife, April, gave birth to their fifth child.

In the late summer of 2005, their family sold their house in Gulfport, Mississippi. Two weeks later, Hurricane Katrina destroyed their former residence along with much of Gulfport. Mahmoud had already moved to Atlanta. He rented trucks and drove supplies back to Mississippi several times during those early days, after the devastation.

Just like when I called him for the "Follow-Thru Fund" all of those years before, if you need Mahmoud in spite of all that went down between us, he's there.

SHARIF NASSIR, in spite of the obvious great job he did while trying to cut his teeth on Mahmoud's career, was never heard from again.

10. The Squeaky Wheel Goes to Greece

EFTHIMIOS RENTZIAS has been a client for ten years. Even though he was drafted in the first round of the NBA draft, he has played mostly in Europe and has had a very good, if slightly underachieving career. This was due primarily to some chronic knee problems. He did make it to the NBA after we negotiated a three-year guaranteed contract with the Philadelphia 76ers. He only lasted through one year. As I was finishing this, Efthimios called to tell me that he was retiring from the game because of his knees. He is twenty-nine years old. He told me he didn't want to play solely for the money.

The primary word I would use to describe Efthimios and his family after having the pleasure to represent them for eleven years is *loyalty.* They stayed with me all of the way. There were ups and downs, but they never sought to blame me for the downs. They knew I was trying, and that was enough for them.

TED still lives in Greece and is very active and well-respected in Greek basketball and here in the United States. We speak on a fairly regular basis. In the past ten years since he waited for me in the lobby in the Holiday Inn in Portsmouth, Virginia, we have collaborated on exactly one additional player besides Rentzias. This proved to me that Ted was not like the others who were just looking to be cut in. He only contacts me when he thinks a particular kid can benefit from signing with me.

12. The $706 Million Bronze Medal

QUINCY DOUBY took my advice in spite of many opinions to the contrary. He remained in the 2006 NBA draft. He was selected nineteenth overall in the first round by the Sacramento Kings. His initial three-year contract is worth potentially over $9 million. He was the highest drafted player to come out of Rutgers University in over twenty years.

I never to this day have received that promised e-mail from the NCAA. If anyone from that organization is reading this, they can relax; he no longer needs a ride to the Knicks facility.

THE U.S. BASKETBALL TEAM dusted itself off after the debacle in Athens. They reorganized and did many positive things to improve not only the United States's performance on the floor, but off it as well. We were rightly perceived in Athens as arrogant and disrespectful of our opponents and of the game itself.

This time Mike Krzyzewski was named the coach, replacing Larry. This move was hailed all during the World Championships held in Japan in September 2006. The press and the players were constantly extolling the virtues of Coach K. The obvious implication being that they were now freed from the burdens of playing for Larry.

This time we didn't get beat in Greece. We got beat *by* Greece. The bronzing of America continues. What the powers that be still don't fully get is that until our entire system of developing basketball players and human beings is dealt with, we will remain a talented, arrogant, and selfish bunch who will wallow in mediocrity.

Three weeks after these World Championships, I spent some time in Venice, Italy, with one of my favorite players, Nikos Zisis. Nikos is a member of that terrific Greek national team that had beaten the United States the month before. He is Greece's best point guard and didn't even get the chance to play in that game against the United States. He had been intentionally and maliciously elbowed in the eye by Andersen Varajao of Brazil. Nikos had watched the game against the United States from a Japanese hospital bed. He would later have two plates and four screws surgically implanted around his eye socket.

Varajao, who is also a member of the Cleveland Cavaliers of the NBA, rather than apologizing to Nikos, claimed that he did it because Nikos "didn't show me respect." As I have previously said, NBA entitlement knows no borders. Maybe if the Brazilians hadn't been down seventeen points to the Greeks at that time of this assault, Varajao would have received a little more of his desired respect.

At dinner overlooking the Grand Canal, Nikos, Aylin, and I discussed what to do about the Varajao incident. I also wanted his reaction to the victory over the United States, which is still being celebrated in song in Greece. The first thing he said to me said it all. He still spoke with respect and almost laughingly acknowledged our athletic superiority over the rest of the world. But he referred specifically to Coach K's press conference after the U.S. team's loss. How he said that Number 4 was a very good player. Number 7 could really shoot it. Number 13 was a great defender, and on and on. This angered, yet interested, the Greeks very much.

Me, too. Maybe when we finally realize that Number 4 is Papaloukas, Number 7 is Spanoullis, and Number 13 is Diamentides, we can stop losing to them.

And, by the way Mr. Varejao, Number 6 is Nikos Zisis, and the respect should be going in his direction, not yours.

14. And Here Come the Elephants

ISIAH THOMAS is the new head coach of the New York Knicks as well as its president and general manager. He will begin his first and, according to his owner James Dolan, possibly only season, as head coach. He will coach a roster of players with the highest salaries in the league. That roster will consist of players entirely selected by him.

LARRY BROWN was fired by the New York Knicks on June 22, 2006. It was the same day as my parents' sixtieth wedding anniversary. Congratulations! I don't think that was planned by James Dolan and Isiah, but considering the overall atmosphere of this episode, who knows. And they didn't send a gift, either.

Commissioner David Stern was specifically selected to be the arbitrator in case of any dispute in the contract my father negotiated and Larry signed with the Knicks. This case actually did go before the commissioner in late September 2006. Mr. Stern found himself in an extremely difficult position. On one hand, he is basically employed by the owners, and one of them was trying to get out of paying his coach $40 million. On the other hand, it was obvious that he couldn't possibly rule against Larry. I think I can safely say, without hurting Larry's feelings, that he did not do his best work for the Knicks. It's also clear to me that he had not breached his contract by doing a subpar job. Any lawyer should agree. What the Knicks were trying to do was going too far. If David Stern ruled against Larry, then he would basically be allowing any team to back out of a guaranteed contract with a coach if they didn't like the results. In the real world, this might seem fair, but it is not the way guaranteed contracts operate in the NBA.

The Knicks said they had fired Larry "with cause," claiming that he had somehow breached his contract. They alluded to claims of insubordination concerning his public criticism of his roster. They also claimed he didn't follow the Garden's protocol in speaking with the media. The claims were vague at best and kept shifting with the season. In my opinion, they had little or no evidence to support their position. But there it was, out in the papers for everyone to see. Larry's entire ten-month relationship with the Knicks troubled me from the beginning and still does. The reaction to Larry's potential and actual hiring was so overblown that it made me uncomfortable—that Larry was the savior brought in to save the franchise.

The reactions of the journalists as well as the fans illustrated to me how far out of whack things have gotten when it comes to sports in our country—not only in terms of the money being spent, but also the attention paid to these hirings and firings. Larry was brought in to coach the Knicks, accompanied by newspaper accounts of his and his family's every move. There was incredible TV and radio coverage as well. When he was finally introduced at the press conference at the Garden, there were hundreds of media people present, complete with a video tribute to Larry and his "coming home" to New York.

Nine months later the send-off was a little different. No parties, no streamers, no balloons. Just as the buildup was exaggerated, now the bashing of Larry took on similar over-the-top proportions. Everyone took a shot at Larry. According to some, he is to blame for everything. High gas prices, people talking on cell phones in movie theaters—you name it. Stephon Marbury took every opportunity available to criticize Larry. Larry's practices were picked apart daily, as if he never knew how to coach or had apparently forgotten everything that had made him one of the best coaches in the league.

The spin in both directions is absurd, of course, but when we build someone up higher than we should, we feel the need to drag him down in a similar disproportionate way. Larry was and is a basketball coach. He doesn't play anymore. He has received and accepted a lot of credit and many accolades over the years, and now I guess he has to suffer the indignities as well. But that doesn't make it right. Just to set the record straight before it comes out in the New York media, Larry had nothing to do with the war in Iraq and had very little involvement in any of the space shuttle mishaps . . . that I know of.

On October 30, 2006, my father spent some ten hours finalizing a settlement with David Stern and the Knicks. Larry would end up being paid very well indeed for his ten-month tenure with the team that he grew up watching. Ten minutes after the settlement was announced it was Halloween.

The parties involved were specifically told not to discuss the details of

the agreement. However, on November 9, 2006, the Knicks' parent company, Cablevision, filed their quarterly report. This release would by law
include the terms of the settlement with Larry. The New York media
somehow learned of the release even before it had happened. The reported
amount was all over the airwaves within minutes. The number reported
was $18.5 million. Without verifying that number it should be added that
the deal allegedly included payment in one lump sum and also included
the elimination of any buyout clause in Larry's contract as well. This, while
not reported in Cablevision's release, was a significant point for Larry and
my father. In the course of the next three years it could potentially be
worth twelve to eighteen million additional dollars.

Larry will be all right. As I gaze into my crystal ball, I predict that
Larry will coach again, probably in the NBA. And he'll coach very well. It
is, after all, what he does.

ACKNOWLEDGMENTS

In looking back on what I have written in this book, I am at first struck by the fact that a very small portion of my experiences in being an agent are reflected herein. The vast majority of the players that I have represented are not even mentioned. Since they number way over one hundred, I want to acknowledge them as well. This book has thirteen chapters. The only players whose stories appear here are the "unusual" ones. The rank and file of my guys were equally as important to me throughout my career. In fact, some of my favorites don't get a sniff in these pages. They know who they are and hopefully will understand what I tried to do here.

Even though my father is featured in several of these chapters, I would be remiss if I didn't acknowledge that we began this enterprise together. We had a plan after I left UCLA to represent and manage NBA players. It wasn't always smooth but I think we did all right. In the grand scheme of things, to acknowledge my father in a business context trivializes what he and my mom have meant to me in life.

In the actual production of this book I have had help as well. First I want to thank my editor, Doug Grad. He has believed in this project for eight years. Without his encouragement I never would have had this chance. I also want to thank HarperCollins for making this book a reality.

My friend Bill Handleman, a writer from the Jersey Shore, helped me years back in formulating the chapter on Tommy Hamilton, which later became part of my "Running For Your Life" chapter.

I need to acknowledge my wife, Aylin. When I sat down to write this I became consumed by it. I know how much time it took me away from her. She never complained except if she thought I was going at it too hard for my own good. Just as with my parents, I can't possibly acknowledge everything that Aylin means to me and it would be silly to try.

Since I'm not a writer by trade, I sent my first raw chapter to my oldest daughter Sami for her to read. What I forgot was that she was a third grade schoolteacher. Instead of merely reading the story she sent me back 192 corrections . . . in red. She was plainly furious with me about my grammar and simply could not let it pass. I sent her every chapter after that for her to edit, even though she was teaching full time and pregnant as well. She worked on my book at night for hours in her "spare time." I couldn't have done this without her. I miss my "Sami Edit" emails. They have, however, been replaced by pictures of my first grandchild Dylan, which has cushioned the blow. Dylan has contributed nothing to this book, but for some reason everybody is wild about him and Sami wanted me to give him some credit.

In that same vein, I was shocked at the input and interest of my son-in-law, Joe Passo, in this endeavor. I want to thank him as well for his reading and constructive thoughts as I was writing this. He has proven to be much more intelligent that I previously thought.

I also realize that I was probably a pain in the ass to all my five kids in the writing and researching end of things. They all at some point had to help their dad with the computer. I know it annoyed them but I'm worth it.

In the end, I want to acknowledge everybody who had an impact who thinks I forgot them.

I haven't.

KEITH GLASS